Hollywood in the Klondike

HOLLYWOOD
IN THE
KLONDIKE

DAWSON CITY'S GREAT FILM FIND

Michael Gates

LOST MOOSE

COPYRIGHT © 2022 MICHAEL GATES

1 2 3 4 5 — 26 25 24 23 22

ALL RIGHTS RESERVED. No part of this publication may be reproduced, stored in a retrieval system or transmitted, in any form or by any means, without prior permission of the publisher or, in the case of photocopying or other reprographic copying, a licence from Access Copyright, www.accesscopyright.ca, 1-800-893-5777, info@accesscopyright.ca.

HARBOUR PUBLISHING CO. LTD.
P.O. Box 219, Madeira Park, BC, VON 2H0
www.harbourpublishing.com

EDITED by Arlene Prunkl
INDEXED by Audrey McClellan
DUST JACKET AND TEXT DESIGN by Libris Simas Ferraz / Onça Design
PRINTED AND BOUND in Canada

Harbour Publishing acknowledges the support of the Canada Council for the Arts, the Government of Canada, and the Province of British Columbia through the BC Arts Council.

LIBRARY AND ARCHIVES CANADA CATALOGUING IN PUBLICATION

Title: Hollywood in the Klondike : Dawson City's great film find / by Michael Gates.
Names: Gates, Michael (Historian), author.
Description: Includes bibliographical references and index.
Identifiers: Canadiana (print) 20220246351 | Canadiana (ebook) 20220246432 | ISBN 9781550179965 (hardcover) | ISBN 9781550179972 (EPUB)
Subjects: LCSH: Motion pictures—Yukon—Dawson—History. | LCSH: Silent films—Yukon—Dawson—History and criticism. | LCSH: Motion picture film collections—Yukon—Dawson—History. | LCSH: Motion picture film—Preservation—Yukon—Dawson—History. | LCSH: Dawson (Yukon)—History.
Classification: LCC PN1993.5.C3 G38 2022 | DDC 791.4309719/1—dc23

This book is dedicated to my wife and life partner, Kathy, whose contributions to this project have been many, and whose support is immeasurable.

TABLE OF CONTENTS

PREFACE 1

INTRODUCTION   Discovery 10
CHAPTER 1   Two Worlds, 1894–1896 23
CHAPTER 2   The Gold Rush Begins, 1897 35
CHAPTER 3   The Boom Year, 1898 54
CHAPTER 4   The Busy Years, 1899–1900 103
CHAPTER 5   The Twilight Years, 1901–1914 129
CHAPTER 6   Movie Night in Dawson, 1915–1979 179
CHAPTER 7   The Klondike and Hollywood 201
CHAPTER 8   Recovery, Restoration and Inspiration 234
EPILOGUE 251

APPENDIX   Gold-Mining Techniques and Terminology 256
ACKNOWLEDGEMENTS 261
BIBLIOGRAPHY 264
INDEX 270
NOTES 278

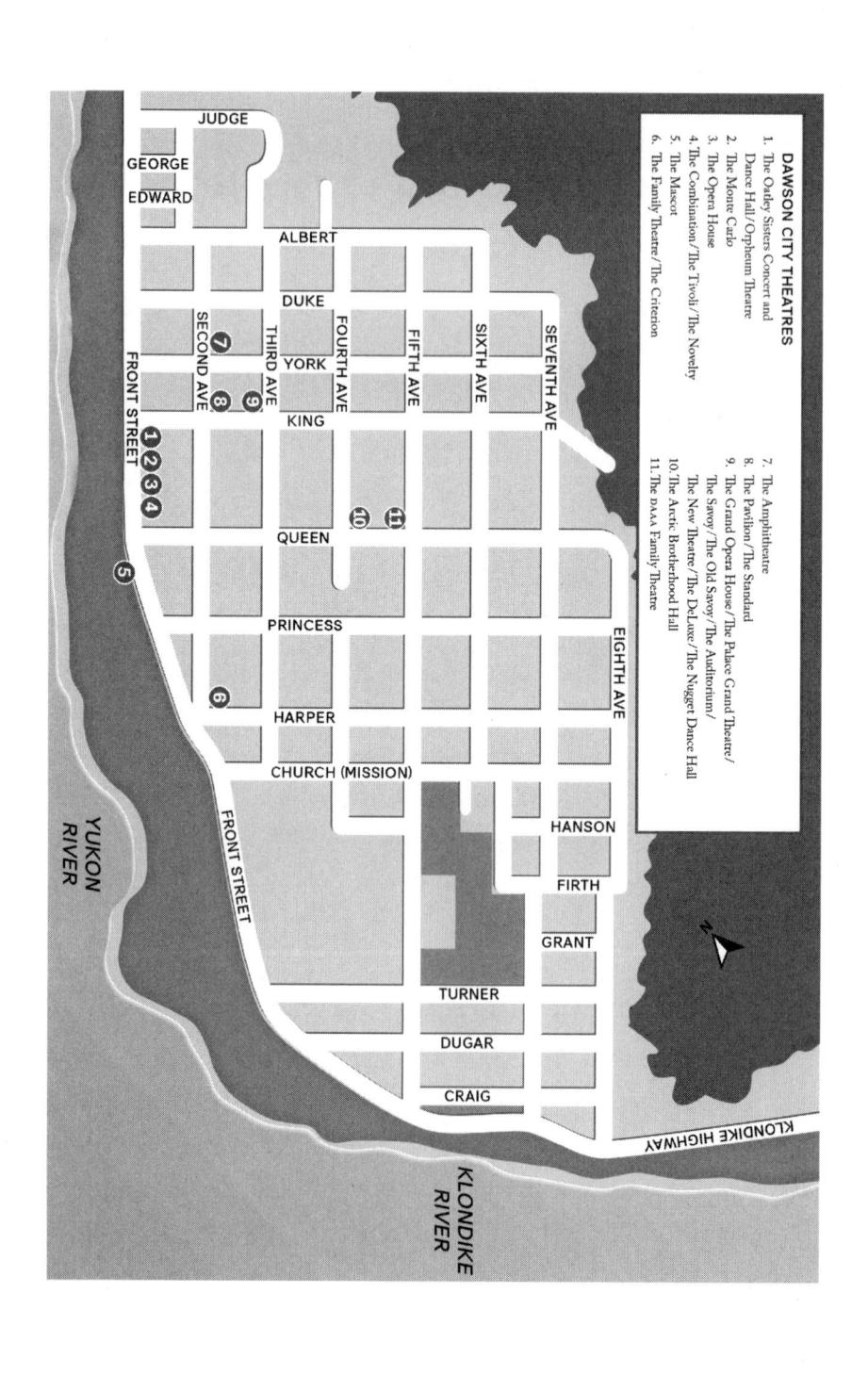

DAWSON CITY THEATRES

1. The Oatley Sisters Concert and Dance Hall/Orpheum Theatre
2. The Monte Carlo
3. The Opera House
4. The Combination/The Tivoli/The Novelty
5. The Mascot
6. The Family Theatre/The Criterion
7. The Amphitheatre
8. The Pavilion/The Standard
9. The Grand Opera House/The Palace Grand Theatre/The Savoy/The Old Savoy/The Auditorium/The New Theatre/The DeLuxe/The Nugget Dance Hall
10. The Arctic Brotherhood Hall
11. The DAAA Family Theatre

PREFACE

As you will read in this account, Dawson City, Yukon, during the Klondike gold rush of the 1890s was a dynamic, bustling place. The area was named after the Klondike River, into which many of the richest gold-bearing streams flowed, streams with names such as Bonanza, Eldorado, and Bear and Hunker Creeks. People's ambitions and dreams were fuelled by the lust for gold, though not everybody left there with a pocketful of nuggets. Theatres, and all the associated activities they came with, became the centre of social life during the hectic but peaceful heyday of the stampede. Many of the people who participated in this grand adventure and worked in these temples of amusement never set foot in the goldfields. Many of them went on to great careers in film or related industries.

Eighty years later, a hoard of silent movies was uncovered from permafrost beneath the frozen ground of Dawson City. The discovery caused quite a stir, and some of Hollywood's greatest performers, who were featured in the more than five hundred titles salvaged from the icy rubble, started their careers in Dawson City, or they were connected to someone who had. The Film Find would not have happened at all if Dawson City hadn't been built upon permafrost. During the recovery of these films, the circumstances surrounding how they came to be buried in the permafrost came to light. This too reflected the unique situation in Dawson City and will be revealed later in this account.

Why did I write this book? First, I was personally involved in the recovery of the Dawson Film Find, so I have first-hand knowledge of the events. To reconstruct them, I referred to my extensive file of notes, newspaper articles, correspondence, photos and other sources that I have gathered over the years. Had I known that the Film Find would become such a significant discovery, I would have paid more attention to it at the time. In October of 1977, I was hired as curator at Klondike National Historic Sites in Dawson City; I was in Ottawa at the time and didn't move to Dawson until the following March. Spring of 1978 was my first season as curator, and everything seemed new and exciting to me. The Film Find was only one of many things I had to deal with that year.

Second, over the past four decades, I have heard the circumstances surrounding the Film Find rendered in highly colourful and inaccurate second-hand accounts. I wanted to set the record straight for future reference.

To place the films in the context of the gold rush, I turned to early books, articles and diaries about Dawson's first theatres and moving pictures. The latter appeared in Dawson City at the height of the Klondike gold rush, but only as a novelty. The fledgling film business took a long time to become the major industry of later years. The theatres in which the early films had been screened in Dawson became part of my story. Tracing their growth and evolution over the decades reflects the history of Dawson City, from its inception as an early gold camp to a boom town, to a respectable settlement, to a ghost town, and then to the vibrant community it is today. Theatres played an important and changing role in the social life of the community over the century that followed the original discovery of gold in 1896.

As I dived into the historical record, I decided that the full story of the Dawson Film Find could not be told without placing it in the historical context of Dawson City, especially the theatres that eventually became the popular movie houses and gathering places in the community. So this is really a story in two parts, with the historical context of the past 125 years sandwiched between the discovery of the films at the beginning, and the recovery and restoration of the films at the end.

There were a number of questions to be explored in this account. What was the theatre world like in Dawson City during and after the Klondike gold rush? How does the transition from live theatre to moving pictures reflect the evolution of Dawson City over the century that followed? Who were the characters involved in the entertainment world of the gold rush, and who were those individuals who later became prominent in Hollywood? How did the gold rush shape Hollywood's later perception of the North? Conversely, how has Hollywood shaped the public perception of the gold rush?

How I became involved in the Film Find project is another part of the story. After being hired as curator at Klondike National Historic Sites, I packed my belongings and my cat, Fritz, into a new pickup truck and made the long journey from Ottawa to Dawson City in the Yukon. I was to care for and curate a huge collection of gold-rush artifacts. I was not a film historian, nor did I qualify as a curator of film. I became involved in the discovery of the Dawson City Film Find not because of my qualifications, but because I was there in 1978, and no one else chose to handle the discovery.

If I had encountered this discovery later in my career, my adventurous spirit and enthusiasm might have been tempered or even tamed by the ever-present government bureaucracy and the chain of command. The health and safety issues alone might have been enough to scare me away from involvement in the project. My boss kept asking me: What does this have to do with our mandate? The answer was nothing, which is why I tried to devote most of my attention to the project on my own time, outside my regular hours of work. But I was new to the job, young and full of energy and confidence in what I was doing.

In the end, my involvement in the project was merely as flame-keeper for a short while; the torch was quickly passed to others, including the Dawson City Museum, the National Film, Television and Sound Archives in Ottawa and the Library of Congress in Washington, DC. On the other hand, if I hadn't taken that single step forward, then none of the other events that followed would have happened. I am pleased that things worked out so well. Like a ghost, the Dawson Film Find frequently rose from the grave (or the permafrost) to haunt me during my career. It deeply impacted me at both a professional and personal level, especially the latter, and in due course I will explain that too.

I was curious about how this single event fit into the story of the gold rush and the consequent development and then decline of Dawson City. I went back in time to the gold rush to explore the theatre world and chronicle the place of theatres and the people associated with them in their historical context. It seemed that in the early days, with little to occupy their spare time, the gold seekers were hungry for entertainment, which is why entertainers and theatres featured prominently and flourished in the colonization of the North, even before the gold rush.

The Klondike gold rush was an event in the most unlikely of places and circumstances, so unique in the history of Canada and the development of the North that Dawson City has become enshrined as a complex of national historic sites. I referred to the records of the Historic Sites and Monuments Board of Canada a few years ago. Dawson City, with a population of twenty-two hundred souls, had a complex of eighteen national historic sites, more if you include sites such as the ss Keno, Dredge Number Four and the First Nation site of Tr'ochëk. The last time I checked, Calgary, a city with a population of one million, had three historic sites. Throw in the numerous commemorative plaques mounted on boulders scattered around town that commemorate the people of national significance associated with Dawson City, and you realize there is something special about the place. If you walk around the community, you are constantly stubbing your toe or grazing your shin against one of these boulders, or bumping into one of the historic buildings.

There is a lot of fiction entwined with the historical facts of the gold rush. Many of these stories have become legendary and enshrined in the collective consciousness. Stories such as the one about Swiftwater Bill, Gussie Lamore and the eggs are told and retold. Most are based upon actual events but have been sculpted over time into widely accepted, colourful narratives. Many gold-rush participants later wrote memoirs, and they embellished their stories and added details that contradict the facts.

Another example of historical misinformation: in his biography of Roscoe "Fatty" Arbuckle, Stuart Oderman reported that Arbuckle went north with Marjorie Rambeau in 1906 to perform in Anchorage, Alaska, with an option of playing in Fairbanks if they were successful.[1] But Anchorage wasn't founded as a railway construction camp until 1914.

Actress Marjorie Rambeau later recalled this northern venture to "Dawson, Alaska." When the theatre company went bust in Dawson, the "governor" (a man she said was appointed by us president Theodore Roosevelt) persuaded her to remain in the gold-rush town. Fifty years later she reported in an interview with Hedda Hopper, an American gossip columnist and actress, that when she left Dawson the following year, 1907, Robert Service was there to see her off.[2] That would have been a remarkable feat, as Service had yet to set foot in the Klondike, nor was he at that time a best-selling author but a bank clerk in Whitehorse. Rambeau wasn't the only one who misremembered encounters with the likes of Jack London and Robert Service. It was a well-established tradition in the decades that followed the gold rush for the stampeders to embellish memoirs with fictitious encounters with such noted gold-rush figures.[3] American accounts frequently refer to the Klondike as being in Alaska, a falsehood that would have been apparent to anyone who visited Dawson City. In some instances, such geographical confusion was purposeful misdirection. Many Americans at the time felt that the Yukon should have been part of American territory in the North. As a result, in these historical accounts Dawson is often identified as an American city, located on American soil, in Alaska.

To get to the story of what happened in Dawson City during the Klondike gold rush, you must unmask the much-varnished stories to reveal events that are every bit as interesting and often more exciting than the legends that were created over the years. (Some may take exception to my remarks regarding Kate Rockwell, popularly known as "Klondike Kate." She was never known as Klondike Kate during the gold rush or for several decades after.) The newspapers of the period were of great help in setting the record straight about certain details. Today they are more accessible and searchable than they were to previous generations of historians.

During the gold rush, Dawson had several newspapers as well as its own Fleet Street. King Street between Third and Fourth Avenues had three newspaper offices facing each other. There was the *Sun*, which published its first issue on June 11, 1898, followed by the *Klondike Nugget* five days later. The *Dawson Daily News* started publishing the following year, eventually outlasting all the others by five decades. Then there were the *Klondike Miner and Yukon*

Advertiser, the *Yukon World*, the *Dawson Record* and the *Free Lance*. The *Nugget*, the *Sun* and the *Daily News* covered the theatre scene in detail during the heyday of the gold rush and provide considerable substance for today's historians. I wasted a lot of time during my research distracted by the many interesting articles in the newspapers not related to theatre. These diversions were fascinating, and I know few people who have been able to resist the temptation to stray from their research project to absorb some of these stories. The gold-rush newspaper coverage seemed to give a more comprehensive account of life at the time than newspapers do today.

Some authors have covered the theatre scene, including Booth (1962), Evans (1983) and Stevens (1984). The latter compiled several appendices that list plays and actors active in the gold-rush theatre scene. Because of his effort I deemed it unnecessary to compile the name lists that have accompanied some of my previous works.

I would like to mention a few things to make it easier for people to understand my writing. First, there is the price of gold. During the gold rush, gold was pegged at roughly twenty dollars a troy ounce. The gold that came out of the ground was not in its pure state, and the accepted rate of exchange for raw Klondike gold was sixteen dollars per ounce, although the purity and quality varied from one creek to the next. A troy ounce used for measuring the weight of gold is different from the avoirdupois ounce that is commonly used as a measure of weight. The former is roughly thirty-one grams; the latter is 28.35 grams. If you add in an inflation factor of roughly thirty-five, today that same ounce of gold would be worth nearly five hundred dollars. But in addition to inflation, gold has increased in value since then, and in Canadian dollars as I write this, is valued at roughly four times that amount.

Until recently the Yukon was difficult to reach. Before roads were extended to communities such as Mayo, Keno and Dawson

City, they were reached by riverboat in the summer and by horse-drawn sleighs in the winter. The latter trip could take as long as five days to complete, with passengers wrapped in heavy robes, sitting in open air during the daily travel at temperatures that sometimes reached –50° Celsius. With only a few hours of half-light in the depths of winter, these communities drew inward during the cold, dark months. Places like Vancouver, Toronto, Seattle or San Francisco were reached with great difficulty, great cost and often great hardship. These places, and anywhere beyond the territorial boundary, were referred to as *outside*, a term that was still in common use when I first arrived in Dawson City. Although times are changing, and transportation at any time of year is better than it once was, many people still refer to those distant places as *outside*. Like Newfoundlanders referring to people who don't live on their rocky island as *from away*, Yukoners refer to visitors as *outsiders*. I ask the reader to understand this distinction when the term *outside* is used in this book.

To avoid repetition, I use Dawson and Dawson City interchangeably. Over the years, Dawson's most durable newspaper, the *Dawson Daily News*, changed with the times to the *Dawson News*, and finally, the *Dawson Weekly News*. In my notes, I use the initials *DDN* to cover all these variations as they are all the same business over a period of fifty-five years.

I refer to characters in this book mainly with reference to their time in Dawson City. Consequently, I have not always traced the details of their later lives and their careers that followed the gold-rush period. Perhaps my work will stimulate someone to write more comprehensive histories about the careers of these individuals. There are some fantastic stories hidden there. Some have already been written about—Joseph "Joe" Boyle, Sid Grauman, Alex Pantages, Kate Rockwell, Roscoe Arbuckle and William Desmond Taylor are but a few of them. They make fascinating reading for those who are interested. Others remain rather mysterious and have not been the focus of biographies of their own—Cad Wilson and Lillian Hall, for example. "Diamond Tooth" Gertie Lovejoy lived a rather ordinary life after the excitement of the gold rush. But they are all tightly woven into the fabric of the remarkable story of Dawson City and the Klondike gold rush.

Plenty of books have been written about the history of Hollywood and its players. I am guilty of bias; my account looks on the events described from a Yukon perspective. I do that because I write about Yukon history, but I also do it because outsiders often get the details of our history wrong or interpret them from a distant perspective.

Language found in some of the quotations included in this volume may contain words or phrases that some readers may find offensive by current standards. I have not tried to expunge these. They are a reflection of the values expressed by people during the time period I am writing about, and they give us an opportunity to reflect upon how much social values have changed over the past 125 years.

This book was crafted during the COVID-19 pandemic. For the greater part of my work on this project, I was confined to home. I could not travel to other institutions for the purposes of research, nor in some cases could I correspond with them. Because of COVID, many institutions were not able to supply me with photographs that would have enhanced this account. Fortunately, I have extensive research files and a large home library to refer to. The advances in internet technology made it possible for me to access valuable sources of information at my fingertips. Not as exciting, but practical. It's my hope that this account has not suffered greatly from these constraints.

INTRODUCTION

DISCOVERY

Responsibility for the discovery of the Dawson Film Find rests on the shoulders of Frank Barrett, without whom the most improbable sequence of events that followed would not have occurred. If any of a long sequence of decisions and actions had not been taken, if any link in the chain of events had been broken, this story would have come to nothing.

In 1978, Dawson City, with a population of eight hundred, was a virtual ghost town, a mere shadow of its former self, filled with relics from the Klondike gold rush of 1898. Decaying buildings leaning this way and that could be found everywhere. Abandoned machinery stood on empty, weed-clogged lots. The contents of many buildings remained untouched after decades of abandonment. Long isolated from the outside world, the town had remained a living museum of the gold rush. But as many of the old-timers would tell you, after a road was completed in 1955 to connect the former capital of the Yukon Territory with Whitehorse and the outside, the town changed swiftly and the relics began to disappear. Tourists started collecting souvenirs from the derelict buildings. Collectors gathered truckloads of old artifacts and hauled them away. Old-timers took things to the dump or burned them or threw them in the river. The

The skating rink in Dawson City was demolished in 1978 to make way for a new recreation centre. Gates collection.

sagging buildings were gradually demolished, having been deemed by forward-thinking residents as an embarrassing reminder of the city's faded past. But unknown to many, buried beneath the buildings and the streets of Dawson City were artifacts that remained in a state of suspended animation, encased by the permafrost that is found everywhere in the North, and perfectly preserved.

Permafrost is the ground beneath the surface that in northern Canada remains frozen year-round, which has been the case for hundreds of thousands of years. With each excavation in Dawson and the adjacent goldfields, more relics from the gold rush are released from their frozen state, and such was the case with the hoard of silent movies that was unearthed in Dawson City on July 4, 1978.

Frank Barrett was an alderman and deputy mayor of Dawson City in 1978. Red-headed and stocky of build, he was the pastor of a local church and a family man, but on this day he was working in an

INTRODUCTION

Some of the film uncovered from the permafrost at the demolition site of the old skating rink in Dawson City was still in the metal shipping containers.
Kathy Jones-Gates

official capacity for the town of Dawson. He had gone to the site of the proposed new recreation centre, vacant lots located between King and Queen Streets that intersected with Fifth Avenue behind Diamond Tooth Gerties Gambling Hall.

The skating rink previously standing on the site had been demolished the summer before. It had been little more than a large, barn-like structure clad with corrugated metal. Alderman Barrett hired a backhoe and operator to dig some exploratory holes at the site to determine the extent of the permafrost. As he stood nearby observing the excavation at the site, the bucket of the excavator brought up a metal box that, upon examination, was found to be filled with reels of 35-millimetre black-and-white film. He stopped the excavation and had the operator move to a different spot to try again, and when the bucket pierced the ground, it brought up more loose films and other stuff. At this point, Barrett faced a dilemma: Should he carry on with his excavation as he had planned, or should he stop?

Barrett put the digging on hold. He contacted Parks Canada and asked them to come and look at what had just been exposed. As the owner of more than two dozen historical properties within the townsite, Parks Canada had ambitious plans of a major restoration project that would rejuvenate numerous gold rush-era buildings in Dawson City. A team of Parks Canada archaeologists was currently working in Dawson under the supervision of the project archaeologist, David Burley. Burley was dispatched to the site to assess the film discovery.

Burley quickly determined two things: first, that what he saw was not on Parks Canada property; and second, that he did not see a link between this scattered array and the Parks Canada mandate of national commemorations. He returned to the old courthouse, where I met him at the front entrance as I was about to leave. The building, a two-storey structure of classical design built in 1901 and designed by federal architect T. W. Fuller, was being used as Parks Canada's Dawson headquarters. Burley told me about what he had just examined and repeated that it did not seem relevant to the federal mandate, but suggested that I might want to look at the site anyway.

I had been in Dawson City for only three months at that time but already had a strong impression of the town, its unique place in history and an understanding that unusual things were regularly uncovered. The territorial government had financed the installation of a new water and sewer system in Dawson and were digging up the old system of redwood stave piping that distributed water to and carried waste from Dawson City homes. During excavation, they frequently uncovered interesting artifacts dating back to the gold-rush era eighty years before.

INTRODUCTION

Despite the film being buried in the ground for fifty years, the image content on many of the reels was largely preserved. Gates collection.

I immediately made my way to the site, which lay open and bare. The rubble of the old skating rink had been removed, and debris was scattered about the two holes dug by the excavator: bottles, broken glass, chicken wire, rotting wood planks, skates and broken curling rocks. There were also metal cannisters, each capable of holding several reels of film, and reels scattered everywhere. Amid the rubble, loose film lay unreeled on the surface. The metal reels upon which the film was wound were badly rusted. Some of the rolls of film had been pushed out of shape, leaving them looking more like bowls than discs.

I picked up a segment of film that was clear of any emulsion and applied a match to one end. It flared up with great intensity and burned so fast that I nearly singed my fingers, confirming that the film was of older cellulose nitrate (celluloid) stock. Nitrate film had admirable qualities for the film business, including durability and low cost, which made it ideal stock upon which to lay the images of motion-picture film. But the film was extremely flammable and burned with sudden and frightening intensity. Nitrate film is known to have caused fires in a Dawson theatre, and was singled out as the

Some of the reels recovered were bowl-shaped and distorted. Rust, dirt and dimensional distortion were challenges when the film was later copied to a safer, more permanent format. Kathy Jones-Gates

source of the fire that destroyed Dawson's recreation centre in 1937. Nitrate film was replaced by non-flammable acetate by 1951. Tests I made with fragments later confirmed how flammable this film was. In one, I set alight a two-metre length of nitrate film and dropped it into a galvanized metal garbage barrel. The flames from the film shot almost three metres into the air, and I later noticed that the heat of the fire had melted the galvanized coating from the barrel and caused it to trickle down the sides in rivulets.

Worse, however, is that when this film decomposes under the wrong conditions of high temperature and humidity, it can spontaneously ignite. These traits had been the cause of numerous fires in warehouses where hundreds of thousands of the old silent films were archived. The silent film treasury is now largely incomplete as a result.

INTRODUCTION

> **Tomorrow Night**
> At the D.A.A.A.
>
> **THE STRANGE CASE OF MARY PAGE**
>
> With HENRY B. WALTHALL, the Greatest Emotional Screen Actor, and EDNA MAYO, the Most Beautiful Actress of Photoplaydom
> The First Number
> Admission, 25c and 50c

One of the first reels of film examined was the film *The Strange Case of Mary Page*. It was shown in the Dawson Family Theatre in October of 1917. *Dawson Daily News,* October 10, 1917, p. 4, Yukon Archives.

I examined one of the reels that appeared to be more intact than the others, and by unspooling the lead end of the reel, I found a frame that held the title of the film: *The Strange Case of Mary Page*. Clearly, the images on some of the reels had not been destroyed by burial in the ground.

My training as a museum conservator had made me sensitive to the possibilities of restoration, and I thought this film might have some potential for duplication—if the images were intact. So I began making telephone calls across the country, inquiring whether anybody would be interested in what had been discovered in Dawson. Time was of the essence as construction was due to begin shortly. Calls to the National Film Board and the Canadian Conservation Institute failed to arouse any interest. Each call led me to other institutions, including the Public Archives of Canada (now known as Library and Archives Canada). At the Public Archives, I contacted Klaus Hendriks in the conservation department. Klaus suggested that I talk to Sam Kula, the director of the National Film, Television and Sound Archives (NFTSA), and he gave me Kula's phone number.

Over a long-distance connection, I explained to Kula what we had found in Dawson City. He showed considerable interest in what was being uncovered, but he said I would need to supply him with a more detailed description of what I had seen before he could know how to respond. I promised to do so, but set the project aside briefly to attend to my regular curatorial work. In the meantime, while doing research on another project, I found, purely by chance in the October 10, 1917, edition of the *Dawson Daily News*, an advertisement for the screening of the film *The Strange Case of Mary Page*. The film was to be shown the following night in the Dawson Amateur Athletic Association theatre. This chance discovery made the films vitally real. I could pinpoint a place and time when one of these reels was screened in a Dawson City theatre, and sensed that this made a difference. I tackled the film discovery with renewed energy, revisiting the site and examining the reels that had been exposed by the backhoe. On July 14, I sent a teletype message to Kula that read:

OLD NITRATE 35 MM BW FILMS

WHEN I SPOKE TO YOU BY TELEPHONE EARLIER THIS WEEK, I TOLD YOU THAT THERE WERE CONSIDERABLE NO. OLD MOVIE FILMS BEING EXCAVATED FROM VACANT LOT IN DAWSON. FURTHER TO THAT I CAN PROVIDE YOU WITH THE FOLLOWING INFORMATION:

1) THE FILMS ARE ALL APPARENTLY CELLULOSE NITRATE.

2) ONE DATES TO AS EARLY AS 1917 TITLED "THE STRANGE CASE OF MARY PAGE," WHICH I EXAMINED, WAS SHOWN IN DAWSON IN SEGMENTS THRU OCTOBER AND NOVEMBER 1917. OTHERS ALSO APPEAR TO BE SILENT FILMS.

3) WE HAVE ABOUT A DOZEN BOXES FULL OF FILM REELS CURRENTLY IN STORAGE. POTENTIAL FOR BUT NOT CONFIRMED HUNDREDS MORE STILL IN GROUND. OF THOSE IN STORAGE, FIVE WERE SAMPLED. ON THREE IMAGES ALMOST TOTALLY LOST.

HOPE TO TEST THE AREA WITHIN TWO WEEKS TO CONFIRM THE NUMBER OF FILMS PRESENT.

4) SEE TWO ABOVE AND ONE SEAFARING MOVIE. DIFFICULT TO DETERMINE CONTENT OF OTHER FILMS.

5) CONDITION: ARE EXCAVATED TOTALLY WET. METAL REELS ARE EXTENSIVELY CORRODED. FILM WET. EMULSION EXTENSIVELY LOST IN SEVERAL CASES. FILMS CURL WHEN DRY. AM SENDING SAMPLES.

ONCE YOU EXAMINE FILM SAMPLES PLS ADVISE ME IF YOU ARE STILL INTERESTED.

M GATES
FOR PROJECT MANAGER
LAND PARKS DAW
NATLIB OTT

It had been a hot, dry summer and forest fires were ablaze across the Yukon, causing interruptions in the microwave system that controlled our telecommunications. In a moment of connectivity, however, I received a response from Kula:

ARR. DAWSON ON NORTHWARD 41 25 JULY 9:15 AM

WOULD APPRECIATE OPPORTUNITY TO EXAMINE NITRATE FILM EXCAVATION.

DUE TO FIRE IN EXCHANGE TELEPHONE LINK W/DAWSON IS OUT. WOULD YOU PLS BOOK SINGLE 25 26 JULY PLAN TO LVE DAWSON 1700 HR 27 JULY.

SAM KULA
NATIONAL ARCHIVES

I met Kula at the airport. We went directly to the film site before checking into the hotel and began examining the films still lying in disarray on the ground. Discussions took place as we poked through the debris. The condition of the films that had been uncovered was poor, with little evidence of the images surviving, but Kula was willing to gamble that what lay beneath would be in better condition and worthy of salvage.[1] He quickly concluded that the potential of finding important film footage was strong. Notable among the gaps in the film record is the work of Theda Bara. Bara was one of the most popular actresses of the silent era and one of cinema's early sex symbols. She made more than forty films between 1914 and 1926, but most were lost in a fire in 1937 at the Twentieth Century Fox film storage facility at Little Ferry, New Jersey, including what is

Sam Kula inspects the demolition site of the old skating rink where the film was buried before checking into his hotel.
Kathy Jones-Gates

considered her most successful work, the film epic *Cleopatra* (1917). The films of other important actors from Fox Studios were also destroyed, including those of Tom Mix, William Farnum and Buster Keaton, leaving little by which to know their work. To find a reel of film featuring Bara or other silent film actors would be a virtual gold mine. It was worth it, he said, to try to recover and restore these films.

Kula felt that any film with salvageable images could be transferred to Ottawa, where they had the facilities to store the material and the means of copying the images from the unstable nitrate film onto safety film. As we stood amid the rubble on the lot behind Diamond Tooth Gerties, the discussion turned to how the films would be retrieved and processed. I made notes on the back of office memos on a clipboard I had brought with me. Sam said it would be too difficult working with another government department, so could I suggest anyone else who might be able to tackle the recovery work? I contacted Kathy Jones, director of the Dawson City Museum, and invited her to join us.

That afternoon, Kathy Jones met us at the site. A shovel was produced, and more films were unearthed for examination. We talked about the potential and how to deal with the recovery. We went out to Bear Creek, an abandoned industrial mining complex of more than sixty old buildings owned by Parks Canada and located ten kilometres from Dawson. There, a Parks Canada archaeological crew had moved dozens of boxes containing hundreds of reels that they had already salvaged from the old skating rink site into an old sod-covered root cellar.[2] Even at the height of the summer, ice still covered the walls of this building. Standing at the entrance of the root cellar, we examined samples of the salvaged films and Sam Kula got a full sense of the magnitude of the collection.

Hundreds of reels of film were already stored in an old root cellar outside of Dawson City when Sam Kula arrived. Kathy Jones-Gates

The following morning Sam joined me in my office, and over the telephone to Ottawa he dictated the terms of a contract for the recovery and cataloguing of the films, to be placed in the mail immediately and sent to the Dawson Museum. Parks Canada would provide the workspace to examine the films and for storage until they were shipped to Ottawa, and would provide technical support in the execution of the work. When the films arrived in Ottawa, said Kula, the process of copying them would begin.

Kathy Jones was insistent that the collection should henceforth be referred to as the Dawson City Film Find, and that the first showing of any restored films should take place in Dawson City. Kula agreed. Before that time, however, much work would be required. Some big questions would need to be answered: How many films of those excavated from the rubble on Fifth Avenue

Sam Kula (left) and Michael Gates (right) examine reels of the recovered film at the front of the root cellar where they were stored. Kathy Jones-Gates

would be worth saving? What was the content, and most important of all, how did they come to be buried in the ground in the first place? A way had to be found to ship them to Ottawa. In July of 1978, nobody had the answers to these questions; nobody could realize what an impact these rusty, buried reels would have on the film world. And I had no idea of the life-changing effect this discovery would have on me.

To fully understand the impact of the Film Find, we have to go back in time 125 years to explore the remarkable story of live theatre during the Klondike gold rush, and the gradual transition to movie theatres that followed. It was an extraordinary period in history, full of memorable exploits and filled with people who would later be catapulted into cinematic prominence. Charting these changes also charts the history of Dawson City.

CHAPTER 1

TWO WORLDS

1894-1896

The First Moving Pictures

This story begins with two events on opposite sides of the hemisphere. In Lyon, France, brothers Auguste and Louis Lumière were perfecting the first motion-picture camera. In 1894, their father Antoine had visited Paris and attended a demonstration of Thomas Edison's invention, the Kinetoscope. Edison's device was able to run a continuous loop of moving film through a device that could be viewed by one person at a time. Kinetoscopes were being installed for commercial use in amusement parks and other public locations.

Auguste and Louis, who were both scientifically inclined, set themselves to the task of improving on the concept. The following year, they patented their creation, calling it the cinématographe, and the first demonstration of their invention took place in Paris on December 28, 1895. The film *La Sortie des ouvriers de l'usine Lumière* (*Workers Leaving the Lumière Factory*) is the first motion picture ever produced. The machine, which was lightweight, could be used both for taking pictures and for projecting them in front of an audience. By 1896 the Lumières were sending trained crews of cameramen-projectionists to cities throughout the world to show films and shoot new material.

In America, Thomas Edison had advanced the technology by producing the Vitascope and distributing it in 1896. Imitators quickly appeared, including the Mutoscope peepshow device, the Animatograph and the American Biograph camera and projector. These new inventions quickly became novelty features in vaudeville houses and in travelling exhibitions at fairgrounds and lecture halls. At first they were regarded as animated photographs, but within a few years they developed storylines. Thus, the modern motion picture was born. Within a decade, the moving picture had evolved into mass-market entertainment.

Half a world away, in the Yukon Valley, people were unaware of these new developments. For nearly twenty-five years, a growing number of enterprising prospectors had been spreading out through a remote river basin in the interior of Alaska and the adjacent British territory, the Yukon, looking for gold. The region encompasses a land area of nearly two million square kilometres and straddles the Arctic Circle. It is a land of extremes, characterized by nearly constant daylight in the summer and short hours of daylight or total darkness (north of the Arctic Circle) in the winter. The temperature ranges from the mid-thirties Celsius in the summer to minus fifty degrees and colder in the winter. The region has been inhabited for thousands of years by Indigenous peoples who lived a nomadic lifestyle, shifting from one area to another during the year to exploit available food sources.

The First Yukon Prospectors

The first Europeans to arrive in the area were traders or missionaries; the first prospectors arrived in 1873. Optimistic of finding another big gold discovery like those that had been found along the spine of the Rocky Mountains from California in the south to the Stikine district in northern British Columbia, they spread out and tested the bars of the major rivers and their tributaries. For these intruders, the lifestyle was harsh and brutal. Living conditions were at first squalid, and many of the prospectors suffered from starvation, scurvy, tuberculosis and frostbite.[1]

In the years that followed, a growing number of prospectors spread throughout the Yukon River basin with hopes of finding the next big placer field. The first gold was mined from the bars of the Yukon, then from its tributaries, the Stewart, Fortymile and Sixtymile Rivers in British territory, and at the town of Circle in Alaska. Each new find heightened the interest in gold and attracted a growing number of gold seekers. Using simple tools and crude devices powered by manual labour, early prospectors extracted gold from the rocky stream bottoms throughout the district. By 1896, as many as sixteen hundred prospectors were scattered throughout the region.

The first significant settlement born of gold in the interior was Forty Mile, established in 1887. Gold had been discovered the previous autumn along the bars of the Fortymile River. The town was situated on the flat on the southeast side of the junction of the Fortymile and Yukon Rivers. Directly at their intersection was the trading post of the Alaska Commercial Company, a two-storey log structure about ten by twenty metres in size, in front of which the river steamers would land to discharge their cargoes.

It was the worst jumble of buildings one could imagine. The main businesses, such as saloons, ran parallel to the bank of the

CHAPTER 1

The first theatre in the Yukon, established in 1894, was located at the mining camp of **Forty Mile.** Veazzie Wilson photo, Gates collection.

Fortymile River. Behind them stood a collection of other businesses and log cabins huddled together without any order. One man described it as a

> collection of eighty or ninety dismal-looking log huts on a mud-bank. The shanties [were] scattered without any attempt at regularity, the marshy intervening spaces being littered with wood shavings, empty tins, and other rubbish, while numerous tree stumps show the recent origin of this Northern mining camp ... Huge placards with the words "Hotel," "Saloon," and even "Opera House" (the latter a "dive" of the lowest description) adorn some of the larger dwellings where, though bread is often lacking, whiskey is never scarce.[2]

The miners' log shacks were covered with sod roofs, which were used as gardens. There were no public services such as water or sewer. If water was required, it was drawn from the river. In the winter, this involved chopping a hole through a metre or more of ice, which froze over immediately after it was abandoned. There was no government presence until 1894; in fact, until that time, it wasn't clear whether Forty Mile was in Alaskan or British territory. The following year a detachment of twenty-two members of the North-west Mounted Police arrived at Forty Mile.

Even in these early and primitive times, the miners sought out distraction from their brutal living conditions. They frequented the saloons in the early Yukon mining towns, where drinking and gambling were among the most popular activities. From 1894 on, there was also live entertainment, though not of the high quality found in theatres in big cities.

The First Theatres in the Yukon

The first theatre was established in 1894 by George T. Snow, an actor from the coastal Alaskan town of Juneau who had prospected in the Yukon in 1888. Born James Fink in Boston in 1857, he later lived in Port Townsend, Washington, and Victoria, British Columbia, before moving north to the new mining town of Juneau in 1887. He made his first trip into the Yukon the following summer and again in 1892 before making the journey to Forty Mile in 1894 with his wife and young family and a small theatre troupe.

One observer described their performance:

> The entertainment was really excellent, especially the dancing of one or two of the girls. Some of the scenery was

really elaborate; one of the favourite turns—a drama in two chapters—in which, by the way, not a soul appeared on the stage from the first to the last[—]had for its setting a richly furnished and upholstered room with table, Chippendale chairs, heavy curtains and richly carved buffet with pier-glass complete! ... After the performance, the audience and performers could adjourn to the nearest saloon and continue to make things "a bit lively" in the course of the night. But although they were noisy—often boisterously so—and there was a rough and ready unconventionality about some of the subsequent proceedings, I never saw anything the least bit objectionable take place.[3]

The female entertainers had a hard time in the wilds of the subarctic forest, but they were also amply rewarded by the miners for the display of their talents. They were certainly a change from the Indigenous women, to whom most of the miners were accustomed, and to whom many were married. One of these actresses boasted of receiving a gold nugget from a miner for a date with him. To her embarrassment, the nugget weighed out at a value of eighty-five cents, and she was forever after known as Six Bits. Another, the youngest of the troupe, was lovingly known as the Virgin because, the miners thought, she had seen one.[4]

The following year, he relocated his theatre troupe to Circle City, Alaska, several hundred kilometres farther down the Yukon River, where gold had been discovered the year before. Circle's main street, which was fifteen metres wide and faced the river atop its bank, was dominated by the trading posts and warehouses of the rival North American Transportation and Trading Company (NAT&T CO.) and Alaska Commercial Company. These were flanked by several saloons and dance halls, of which there were said to be twenty-eight of the former and eight of the latter.

Surrounding this core of buildings was an array of log residences, each with its anti-mosquito smudge in front of the door during the summer. Among the amenities in Circle were two churches, a hospital, three blacksmith shops and a library of two thousand volumes, which were brought from Forty Mile by trader Jack McQuesten.

Circle had two theatres in the winter of 1896–97. George T. Snow's family troupe performed in the Grand Opera House. Snow and his partner, Byron Allison, started building the theatre in the spring of 1895, and eventually took the Alaska Commercial Co. in as a partner in order to complete the construction. In addition, the Circle City Miners' Association had their own log "opera house," the Tivoli, where they sponsored minstrel shows and other entertainment presented by such people as James "Nigger Jim" Daugherty (thus named for his blackface performances) and Casey Moran. These theatres were the germ of a robust entertainment industry that would soon develop in the Yukon with the discovery of gold, and the region would become known as the Klondike.

The Tivoli was constructed in March of 1896. The first professional troupe to play there was a group of six women and five men. The Tivoli was touted as being the most northerly "temple of amusement" in the world; the price of admission was two dollars and fifty cents. Despite the novelty of having live theatre in Circle, the patrons soon tired of the performance, as the same program was offered every night for seven months.

CHAPTER 1

Discovery of the Klondike

In the summer of 1896, prospector George Carmack was camped with his Indigenous wife Kate (Shaaw Tláa) and daughter Gracie several hundred kilometres above Circle City, in the shadow of the Moosehide Mountain, where the Klondike River joins the Yukon. The mountain is easily recognizable as one floats down the Yukon toward it because of a scar on the hillside that resulted from an enormous landslide that had occurred hundreds of years before. To local observers at the time, the scar was reminiscent of a Moosehide stretched out to dry, and the name stuck.

Carmack's fish camp was on the bank of the Yukon River, a short distance below the mouth of the Klondike at the foot of what would later become King Street. On the opposite side of the mouth of the Klondike River was the traditional fishing camp of the Tr'ondëk Hwëch'in, who had occupied the location seasonally for hundreds of years or longer. Later in the summer Kate's brother Skookum Jim (also known as Keish) and his nephew Tagish Charley (Káa Goox) joined them.[5] Carmack and Skookum Jim had prospected and mined together before, so they were no strangers to the enterprise. After a visit by a prospector from the Canadian Maritimes named Robert Henderson, they trekked to his camp on what Henderson had named Gold Bottom Creek, a tiny tributary whose waters eventually emptied into the Klondike River about nineteen kilometres upstream from its mouth. Carmack staked a claim there on August 11, but after hostile treatment of Jim and Charley by Henderson, they decided to return to the fish camp on the Yukon River.

The party climbed the ridge that separated Gold Bottom from Rabbit Creek, another small tributary that emptied into the Klondike about one and a half kilometres from its mouth. Running short of food, they shot a moose, and while encamped on Rabbit Creek Jim panned the creek bottom, finding gold. They tested the creek bottom up and down the valley until they selected what they felt was the most promising location, then staked four adjoining claims, with Carmack staking a double discovery claim for himself. While Jim remained at the site of their new discovery, Carmack and Charley decamped and headed for the Mounted Police headquarters at Forty Mile to file their claims with Inspector Charles Constantine, who also acted as the mining recorder. Along the way, they directed prospectors they encountered to try their luck on this new creek. Good fortune befell many of those who took their advice and staked on this Klondike tributary, which was renamed Bonanza Creek a few days later at a miners' meeting on a hill overlooking the tiny stream.

But winter was quickly coming on, and these men were trapped in the sub-zero confines of the Yukon and could not leave for the coast except at their peril. So they continued their toil, burrowing into the frozen ground and stockpiling their pay dirt until the spring thaw would allow them to sluice their winter's labour. They used the tried-and-true methods that had been perfected by veteran prospectors for mining in the permanently frozen gravel. During the winter of 1896 they set fires daily. When the frozen muck and gravel thawed, they shovelled it onto a stockpile or "dump" and started another fire, repeating the process and digging down until they reached the solid bedrock, upon which they hoped lay the gold they dreamed of. If they were lucky, it was there that they would find the gold Mother Nature had winnowed from the surrounding rocks and concentrated for millennia. This was known as the pay streak, and the gold concentrated there was so abundant that once they found the yellow nuggets, raw gold would become the standard of exchange in the Klondike for many years to follow.

CHAPTER 1

Dawson City is Established

Meanwhile, at the mouth of the Klondike River, a small cluster of log cabins developed like those at Forty Mile and Circle. One of the traders, Joe Ladue, who had a trading post eighty kilometres upstream, had the foresight to realize there would soon be a demand for lumber, so he moved his trading supplies and sawmill down to the moose pasture below the mouth of the Klondike. He applied for title to 160 acres of land at this site, had it surveyed by the government surveyor William Ogilvie and named it Dawson City in honour of George Mercer Dawson, the famed Canadian geologist who had explored the region nine years before.[6] Dawson had predicted that a great gold discovery would one day be made. Aside from the Mounted Police who had been stationed near Forty Mile the year before, Ogilvie was the only government official placed on duty in the Yukon at the time.

They didn't know it then, but the miners were digging into what would become the richest placers the world had ever seen. In October, a prospector named Louis Rhodes reached bedrock five metres below the surface on Claim Number 21 Above Discovery[7] on Bonanza Creek. There he found a gravel pay streak studded with gold nuggets. Soon other prospectors along Bonanza and its main tributary, Eldorado Creek, were hitting bedrock with similar results. Eldorado proved to be the richest creek of all. The men who staked the first forty claims above its mouth became instant millionaires. By January of 1897, five hundred claims had already been staked on this new watershed.

The Klondike miners were cut off from the outside world by ice and snow, distance and treacherous terrain. They were short of everything—except gold. There was little amusement and less for the men to do other than dig up more gold. Labourers could demand extraordinarily high fees for their services. Food was in short supply. Flour cost a dollar a pound—if you could find any. About the only thing for sale was beans. Shovels and other mining instruments were literally worth their weight in gold, but there were no sellers. And they couldn't get the gold out of the ground fast enough. Lack of labour and a limited supply of tools all conspired to slow down the mining, yet miners were still grubbing out gold in quantities that beggared avarice.

Miners from Forty Mile were soon in on the action, and a slow trickle of miners from Circle were making their way up the frozen Yukon River. With spring breakup, steamers at last began to arrive with supplies of all sorts. The first to arrive was the *Bella*, pushing a load of supplies that included whisky and gambling equipment from Circle. After a long, impoverished winter and laden with more gold than they had ever imagined, miners from the creeks began to celebrate twenty-four hours a day.

Reports of the new discovery had trickled from the Yukon during the winter and had made their way into newspapers across Canada and the United States. Dawson City grew exponentially as more newcomers arrived, pursuing the rumours they had heard in towns like Juneau, in accounts they had read in newspapers or in letters from friends. Soon there were a thousand men—and a few women—on site, feverishly building cabins and stores, saloons and dance halls. That number increased to two thousand, and then three thousand.

And even as the hopeful were arriving by the hundreds, those claim owners who had been gathering gold through the long dark winter months were eager to carry their new-found wealth outside to civilization. Outside the Yukon, interest in the gold strike was already smouldering when the first Klondikers reached Seattle and San Francisco in mid-July. The arrival of a rag-tag gathering

CHAPTER 1

of Klondike claim owners laden with the precious metal added gasoline to the embers, and the Klondike gold rush turned into a frenzied, manic stampede. The Klondike gold rush had become front-page news.

CHAPTER 2

THE GOLD RUSH BEGINS

1897

Growing Pains and Pleasures

The arrival of spring in 1897 in the Klondike brought a flood of humanity into Dawson City. The new town, less than a year old, was quickly taking form. Sounds of construction echoed across the valley. Along the waterfront tents were quickly erected, soon to be replaced by log cabins displaying signs offering every kind of product or service. As the wealth and population exploded, so did the value of waterfront property. Lots that sold for a few dollars in the fall of 1896 now sold for a thousand times more. The heart of the city was the avenue fronting the river between King Street to the north and Princess to the south. Two-storey log buildings stood shoulder to shoulder, interspersed with small cabins and tents bearing signs proclaiming saloons, hotels, restaurants and other services. Backing upon the river and facing Front Street was a "motley assemblage" of

CHAPTER 2

In the summer of 1897, Dawson City, less than a year old, was a beehive of activity. Sounds of construction echoed across the valley, and along the waterfront, tents were replaced by log cabins that displayed signs offering every kind of product or service. Library of Congress Reproduction Number: LC-DIG-ppmsca-08703.

crudely erected tents and slab buildings. In the alley between Front Street and Second Avenue was a row of cribs named Paradise Alley, housing prostitutes.

The atmosphere in Dawson was one of excitement mixed with fatigue. One observer described it as the toughest town in the country: "It was a wilderness of tents, bog over your rubber tops and log houses, saloons and dance houses until you can't rest and the general paraphernalia that goes with a mining town."[1] The gold miners, who came to town with caravans of packhorses carrying the yellow stuff, had worked tirelessly month after month underground in brutal sub-zero Arctic darkness. Now they sought their reward with gold

> **WHEN YOU ARE BLUE**
> ....GO TO....
> # The CLONDYKE,
> Good Music,
> Good Fellowship,
> and Wines.
>
> **HOLDEN & STEVENS,**
> PROPRIETORS.
> DAWSON CITY, D. C.
>
> ---
>
> **...The Palace**
> **SALOON AND DANCE HALL**
>
> Our Scales do not cheat the Miner.
>
> *POKER TABLES ALWAYS OPEN IN OUR CARD ROOMS.*
> **DAWSON CITY, - - D. C.**
>
> ---
>
> We have just received a consignment of
> **MOOSE AND CARIBOU**
> FROM THE INTERIOR.
> *Opp. News Office.*   DAWSON CITY.
>
> ---
>
> # BECKE & WILSON
>
> We Run a First Class
> *DANCE HALL and SALOON.*
>
> **For an Exciting Game Our Card Rooms Cannot be Beat.**
>
> Opp. Commercial Co's Store, DAWSON CITY.

The earliest newspaper published in Dawson City was the *Clondyke News*. In 1897, it was already advertising music and dancing in some of the Front Street establishments. *Clondyke* News, July 17, 1897, Yukon Archives.

to buy everything Dawson had to offer. Often these offerings were made in the crudest of conditions. According to W. S. Dill:

> The camp was still in its infancy when "Eye and Ear Entertainment" began to take its place in the list of primitive diversions. Performances were given in the dance-halls, without stage, footlights, scenery, or any of the usual theatrical accessories. The performers were recruited from the

various halls, and although a few of them had "done a turn" before coming to the Yukon, in the aggregate they were waitresses, box-rustlers, scales men, tin-horn gamblers and the usual hangers-on of a mining camp. Genius was served by cake-walking, the occidental occupation of oriental grace, and kicking hats off a dozen men's heads.

As a rule, the shows were terrible, despite which they ran for weeks to crowded houses. We went to the halls, anyway—it was no trouble to sit through the vaudeville while warming up for a dance ... Now and again, however, there would be offered something (for men only) that was startlingly fresh—so fresh in fact that the police would step on it and take it from the boards ...

It is difficult to trace the history of dramatic expression in Dawson, from the nights of dance-hall entertainments to the time when regular stock companies played for months in the Orpheum ... in the early days there were no organized productions. The girls gathering together a group of performers—anyone they could find—and prompted by the management, simply muddled through a programme. At that, however, there were outstanding exceptions to the general rule.[2]

In the energy and bustle, there was no time yet to build a theatre. Joe Ladue was asked whether he could mill fifty thousand board feet of lumber for an entertainment hall, but his sawmill was too busy to fill the order. He noted that George Snow's theatrical company had arrived from Circle, Alaska. "His wife is the leading lady," reported Ladue in direct language. "They are real good. They have all sorts of plays, 'Uncle Tom's Cabin' one night, 'Old Kentucky' the next, 'Camille' the next. It is a repertory company. They will have a theatre in Dawson this winter."[3] But it would be several months before one was constructed.

The streetscape of Dawson grew quickly as the gold poured in from the creeks and a continuous stream of humanity arrived on the Yukon River from outside. Tappan Adney, a journalist sent to the Klondike to report on events for *Harper's Magazine*, described Dawson as he saw it, at the beginning of November:

> First, or Main Street, the one skirting the river, sixty-six feet back from high-water, is practically the only one used. Along this street, beginning towards the barracks, the buildings consist, first, of a few small earth-covered log dwellings; then several two-story log buildings designated "hotels," with conspicuous signs in front bearing such names as "Klondike," "Dawson City," "Brewery," with more dwellings between them and caches behind; then more large houses—the "M. & M." saloon and dance-hall, the "Green Tree" hotel, the "Pioneer" or "Moose-horn" and the "Dominion" saloon, the "Palace" saloon and restaurant and the "Opera-House," built tolerably close together, the space between being filled with tents and smaller cabins used as restaurants, mining-brokers' offices, etc.[4] On the river's edge, facing this irregular row, are tents, rough buildings hastily constructed out of slabs, scows with tents built over them and warmed by Yukon stoves, and used as offices and restaurants or residences, etc. a ragged, motley assemblage ...
>
> As one walked for the first time down the smoothly beaten street, it was an animated scene, and one upon which the new-comer gazed with wonder. The Klondike had been frozen for three weeks. Snow ankle-deep lay on the ground and on the roofs of buildings. Smoke curled upwards

from bits of stovepipe in the roofs of cabins and tents. The saloons and stores and bit of sidewalk were thronged with men, more than half of whom were stamped as late arrivals by their clothes and manner. The new-comers were mostly dressed in Mackinaws with heavy cloth caps, but oldtimers were marked usually by coats of deer-skin, or the more typical parka of striped or navy-blue twill, with light fur caps of lynx, sable, mink, or beaver, unlike in shape those worn anywhere else, and big blanket-lined or fur-lined moose-hide mittens, with gauntlet tops. Men were coming and going, both with and without packs, and now and then a woman, in deer-skin coat or curiously fashioned squaw's parka of mink or squirrel skins all trotting or walking with an energetic stride, probably begotten no less of the sharp temperature than of the knowledge that the darkness of Arctic winter was fast settling down. Dogs, both Native and "outside," lay about the street under every one's feet, sleeping as if it was furthest from their minds that any one should hurt them or else in strings of two to ten were dragging prodigious loads of boxes or sacks intended for the mines or for fuel, urged on by energetic dog-punchers. Prices at which goods were selling were gathered by inquiry and from bits of paper posted on the sides of saloons or the bulletin-board at the Alaska Commercial Company's corner.[5]

The sudden population growth had outstripped the supplies that were delivered by steamers from St. Michael at the mouth of the Yukon River. Many of the new arrivals, in a hurry to reach the Klondike as quickly as possible, arrived ill equipped and without sufficient food for the long winter that loomed. Despite the gloomy prospects of famine, Dawson City had already taken on the persona of the gold-rush town by which it would forever be remembered. Tappan Adney shared his impressions:

> The stores were full of men warming themselves by the stoves and appearing to have nothing to do. The stock of goods was of course considerably larger than at [Fort] Selkirk, but there were whole rows of empty shelves where groceries should have been. The Alaska Commercial Company was selling axe-handles and sugar, that's about all. The North American Transportation Company was doing somewhat better. The warehouses, however, looked full, and men in parkas with dog-teams were sledding stuff away from piles marked with their names; but every one else was growling and cursing this or that man whom he thought responsible for the shortage, or was anxiously watching developments. It was certain that between five and six hundred persons had been forced down river, where the nearest supply of grub was said to be; several score had started up river in canoes or along the shore-ice, and no one knew how many were only waiting for the river to close to start up river. To go either way at this time, the old-timers regarded as certain death, by the ice in one direction, from cold or starvation in the other, unless help reached them on the trail.[6]

Fortunately, the famine that threatened the community early in the fall of 1897 never materialized, although many experienced shortages and hardship.

CHAPTER 2

Dawson's First Theatre Opens

By the fall of 1897, Dawson City could boast its first purpose-built theatre, the Opera House. With the growth of Dawson, real estate values escalated dramatically. The lot on which the Opera House stood on Front Street, centred between King and Queen Streets, was one of the most valuable pieces of real estate in the bustling infant town. It had sold for five dollars the previous year; in July of 1897, it was sold for $8,000; by the fall, it was valued at $15,000, and double that by Christmas.

It opened in late October, with performers previously from Circle, to much fanfare, as one observer described:

> A few nights after my arrival in Dawson I visited the theatre, which, for a week or more, had been advertising a grand opening by means of home-made posters made by daubing black paint on sheets of wrapping paper. The programme was of a Vaudeville nature, and included half a dozen song-and-dance "artists," a clod dancer, a wrestling match, and, I believe, a boxing match between Jim [Frank] Slavin, an old-time fighter, and Pat Rooney, a Canadian. The interior of the little theatre was crowded to the walls with an audience composed almost entirely of men dressed in gaudily coloured mackinaw clothes and fur coats and caps. The orchestra consisted of a piano, a violin and a flute, and the footlights were tallow candles, whose faint light was reinforced by oddly shaped reflectors made from stray bits of tin. The low ceiling was of hewn logs, and the walls on either side were lined with boxes, to which the miners could gain admission by paying double the price for liquors and cigars. The stage was a narrow affair, and very little space

intervened between the blue denim drop curtain and the back wall of the building.

The play began at the conclusion of a medley of popular airs by the orchestra, and during the ensuing performance the audience shouted and cheered at the men and women on the stage, all of whom seemed to appreciate the laughable burlesqueness of the thing, and made it seem all the more ridiculous by lending extra colour and energy to their individual efforts. The programme was concluded with the prize fight, which was quite naturally decided by the referee to be a draw, this being the only realistic event of the whole performance. While the show was going on, one of the song-and-dance artists, who enjoyed considerable popularity with the miners, was encored heavily upon singing one of the latest songs, and the miners attested their enthusiasm by greeting her with a shower of nuggets thrown on the stage.

One of the proprietors of the place mounted the footboards when the performance had ended, and announced that as soon as the hall could be cleared of the wooden benches that had served as seats, a dance would take place, to which every one was invited. The audience moved slowly out into the gambling room, the benches were piled along the walls, and the music struck up a lively waltz. The women who had performed on the stage, and others who were employed by the management to dance with the miners, went among the little groups of men who stood about the floor and along the walls asking them to dance. In a few moments the floor was crowded with a whirling, animated throng of men and women, the men making a curiously striking appearance in their furs and moccasins and bright-coloured mackinaw suits. The women were dressed in ordinary English and American costumes. The ease and grace with which many of the miners danced were rather surprising, their activity being due to the manner of life led by them, and, in a great measure, to the lightness and flexibility of their moccasins and muck-lucks.

At the conclusion of the dance the couples promenaded to the bar, where the men drank liquor or smoked cigars, and then handed their gold sacks to the cashier behind the bar, who weighed out four shillings (or one dollar), in payment for the liquor and the privilege of the waltz. The women were given a check, which would afterwards be cashed by the management for a shilling (or twenty-five cents), and in addition to this each one was paid a weekly salary varying from two to ten pounds (or ten to fifty dollars). The women in the dance-halls were always well behaved, and the ribald scenes and shocking familiarity that are popularly supposed to occur in Dawson dance-halls never take place. Those who would see these things must go to cities of the older and more "civilized" countries.

By the time the dancers returned from the bar the caller would be shouting, "Well, where is all them good waltzers? Grab a girl, you fellows, and take a spin roun'," and other pressing invitations hard to resist. The music would probably begin with a polka, and there would soon be witnessed the lively spectacle of a few moments before. Then the floor manager would call for a square dance, and the miners who were unable to solve the mysteries of the mazy waltz were given an opportunity to gyrate. The square dances were always animated and full of life, but the enthusiasm of the dancers never led them beyond the bounds of a common propriety.[7]

The large log structure operated on a business model adopted later by other theatres along the waterfront. It contained a saloon and gambling area at the front and a theatre/dance hall in the rear where vaudeville performances were offered to patrons for several hours each evening before the dancing began.

These dance hall/theatres never closed, although restrictions were eventually put in place by the North-west Mounted Police, who imposed a closure of the drinking, gambling and vaudeville performances from midnight Saturday night until early Monday morning. On Sundays, in place of the usual entertainment, the performers put on "sacred" concerts that would pass the scrutiny of the ever-watchful Mounted Police. For those who wished to carry the usual festivities into the Lord's Day, at least in the summer, a river steamer and barge were chartered, and the revellers would make their way out of town either up or down the Yukon River, where, beyond the long reach of the law, the partying could continue.

On November 25, 1897, fire swept through the business section of Dawson, destroying the newly constructed Opera House as well as the M&N Saloon and Dance Hall, the Dominion Saloon and several other buildings. A masquerade ball was held in the Opera House that night. Dawson had no firefighting equipment, and with the mercury dipping to the bottom of the thermometer there was little water with which to fight the blaze. Firefighters used dynamite to blow up buildings adjacent to the blaze to prevent the fire from spreading. With the Opera House at least temporarily out of commission, the unemployed entertainers found work in other establishments.

CHAPTER 2

Tex Rickard: The Invisible Door

One of the first characters to arrive on the scene was George Lewis "Tex" Rickard. Rickard was born in Wyandotte County, Kansas, on January 2, 1870, but his family moved to Texas when he was four years old. When he was older, he worked as a ranch hand to provide money for his impoverished family. In 1894, he married and was elected city marshal of Henrietta, Texas, but a short time later his wife and infant son both died.

Unattached, in a depressed economy, Rickard headed north to Juneau, Alaska, in November 1895, where he spent his time playing poker. In April of 1896, he crossed the Chilkoot Trail, built a boat and floated down the Yukon River to the tiny gold-rush community of Circle, Alaska, arriving dead broke.

Tex got a job working for "Silent Sam Bonnifield" in his gambling establishment. That day, says biographer Charles Samuels, Tex "walked through the invisible door into that all-male, never-land in which he spent the rest of his life."[8] Tall, slim and soft spoken, Bonnifield was a rarity—an honest professional gambler. Like Bonnifield, Rickard was a better listener than a talker, who "never had two sentences to rub together in his life and he was always like that, Circle City to Coney Island and back."

One piece of advice Bonnifield offered Tex: "Either be a gold miner *or* a gambler. You can't be both."[9] But when word of the Klondike strike reached Circle early in 1897, the twenty-six-year-old Tex partnered with Harry Ash, and in February of 1897 they assembled a dog team and headed off through the ice and snow to get in on the action. It took twenty days for the two men to haul a heavily laden sled up the Yukon River to the new strike. Once they arrived, Tex acquired an interest in Claim Numbers 3 and 4 Below Discovery on Bonanza Creek, just below those staked by George Carmack,

Skookum Jim and Jim's nephew, Tagish Charley. He quickly flipped them for a cool $60,000. With this money, he partnered with Tom Turner and established The Northern, a saloon and gaming hall.

In just four months they made $155,000, but in one bad night at the gaming tables, they lost it all, including The Northern, and Tex was broke once again. For the next fifteen months, he tended bar at the Monte Carlo, barely keeping ahead of his debts. Though he was making $20 a day, he frequently went to bed hungry.

Jack London: The Witness

An aspiring young author and newly minted prospector came north, lured by opportunity in the Klondike along with a legion of others. Accompanying a brother-in-law who was much older and less physically fit, Jack London followed the Chilkoot Trail into the Yukon. Having left in late July, his party was able to breach the coast mountains, construct a boat and make its way down the Yukon River before freeze-up in the autumn of 1897. Instead of continuing into Dawson City, however, they established themselves in an unused cabin on Break-up Island at the mouth of the Stewart River. They staked claims on nearby Henderson Creek, then, in mid-October, London accompanied a couple of others downriver to Dawson to file their claims with the mining recorder there.

London spent only a few weeks in Dawson City before returning to Break-up Island on December 7, but he was able to witness the bustling and swiftly growing community before the great stampede that would arrive the following spring. He had an inquiring mind, a sharp wit and a compelling intellect; he found himself talking to the sourdoughs, absorbing their stories like a sponge and engaging in lively discussion with both stampeders and sourdoughs about important social issues.[10] It is unclear how much of his time was spent working on his claim on Henderson Creek, or whether he did any work at all after staking, though it appears that he took the time to construct a log cabin on the Henderson Creek plot.[11]

London may have had plans to stay longer in the Yukon, but he was stricken by the miner's scourge: scurvy. As soon as the Yukon River broke up in mid-May, he was back in Dawson, afflicted with the symptoms of the feared disease. Although his condition worsened, he was able to visit some of the haunts he had frequented during his earlier trip to the town. On June 8, he departed Dawson City by canoe with two others. When they reached Anvik he was given some fresh potatoes and a can of tomatoes to ease his symptoms, but by then, he reported being crippled from the waist down.

London eventually returned to California and recovered from his illness. He set about writing of his experiences in the North. His novel *The Call of the Wild* propelled him to instant fame, and he continued to dig into his Klondike experiences to fuel his creativity. Half the short stories he wrote during his career were based upon his personal experiences in the North, and when he ran out of his own story ideas, he wrote letters to sourdough friends seeking inspiration for more stories.

Many sourdoughs tell of their encounters with Jack London, but few such claims can be verified. It is said that London was often seen drinking with the notorious Swiftwater Bill Gates, but that was physically impossible: Gates had left the Yukon over the Dalton Trail in September 1897, while London came into the Yukon by the Chilkoot Trail, not reaching Dawson City until a month after Gates had fled town.[12]

Swiftwater Bill: Exaggerated Indifference

Bill Gates was one of the most colourful characters woven into the fabric of myth surrounding the gold rush. In 1896, he was a nobody, a dishwasher in a saloon in Circle City, Alaska. Like many others, he heard the siren call of the Klondike and partnered with six other men leasing unlucky Claim Number 13 on Eldorado Creek.[13] Shaft after shaft they sank, each one barren and dispiriting, until Bill found himself alone to pursue the yellow metal on this bad-luck claim. Then he sank a shaft that hit the pay streak. Suddenly, he was one of the richest men in the Klondike, worth hundreds of thousands of dollars (which would be millions today if you allow for inflation).

He went from being a nobody to a celebrity overnight. Everywhere he went, he drew attention to himself with his wild and extravagant behaviour. He gambled with a passion and become known for his pricey and impulsive bets. Bill liked the ladies too, and one lady in particular—Gussie Lamore. Nineteen-year-old Gussie had been an entertainer in Circle City who had followed opportunity to Dawson. Bill wanted her at any price; in fact, at one point, he offered her weight in gold if she would marry him.

When he caught Gussie stepping out on him, even his revenge was of the type that drew attention. Gussie loved eggs, and when Bill saw her with another man, he vowed to deny her that indulgence unless she came home with him. In the dark of the winter of 1897 eggs were hard to find, and those that were available had been on the trail six months or more and were gamey and aromatic, but Gussie loved them anyway. Bill bought up the entire supply in Dawson, and this act became legend. He was forever after known as "the Knight of the Golden Omlette."[14] The number of eggs involved and the price he paid for them varies from one account to the next, but the result was the same. Gussie had the final word on this episode in a newspaper interview a few years later: "I went down to the store to buy some eggs," she said. "Lordy how I wanted some eggs for breakfast. Well, Bill was in the store when I goes in. He sees I want the eggs and while I'm talking with the clerk, see, he buys up the whole consignment at $1 apiece. Then he says to me, 'Now, my dear, if you want eggs for breakfast, come home where you belong.'" She added, "Well, say, I was just dying for them eggs, and I came to my milk like a lady. I goes home with Bill."[15]

Joe Boyle (*left*) and Swiftwater Bill Gates were two of the most prominent figures in the early days of Dawson City. Boyle went on to become one of the richest men in the Klondike. Gates went through several fortunes—and several wives.
Yukon Archives, Oxford Historical Society collection, 84/78 #34.

Bill headed outside to San Francisco in a small party in September 1897, ostensibly to purchase supplies for his partner, Bill Smith, who remained in Dawson, tending to business. Gates was joint owner of the Monte Carlo saloon and dance hall, one of the most famous establishments in the Klondike heyday. Gates left Dawson in the company of Joe Boyle, who would later become one of the richest of the Klondike kings. Their trip out of the Yukon in the fall of 1897 over the Dalton Trail was plagued by an ice-filled Yukon River, blizzards and a harrowing passage on the trail and the Chilkat Pass. They almost perished, surviving mainly because of the iron resolve of Boyle to get them through.[16]

Swiftwater Bill left an unforgettable trail of his travels, for he seemed to thrive on publicity. In Victoria, the *Colonist*, upon his arrival, described him:

> A mixture of buckskin and diamonds was the first impression he gave one as he posed on the *Seattle* with exaggerated indifference and a blasé air, a sort of "don't I look weary" sort of expression on his bearded face. He was dressed in buckskin, while on the bosom of his shirt was stuck a diamond as big as a filbert and a big solitaire glowed on a ring on his finger. Bill has the reputation of being worth a cool million and has an interest in a goodly number of claims. He cut a big swath at Dawson, and while he pretends to be indifferent evidently likes to be talked about.[17]

Arriving in Seattle, Swiftwater Bill was seen dressed in a flashy manner and sporting one of the largest nuggets to come out of the Klondike that fall. In San Francisco, he rented a suite of rooms in the Baldwin Hotel, then proceeded to draw attention to himself by handing out gold nuggets in a conspicuous fashion and tipping the bellboys in the hotel to point him out as the "King of the Klondike."[18] But he was a walking contradiction. Although he dressed the part of a wealthy man in a Prince Albert coat, diamond stickpin and cufflinks, "in spite of his munificence, the illusion was shattered by his small stature, and ragged beard, for Swiftwater Bill was as meek-looking an individual as ever sold ribbon."[19]

Bill was supposed to be in San Francisco to purchase bar fixtures and other supplies for the new saloon that Smith was having built back in Dawson City, but he had other ideas, and his money was disappearing fast. He had chosen San Francisco for this task, not for any practical business reason, but because that was where Gussie was. But she couldn't marry him—she was already married with a three-year-old child—so he married her younger sister Grace instead.

Bill indulged his new bride with a $25,000 mansion in Oakland and showered her with gifts, but the marriage didn't last long.[20] Grace was apparently a pale substitute for Gussie, and she knew it. She was prepared to stand aside and let Bill fulfill his passion for Gussie. "This will be no sacrifice on my part," Grace said, "for I hate the very ground he walks on and abhor him and his name."[21] Soon after, they were divorced.

After all his extravagances, Gates soon found himself strapped for cash, so he found an investor named Doctor Wolf who was willing to advance him $20,000 for ninety days at the exorbitant rate of 100 per cent interest. Bill and Wolf went to Seattle to set up a transportation company. While the doctor attended to business, Bill gathered a bevy of women who were hired to work in the Monte Carlo. He stayed at the Rainier-Grand, one of Seattle's best hotels, where he bathed in champagne for the press and left a whopping bill ($1,500) for damages behind.

Gates returned to the Yukon with Wolf over the Chilkoot Trail. Wolf pushed on ahead over the ice while Bill remained in the boom town of Bennett with his bevy of showgirls. Rumours circulated that Bill had drowned at Lake Bennett—he even paid a reporter $100 to write a story about his drowning just to keep his name in the papers—but as soon the ice broke up on Lake Bennett, he followed Wolf to Dawson City, where he arrived a short time later in a Peterborough canoe "with two scow loads of girls and whiskey in its wake.[22] Swiftwater himself sat in the prow of the canoe, a silk topper cocked on his head, his Prince Albert coat draped across his shoulders, his arms extended in welcome to the crowd that stood on the banks to greet him. Directly behind him a girl was perched on a case of whiskey, and on the scows other girls waved prettily and shouted saucy greetings to the onlookers."[23]

By now, Dr. Wolf was aware of Swiftwater's profligate behaviour. In early June of 1898, Wolf was waiting at the waterfront when the Gates flotilla arrived at the Dawson waterfront. When Swiftwater stepped ashore, Dr. Wolf blocked him. A hush fell over the large welcoming crowd. Wolf delivered an ultimatum: Gates had three hours to come up with the $20,000 and forget the interest. Gates wilted noticeably, but within three hours, he produced the gold. Nobody knows how he procured it, and it was one of the few times that money loaned to Swiftwater Bill Gates ever found its way back into the lender's pocket. Without hope of receiving the interest that had been promised him, Wolf booked passage on a boat headed upriver, thankful to have seen the last of the gold-rush town, and of Swiftwater Bill Gates.

Shortly after this incident, Bill Smith bought out Gates's interest in the saloon, the whisky and the girls. It was temporarily closed, but Dawson was promised that "amicable arrangements were under way for the re-opening."[24] Meanwhile, Gates continued to capture the limelight with one escapade after another. His life was to become a real-life melodrama and ultimately was converted into live theatre. It was the harbinger of things to come: Dawson was about to be transformed into the "Paris of the North" as thousands upon thousands of eager gold seekers converged on the Klondike during the frantic, exhilarating 1898 summer of gold.

CHAPTER 3

THE BOOM YEAR

1898

The Tr'ondëk Hwëch'in

For thousands of years, the mouth of the Klondike River had been a settlement for First Nations people who occupied the land in the Yukon Valley. It was a favoured location for harvesting the annual salmon run, as witnessed by the early prospectors who came into this region in the latter part of the nineteenth century. The Indigenous people, who today call themselves the Tr'ondëk Hwëch'in, set up fish traps at the river's mouth. In fact, the name *Klondike* was a corruption of the Hän language name for the tributary: Tr'ondëk. Their fish camp is known as Tr'ochëk, and as many as two hundred Tr'ondëk Hwëch'in assembled there each year in late summer to capture the returning salmon. They had established cabins and other structures as dwellings, caches and fish smokers necessary to living and procuring food at the mouth of the river.

When gold was discovered on Rabbit Creek (now Bonanza) in 1896, everything about the traditional lifestyle of these people was changed forever. With the introduction of gold mining came new religions, new types of land use that were foreign to them, and a new structure of governance that ignored the Indigenous occupation of the land. In the fall of 1896, the first miners streaming into the Klondike valley saw the strategic advantages to securing land near the mouth of the Klondike River. For a few dollars or a few hundred, the Tr'ondëk Hwëch'in sold their cabins, unaware that this implied the purchase included the land on which the cabins stood. The concept of property ownership, as viewed by the newcomers, was foreign to the Indigenous people's traditional way of seeing the land. In short order, the Tr'ondëk Hwëch'in were displaced by the growing number of miners, so they moved across the Klondike River to south Dawson, where they found that their occupation of the land conflicted with that of the North-west Mounted Police.

Bishop Bompas, the Anglican missionary, championed their cause and applied to the government for title to this land. The exchanges of correspondence between Bompas and the government in Ottawa were interminably slow; by the time the appropriate permission had been granted, a different arrangement had been reached. Bompas and the Tr'ondëk Hwëch'in came to an agreement with Inspector Charles Constantine of the Mounted Police to move to another traditional fish camp five kilometres down the Yukon River at the mouth of Moosehide Creek.[1] Meanwhile, the transformation of the traditional campsite was fast, and the land below Moosehide Mountain was profoundly impacted. By the spring of 1897, Tr'ochëk was the site of several hundred tents, a trading post, a sawmill and two saloons. By the fall of 1897, the presence of the traditional camping site of the Tr'ondëk Hwëch'in at the mouth of the Klondike was obliterated. Even the name had been changed to Lousetown, but it also became known by the more genteel name of Klondike City. For the next two years, the influx of newcomers never stopped, and the Tr'ondëk Hwëch'in culture was decimated. It was not until nearly a century later, with the signing of the Tr'ondëk Hwëch'in Final Agreement with the territorial and federal governments in 1998, that the First Nation again emerged as a force in the community.

Boomtown in a Bog

Meanwhile, gold continued to flow into Dawson City from Klondike mines in unimaginable quantities in 1898. A constant stream of new arrivals crowded the shoreline. Tents sprang up by the hundreds; by mid-July, the Mounted Police counted over four thousand people as well as nearly thirteen hundred log buildings.[2] In the heart of the business section, facing the Yukon River, these simple cabins were replaced with two- and three-storey log structures with false clapboard facades, creating a veneer of sophistication over the rough-and-ready avenue that was rapidly growing. At the south end of the waterfront was the stockade of the North-west Mounted Police. North of that was a long line of hotels, saloons (thirty-three by count), gambling parlours, music halls, restaurants (forty-two by count) and theatres. Beside these were sixteen doctors' offices, six jewellery stores and seven laundries. To the north of these, Front Street was dominated by massive commercial stores of the Alaska Commercial and the North American Transportation and Trading Companies.[3]

Within months, the population of Dawson exploded from three thousand to nearly sixteen thousand. As many as forty thousand were scattered throughout the territory.[4] The city struggled to keep up with the accelerating expansion, and problems including constant construction, a lack of goods and services, a lack of sanitary facilities, and continual coming and going under the midnight sun.

Front Street, August 1898. Two- and three-storey log structures with false clapboard facades created a veneer of sophistication over the rough-and-ready avenue that was rapidly growing on the bank of the Yukon River. Dawson City Museum, 1999.398.58.

The Klondike was a case study in extremes. Dawson City was nestled in the wilderness thousands of kilometres from civilization, yet it quickly became the most modern and cosmopolitan of cities. It was a land of great fortune and bounty for some, failure and hardship for others. Some lived on champagne, while others ate beans. The summer days were long and warm; the winter nights were equally long and bitterly cold. Amid the excitement and aura of gold, men and women were suffering from scurvy, malnutrition and consumption. Typhoid fever reached epidemic proportions, a product of poor sanitation and a lack of clean drinking water.

CHAPTER 3

Crowd on Front Street, Dawson City on July 4, 1899. Thousands of people milled about the waterfront celebrating American Independence Day. One observer likened it to the fair grounds at the World's Fair. Dawson City Museum, 1982.1.82.

The smell of sawdust and shit mingled with the sound of hammers pounding, music playing and the jumble of a dozen different languages. When the weather was warm and dry, the streets were hard and dusty; with a few days of rain, they turned to muddy quagmires that sucked the boots off men's feet and mired teams of horses and their drivers knee deep in the muck. Thousands milled about the waterfront—it was a gigantic carnival. One observer even likened it to the fairgrounds at the World's Fair.[5] Amid it all were the saloons, dance halls and theatres. It was a crazy place. One observer wrote:

> Before they settled down to gaming, dancing, or drinking, men paraded up and down the water front, as they had done in the day time. For in this Arctic city at ten o'clock at night,

the sun still shone brightly. There were no street lamps, no advertisements flashing down on the crowds; but the streets were animated as Broadway or Piccadilly Circus. Up and down the crowd wandered aimlessly, talked, laughed, joked, sang and drifted into saloons. These generally had drawn their blinds, and showed through their opened doors their brilliant interiors, lit up to give a semblance of night and gaiety, enticing all to come in. Outside, scores of people stood watching the scene, greeting friends, or just waiting there, until someone they wanted to see turned up. Through the middle of them a constant stream pushed and shoved their way in or out, elbowing their way to the bars or through the drink saloon to the gaming rooms at the back.[6]

Amid the chaos, the North-west Mounted Police imposed a strict regime of law and order in which handguns and gunfights were forbidden. Front Street thronged with dense crowds, especially for celebrations like the Queen's birthday and the Fourth of July. The population of Dawson was a polyglot assemblage of nations, dominated by Americans on British soil; as much as 80 per cent of the population was American.

In particular, the Mounted Police enforced rigorous oversight on the mining camp; it was even forbidden to chop wood on the Lord's day of rest. At the peak of the gold rush, the Mounted Police injected the stability that made Dawson City and the Klondike one of the most orderly gold rushes in history. Inspector Harper of the Mounted Police reported:

> I consider, taking into consideration the kind of town Dawson is, and the very respectable way in which the music halls are conducted, they are no worse than some of the

entertainments I have seen in the music halls in some parts of London. With the exception of one man who was summoned before me under section 177 of the Criminal Code and fined $50 and cost, there have been no complaints whatever regarding the morality of the entertainments. The dance halls and gambling places are also conducted in an orderly manner, the proprietors of the same being very quick to stop any row or disturbance that may commence in their establishment, knowing that they will be punished, should they allow such a state of affairs to exist.[7]

Thousands of gold seekers arrived over the short summer, joining the seasoned veterans of the mines on the Klondike creeks. Said one veteran miner,

We had earned our fun, earned it by the terrors and hardships of that awful trail, by packing for hundreds of miles, by the horrors of the rapids, by the blinding blizzards that we faced, by the grueling toil of digging day after day on our claims; by the incessant chopping of cord-wood to keep fires burning which would thaw the ground; by suffering from scurvy; by want and by untold privation and loneliness. Yes, we had earned a night of pleasure even if persons might call it a night of orgy.[8]

The new arrivals were voyeurs to this remarkable sideshow. During the summer of 1898, Dawson became the hub, Front Street became the epicentre, and the saloons, dance halls and theatres became the crossroads where friends met, where business was transacted and where men indulged in all the pleasures that the avenue had to offer. Later in the season, when winter beset the Klondike, the miners left their "cold, dark cabins and rough fare and came to town and went into the warm and well-lighted saloons, where there was always music of some sort, dancing and women, that many a man went to pieces and squandered all he possessed."[9]

But during the summer of 1898, there was a general air of excitement, of happening, of adventure. The throng that milled about the streets, seemingly wandering aimlessly from one saloon to another, caused one observer to write, "If a stranger should happen to drop into Dawson during the cool of a pleasant evening, he would almost certainly come to one of three conclusions: either a circus is in town, or a big fire is in process of wiping the city out of existence or else an exceedingly exciting election is pending ... there are so many men that if you wish to make any progress at all, you must leave the sidewalk and betake yourself to the middle of the street."[10]

For those with gold, everything was available to them: booze, women, gambling and entertainment. Those without the glittering metal witnessed a sideshow like nothing they had ever seen before or would ever see again, and the businesses were quick to take advantage. Edward Trelawney-Ansell wrote:

> Dawson in those days was a mixed stew of wild excitement, misery, starvation, debauchery, scurvy, frost bites, colossal fortunes made suddenly, and many suicides from misery and despair. The land we had all hoped for was not a land of gold in the streets, as so many fools had thought. It was a land of want and cold—cold of such severity that few would have believed it possible. The coldest place is not the North Pole: It is the Yukon Valley ... in Dawson ... the saloons and gambling halls were the clubs in which the incoming miners from the creeks met with their pokes full of dust. The saloons were open day and night, always ablaze with light—*and*

always warm. It was the warmth, the light, the liquor and the less than half-clad women which drew the miners, the moths who would get their wings scorched.[11]

When the long summer nights gradually turned to autumn, and then quickly to winter, these establishments became a refuge from the loneliness and cold. While those flush with gold were playing at the gaming tables or buying rounds of drinks, others less fortunate huddled near the stove for warmth. The buildings were hermetically sealed against the bitter cold, with the only means of ventilation being through a small vent in the roof. On busy nights with the men crowded in shoulder to shoulder, the smell of unwashed bodies, smoke and tobacco combined to create a noxious bouquet that was not altogether pleasant.[12] There was always a barrel full of drinking water with a ladle to drink from. As the evening progressed, many of them stretched out to sleep in the warmth, and the proprietors allowed this, knowing full well that today's indigent might become tomorrow's "Eldorado king," a reference to the Klondike's richest tributary.

A Northern Broadway

In addition to the Opera House, which had been rebuilt in the months following the November 1897 fire, other establishments of entertainment were opening. Like Swiftwater Bill, Charlie Kimball had made his fortune with his Klondike mining property, and he then invested one hundred thousand dollars in a theatre he named The Pavilion. Located on King Street between Second and Third Avenues, the earliest version sported a vertical board and batten facade with a large sign across the front of the building. It opened

The Opera House was the first proper theatre constructed in Dawson City. The owners went broke when it was destroyed by fire in January of 1900, and it was never rebuilt. Dawson City Museum, 1984.47.3.

the evening of June 13, 1898, and took in $12,000 the first night.[13] Kimball was delighted at this new way to make money and started to celebrate. Over the next three months, he made and spent $300,000, but when he sobered up from this spree, he had lost his theatre and dance hall and was left with nothing.

Included on the playbill for his new establishment were names that would become theatrical regulars around Dawson: the Newman children, Maude Roselle, Emma Forest, Jacqueline and Rosaline (lovingly known as Glycerine and Vaseline), Caprice, Gracie Robinson, Fred Breen, the midget comedian, Dick Maurettus, Myrtle Drummond and Nellie "the Pig" Lamore.[14]

CHAPTER 3

The Pavilion first opened on King Street on June 13, 1898. Its owner, Charlie Kimball, invested $100,000 in it. He took in $12,000 the first night, but within three months he had lost his theatre and dance hall and was left with nothing. Dawson City Museum, 1962.6.11.

Nellie Lamore got her moniker because the first night she was in Dawson, she

> had a couple of suckers in a box at the Dominion [Saloon] who were buying her champagne. As it cost twenty dollars per pint, she insisted the waiter address her as "madam." He made some crack as to what the title implies, which she resented, so she bit his ear off as they clinched and fell down the steps to the dance floor. Seeing her wallowing in the sawdust with the waiter, some of us dubbed her there and then. She had a little turned up nose, so that she had to wear a broad-brimmed hat in the rain to keep the water off the roof of her mouth. But she was goodness itself, when she wasn't drunk ...[15]

Glycerine and Vaseline once worked Irishman Roddy Connor out of the $50,000 he had made from the sale of his mine. Connor loved to dance, and with his remarkable stamina, there was no girl who could keep up with him on the dance floor, so Glycerine and Vaseline took turns dancing with him. He spent from $500 to $2,000 a night on them until it was all gone.[16]

The Oatley Sisters: "Wonders of Their Kind"

Other entertainment in Dawson was provided by the Oatley Sisters, who were quick to establish themselves on the scene. Lottie and Polly Oatley were veterans of the theatrical circuit in the southwestern United States. In 1890, as young teenagers, they were on the playbill of the Novelty Theatre in Ogden, Utah. Both were said to be the best buck-and-wing tap dancers around, and by October 1897, when performing at the Legal Tender Saloon in Tucson, Arizona, Lottie was heralded as the champion lady dancer of the United States.[17]

Within a few days of their arrival in Dawson, they were open for business. Their first dance hall in Dawson was nothing more than a wooden platform with a frame covered with canvas on King Street near Second Avenue, to the rear of the Bank Saloon. Here, accompanied by a fiddler and a big German American with a pompadour hairstyle and a portable organ and two or three other girls, they started their business. They charged a dollar for a dance that was three rounds of the platform, and at the time it was the best entertainment on offer in town. The sisters would sing, and when a crowd had gathered, the makeshift orchestra would strike up a tune and the girls would begin dancing. After twenty dances, the sisters and the other girls would take a break before starting all over again. Doing this, they were pulling in $500 a week each, and soon they had

CHAPTER 3

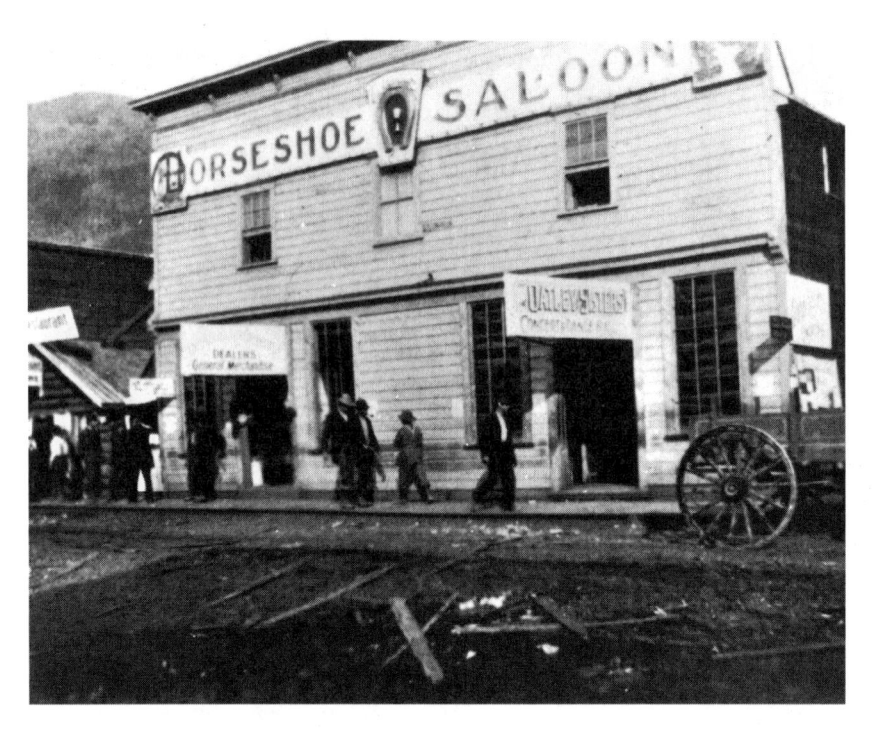

The Oatley sisters rented space for their concert and dance hall in the Horseshoe Saloon. According to stampeder Bert Parker, "I stood there with my mouth open night after night listening to the Oatley Sisters sing those sad ballads. I never knew the sisters personally, but they helped me to put many a lonesome night behind me." Tyrrell collection, Fisher Library, University of Toronto, Brown Album 1898-9 #126.

enough to establish themselves in a more substantial venue.[18] By July 12, they had set up the Oatley Sisters' Concert and Dance Hall in the Horseshoe Saloon, where they were receiving good reviews in the newspapers.

The routine was simple. As described by one witness:

> It was full of menfolk who stood and gawked at one or more couples whirling lustily in time with the fiddler's false music. When the dance ended, a red-haired Irishman, the master

of ceremonies, sang out that all the men should take their partners to the bar, and to the bar they went—this happened after every dance. At the bar the women get a check instead of whisky, which the men usually take; and, when the dancing stops for the night, the women receive twenty-five cents per check from the saloon-keeper. As soon as a girl has received her "treat," she hurries back into the crowd to engage a partner for the next dance because there it is always ladies' choice—and soon we see another miner swinging merrily on his iron-soled shoes or moccasins with a "beautiful" girl in his arms. This means more to the old miners than all the gold in Klondike—and thus the merriment continues until "the small hours" when we may chance to see them again as we go to our work, they having just finished for the night and being on their way to the restaurant or to their little cabins.[19]

Bert Parker, who was in Dawson as a young man during the gold rush, remembered the Oatley Sisters many years later and their impact upon him:

> I stood there with my mouth open night after night listening to the Oatley Sisters sing those sad ballads. I never knew the sisters personally, but they helped me to put many a lonesome night behind me. I take this opportunity of thanking them, if they are still alive. I think of all my recollections of Dawson City, this is the sweetest. Long after the girls and the gold and the gamblers were gone, long after I had stopped selling papers in the gaming houses and settled down in a more prosaic life, the memory of their songs remains. I can remember every word of every verse they sang, just as

CHAPTER 3

In the Dawson City dance halls, after the variety acts ended, chairs were pulled to the side, the orchestra would commence playing and patrons would dance until the early hours of the morning. The girls received a percentage of the take on every dance—and drink. Tappan Adney, Gates collection.

> I heard it half a century ago as an eighteen-year-old kid in the Klondike.[20]

They may have enthralled him with their singing, but others came out simply to witness their capacity for alcohol consumption. One correspondent noted that "their remarkable capacity for drink, if nothing else should attract a good patronage out of mere curiosity to see two girls who are put to bed drunk every night yet retain the bloom of youth, bright eyes, good voice, and lively heels. They are wonders of their kind."[21] Like many other entertainers who became dance hall managers, the Oatley Sisters did not remain managers for long. By February of the following year, they had relinquished their spot in the Horseshoe Saloon and were performing in the Novelty Theatre farther down Front Street.[22]

"Packed to Suffocation"

Front Street quickly became the Klondike's answer to Broadway. On August 1, the Combination Music Hall opened to a crowd that was "packed to suffocation, jammed clean to the doors, through the saloon and out into the street." Featured on the playbill for the evening were Dick Maurettus, Lucille Elliott, Emma Hull and Nellie Lamore, John and Carrie Linton, and John Mulligan.[23] Mulligan and his wife, also named Carrie, had been performing vaudeville and burlesque in theatres all along the Pacific Coast before coming to the Klondike. In Dawson, Mulligan was a multitalented thespian whose "impersonations were apt and his comedy infectious."[24] He turned his talent to writing the scripts for a series of bawdy and satirical productions inspired by local events. He wrote the farce *The Adventures of Stillwater Willie* about Swiftwater Bill and his infatuation with Gussie Lamore. Gussie's sister Nellie played the leading role. Swiftwater Bill, who attended the performance, showed his appreciation from his private box by laughing and applauding. Nellie later won first prize at a costume ball wearing a top hat, a Prince Albert coat and a sign that read "Stillwater Willie, the Mayor of Lousetown."[25] Gates showed his appreciation again later when Mulligan produced a sequel, *Stillwater Willie's Wedding Night*, at the Palace Grand Theatre.

Other Mulligan creations followed: *Casey the Fiddler*, *The Business Block*, *Hotel Life in Dawson* and *Ole Olsen in the Klondike*. *Working a Lay in the Klondike* was performed in the Opera House in December of 1899, while *The Coming Cheechako* was produced by

Dick Maurettus and Fred Breen. *King for a Day*, a one-act burlesque, was produced at the Palace Grand in June of 1900. Although we know where and when they were performed, none of the scripts for these plays is known to have survived.[26]

H. B. S. Marcus, the owner of the Combination, described his operation. The entertainment began at three o'clock in the afternoon and continued for the next seventeen hours. The price of a seat was $2.50, but the main source of revenue came from the drinks sold. Beer cost $6 a bottle, wine $40 per pint and whisky sold for fifty cents a shot. "What we want above all in women," he said, "is voice, and plenty of it, good and strong, for variety business is our long suit, and plenty of singing is required."[27] Just like at other establishments, while the men worked for a fixed wage, the actresses, when not performing on stage, made extra money receiving a percentage of all the drinks they induced patrons to consume. The entertainment lasted until midnight or later, after which tables and chairs were moved aside, and dancing continued until seven or eight o'clock in the morning.[28]

On August 4 the Monte Carlo, formerly owned by Swiftwater Bill, was reopened under the management of W. M. Wilson, with Fred Breen acting as stage manager.[29] The theatre was quite impressive for its day, yet at the same time displayed the characteristics of an isolated and remote boom town, where some items were available in abundance while others could not be had at any price. In addition to the saloon, through which patrons had to pass to get to the theatre, there was a second bar in the theatre itself. Tappan Adney, writing for *Harper's Magazine*, described the scene:

> The stage was commodious, and in some there was real painted scenery, but in others the "scenery" consisted solely of a screen of striped bed-ticking or similar goods, which

was also used abundantly for wall coverings. The audience were seated on boards placed on stools; but "Eldorado kings," government officials, and other "dead game sports" "spending their money," occupied "boxes" on one or both sides of the pit, and raised sufficiently to allow the occupants, who sat upon hand-made board stools, to see over the heads of the common herd. The price of admission was 50 cents ... For the boxes there was no extra fixed charge, but occupants of such were expected to receive female members of the troupe, or any lady friends they themselves might choose to bring in, to help them dispose of champagne, which varied in price from $40 a quart to $40 a pint. At the opening of the Monte Carlo one man spent $1700 for wine during one night. The same evening two girls opened forty-eight bottles of wine, receiving $4 commission on each bottle.

The orchestra consisted usually of piano, violin, trombone, and cornet, and musicians were each paid $20 a day. The actors and actresses received various salaries, $150 a week prevailing ... The show was a succession of vaudeville parts, interspersed with impromptu local sketches, which were changed each week. Some of the performers, who came out of English and American concert-halls, gave a fairly good performance; while their impromptu jibes and horse-pranks would convulse the audience, who were never over-critical, for whom the humor could not be too broad for them to relish, and who never tired of the same performances night after night.

Many of the songs turned on something of local interest, as "Christmas in the Klondike," or "The Klondike Millionaire," and when sung by Freddy Breen, "The Irish Comedian," sounded not badly, but when committed to paper were the veriest doggerel. Of the female vocalists, with one or two exceptions, the less said the better. Untrained, never even second rate, at times they sadly tried even the patient Klondike audience.[30]

The lineup for the opening consisted of several acts known to the patrons of Dawson's Broadway: Freda Maloof, the "Turkish Whirlwind," was hired to perform "all of the Turkish Harem Dances." Jacqueline and Rosaline were featured; also included on the program for the evening were Beatrice Leon, Emma Forest, Caprice, Gracie Robinson, Frank Howard and Fred Breen along with "others all high in the niches of art in their respective lines."[31]

The Newman Children: Family Entertainment

Soon to be a popular attraction at the Monte Carlo were the Newman children, George, Willie and Margie, who had first arrived in Dawson in the spring with their parents. They had been performing at the Theater Royal in Skagway, Alaska, and the Olympia Hotel in Dyea, Alaska, before departing for the Klondike around the end of May.[32] Their first stage appearance was the week of July 5 at the Pavilion, followed a short time later at the Mascot Theatre, also on Front Street, on its opening night. The children were paraded down Front Street on donkeys draped in advertising for the Mascot, which was located opposite the post office. Little is known about the Mascot, which seemed to disappear from the theatre scene without much fanfare.

The Newman children then appeared at a "grand family entertainment" at Belinda Mulroney's Fairview Hotel on August 12, and

The Newman children, especially little Margie, were a popular act in 1898. In early August, 1898, they advertised the opening of the Mascot Theatre by posing on Front Street on donkeys, but the Mascot didn't last long. University of Washington Libraries, Special Collections, Hegg photo 556.

within weeks they were being featured at the Monte Carlo. According to all accounts, the Newman children were regularly showered with nuggets and gold coins when their stage act concluded. While all three Newman children quickly became a featured act, little Margie was clearly the hit of the show, and ultimately the most revered child actor to perform in the Klondike. With her round face and long dark hair parted in the middle and falling to her shoulders in ringlets, ten-year-old Margie plucked the heartstrings of many weary miners, who, homesick and thousands of miles away from family, were reminded of their wives and children when they watched her perform.

One witness to her popularity was George Tuxford, a Saskatchewan farmer who arrived at Dawson in October with a herd of cattle and saw her performance at one of the theatres. The audience had been amused by the Lamore sisters, whom they loved, and they'd been entertained by a large lady in a very short skirt who warbled in a "tiny thin voice." But they were stilled when little Margie Newman appeared. "Just then," Tuxford noted,

> a little tot of maybe ten years old came on the stage, and we were immediately all attention. She was obviously attended by a woman, who was evidently, from our point of vantage, in a state of considerable anxiety, and who, we were told later on, was her mother. The little tot seemed so completely out of place in that gathering of rough and ready men, but she seemed oblivious to any nervousness or fear. She danced, sang, and acted in the most charming fashion. She was a born actress, and when her turn was over, she was vociferously recalled time and time again. She responded in the most dainty manner possible, whilst the crowd shouted its approval, and showered the stage with coins and even nuggets of gold.[33]

Little Margie's parents were also theatrical, and they actively encouraged their children to perform. Mrs. Newman used her skills with a needle and thread to create a pair of matching outfits for little Margie and one of her brothers. Each outfit was half masculine and half feminine. "I went to see the children perform in the theatre," reported one witness. "It was ludicrous when each danced with the partner; this partner was the individual's counterpart; one half male and the other female. The illusion was about perfect, and it brought the house down."[34]

Summer slowly receded as the days grew shorter, and the nights became frosty beneath skies illuminated by the shimmering light of the aurora borealis. The first snow fell September 11. As the steamer *Susie* pulled into her mooring on the Dawson waterfront, her searchlight "revealed the air full of feathery couriers of Father Frost."[35] The following day, the steamer *Joseph Clossit* brought another load of gold seekers. Among them was Miss Mertie Houck of Chicago. As soon as she arrived, she announced that she planned to establish amateur theatre in Dawson as an alternative form of entertainment to that which was currently on offer to patrons.[36] Within a month, the Dawson Dramatic Club put on a performance of *The Three Hats* at the Pioneer Hall. Some of the amateur actors had difficulty delivering their lines on a stage that was much too small for the performance. Nevertheless, the report in the *Klondike Miner and Yukon Advertiser* stated, "One of the things to be desired in Dawson at present is a wholesome form of entertainment for the people—especially now that men are bringing their wives and families to reside in the city—and the excellent effort to provide this on the part of the club is most commendable and worthy of support."[37] But Dawson City wasn't ready to be tamed yet.

The Combination Music Hall changed hands at the end of September. Under the new management of Robert Blei and Joe Cooper, it was renamed the Tivoli. Blei had extensive theatrical experience, having managed professional theatres in Chicago, Portland and Seattle. Blei and Cooper wasted no time in offering a stellar cast of Dawson performers. John Mulligan was stolen away from the Monte Carlo to be the stage manager and star entertainer, while Harry Warnock, who had led the Monte Carlo's tiny orchestra, was the new musical director. There were of course lesser acts whose talents were less formidable, but while the quality of their singing was "dreadfully low," they could kick "dreadfully high."[38] Between

The theatre troupe in the Tivoli Theatre. The Tivoli, formerly the Combination Music Hall, opened in October of 1898. University of Washington Libraries, Special Collections, UW1824.

acts, they sat in the boxes drinking wine costing $30 per bottle, all at other people's expense. The owners of the theatre were shrewd enough to paint the name of some mining region on the facade of each box, such as Bonanza, Eldorado or Hunker, and when one of the gold "kings" came to the theatre, he always sat in the box bearing the name of the district where he had his claims—and whooped it up.

Cad Wilson: "Such a Nice Girl"

Among the sixteen acts on the playbill for October 8 were Caprice, Mollie Thompson, Mulligan and Linton, Emma Forest and Pauline Claire, a Dutch song and dance artist. The performers were billed as "A Galaxy of New Stars," although many of the names were already recognizable from performances at other establishments earlier in the summer. But the featured act was a new arrival who had reached Dawson on the *Ora*, one of the last boats to come down from Whitehorse as winter was looming. Her name was Cad Wilson, and she set the stage afire with her performances during the winter of 1898–99.

She was no beauty, didn't have much of a figure, and her voice was nothing to write home about. Yet the brown-eyed redhead had a stage presence that was hypnotic, and her wardrobe was the most elaborate to be seen on any stage in town. She was soon the best-paid act in Dawson City. Men would compete to bestow her with the biggest gold nugget from their claims. They went mad when she sang, and when she started into "There'll Be a Hot Time in the Old Town Tonight," they pelted the stage with nuggets and jewellery. She would dash about the stage laughing gleefully as she picked them up. When she concluded her act, a little boy would come out onto the stage with a broom and a dustpan to sweep up the remaining golden debris. It was said that if she didn't clean up $500 a night, she left the stage in a pout.

The winter of 1898, Cad Wilson was the queen of the Dawson theatre scene, performing her signature song, "Such a Nice Girl, Too!" Gates collection.

CHAPTER 3

Her performance was a risqué repertoire with an affectation of innocence. Her most popular song, "Such a Nice Girl, Too," which was composed by Arthur Seldon and Hattie Anderson in 1892, became her anthem:

> She told me that she was a "Miss"
> And scarcely had turned twenty,
> She said she never cared to wed
> Tho' offers she had plenty.
> Last week they took her up to court,
> She said, "Judge, be forgiving."
> He answered, "Yes, if you can prove
> You've not three husbands living."
> Such a nice girl, too,
> Such a real nice girl;
> So affable and full of animation.
> All who know her must admit,
> She's a lady every bit!
> Yes, a lady with a spotless reputation.

Cad made no secret of the fact she wanted to separate the miners from their money. Before she came out for her performance, the stage manager of the Tivoli Theatre would read a letter he claimed came from her mother. In it, she admonished Cad "to be sure and be a good girl and pick nice clean friends." He would look out at the crowd and shout, "I leave it to you, fellers, if she don't pick 'em clean!"[39]

One admirer paid for a bathtub to be filled with wine. It is not known if she let him scrub her back, or if he even saw her in her expensive ablutions. One Eldorado king is said to have lavished his attention upon her to the tune of $75,000. And she wasn't choosy. Jack Mitchell, known as the Sawdust King because he made his living changing the sawdust on the barroom floors, had an uncharacteristic streak of good luck, winning $1,800. That was enough to propel him into Cad Wilson's arms temporarily, where "she had one arm around his neck and caressingly stroked his unkempt hair. Each was sipping wine from the other's glass." A few hours later, he was thrown unceremoniously out of the Tivoli, still wanting to spend his remaining $60 on more booze.[40]

Sparks and Flames

In the waning light of the northern autumn, Dawson was soon to be illuminated by electricity. On October 4, the Dawson Electric Light and Power Company threw the switch. Two small steam-driven generators capable of powering 308 light bulbs whirred into action, and the lights came on along a small section of Front Street. The Horseshoe, where the Oatley Sisters had performed, the Monte Carlo, and the Opera House were all bathed in the glow of electric light bulbs. No longer would businesses be dependent upon candles, kerosene, or acetylene light.[41] The steady glow of the bulbs was an improvement over the lamps that required frequent refills and cleaning of their sooty glass chimneys; worse, they posed the constant threat of fire. More generators were on the way but they were stuck in the Yukon upriver, and with the threat of the Yukon freezing solid at any time, they would have to be sledded into Dawson once the ice was thick enough to support the load.[42] On November 4, the river in front of Dawson was covered with ice, and a man was seen to be cautiously crossing on foot, a sure sign that the frozen river would soon be able to support heavy traffic.[43]

In anticipation of the arrival of the larger generators, the light company continued to wire more buildings. The grid was quickly expanded, and within a few months, all the streets in Dawson would be illuminated by electricity. Several people had already been injured falling off the boardwalks of Dawson in the dark, some of which rose more than a metre above the grade of the street. With electric streetlights, these would no longer be a menace to pedestrians. Meanwhile, the Front Street businesses enjoyed the benefits of incandescent lighting. What a difference it made to have a stage lit up with the steady glow of electric bulbs! With the days growing shorter as winter approached, Front Street was an oasis of light whose siren call beckoned lonely miners downtown. Within a few weeks, The Tivoli Theatre was added to the electrical grid, and could proudly advertise: "EVERYTHING NEW—LIGHTED BY 100 LIGHTS."[44]

On October 14, there was another example of the need for electric lighting. Early that morning Tony Page, a drunken prostitute, had left her room in the Green Tree Hotel, located a block south of theatre row, leaving behind a still-lit candle. When the candle burned down a fire started and spread quickly, and the alarm was raised. Mounted Police and members of the militia were quickly on the scene to battle the flames. Fire threatened the post office next door, and men hurriedly carried the mail out of the burning building. A bucket brigade was formed on the street and soon three lines of men were feeding the firefighters with water, but the flames continued to spread, crossing the street and igniting the buildings whose rear facades faced the river. Fear spread that the entire town would be engulfed in flames as nearby buildings were quickly demolished. "At least 200 men were engaged in the work. Ropes were attached to the corners of log cabins and then with a long pull and a strong pull it would be torn log from log. Empty caches were turned over and crushed like egg shells. Frame buildings were hewed and chopped into kindling wood."[45]

The Tivoli

FRED N. TRACY, MANAGER.

EVERYTHING NEW.
LIGHTED BY 100 LIGHTS.

PERFORMERS—

Mulligan & Linten, Charles T. Sagers, Vera Gray,
George Newman, E. J. Gardner, Nellie Lewis,
Willie Newman, Billy Birch, Alex. Schwartz,
Margie Newman, Eva St. Clair, Frank Howard,
The Rodolphes, Marie Thompson, Newman Children,
Byron Way, Emma Forrest.

MOVING PICTURES.

Matinee every day at 3 o'clock; four-act melodrama "T'riss," by the Tivoli Star Company. Admission, 25 cents.

GRAND FAMILY ENTERTAINMENT EVERY SUNDAY EVENING.

The Tivoli Theatre was one of the first buildings in Dawson City to show moving pictures and be illuminated by electricity. *Klondike Miner and Yukon Advertiser,* January 20, 1899, p. 1, Yukon Archives.

Newly arrived firefighting equipment had been stored down the street in front of the NAT&T CO. building, some still in the delivery crates. These crates were quickly broken open and a new fire engine was speedily put into service, with cheers of approval from the men in the bucket lines. In the end, the town was saved, but much of Front Street between Queen and Princess was a smoking ruin. All that remained of some forty buildings was blackened rubble. In addition to the Green Tree, two more hotels, two saloons, the post office, and sixteen buildings on the river side of the street were destroyed. In Paradise Alley behind the hotels and saloons on Front

Street, twelve cabins and their contents were destroyed by the fire. Anything that was salvaged from the cribs was trampled in the streets. Fortunately, there was no loss of life.

The Show Goes On

Reconstruction commenced immediately, while a block to the north the theatres of Dawson continued to operate as usual. Robert Blei announced a reprise of Mulligan's play *The Adventures of Stillwater Willie* at the Tivoli Theatre in late November, starring Nellie Lamore and Nellie Holgate. A few days later, posters went up all over Dawson announcing the opening of yet another theatre. The Family Theatre, located on Second Avenue, was opening its curtains for the first time to a minstrel show on December 13. The announcement proclaimed that this was the first theatre in Dawson not associated with a saloon, and to further cement its claim to wholesome entertainment, it stated, "The patrons can be assured there will be no slang or obscene language used in the stage at any time. The cast will be made up of professional people who will produce plays and vaudeville entertainments far superior to anything ever before produced in Dawson. We have the most comfortable seats in the city."[46]

The Family Theatre continued to offer less risqué entertainment. The Elks Club held a social there before Christmas that included performances by "Professor" George, Jack Crawford, Mr. Noble, Ben Davis, Margie Newman, Leroy Tozier and Mrs. Barlow. Dancing followed and, as the electrical grid had not yet been extended that far, it relied on gaslight for illumination.[47] The newspaper reported that the gas went out twice during the evening, plunging the house into darkness. Two months later, a local dancing club assembled at the Family Theatre with "just enough couples to make dancing a pleasure."[48] The dancing club had been organized because a Christmas Eve party had been spoiled when it was invaded by a horde of dance hall girls.[49] But good clean entertainment did not attract the large audiences of the more popular establishments, and by the following spring, the Family Theatre, renamed the Criterion, was in new hands.[50]

The renovations to the Criterion included a division of space with the addition of a saloon occupying the front nine metres of the hall, which was dominated by a bar extending the length of the room and three metres into the dance hall behind it. The construction of native wood was completely hidden beneath white enamel and gilding, with French plate mirrors mounted on the walls behind the bar. The dance hall behind the barroom extended another twelve metres, with two parlour rooms behind that. Behind the semicircular stage at the far end of the hall was a backdrop painting of Five Finger Rapid, with smaller northern scenes on the side walls. Frank Swanson, the new proprietor, was forecasting that the Criterion would become one of the leading establishments in Dawson.[51] Within weeks of its opening, however, the Criterion

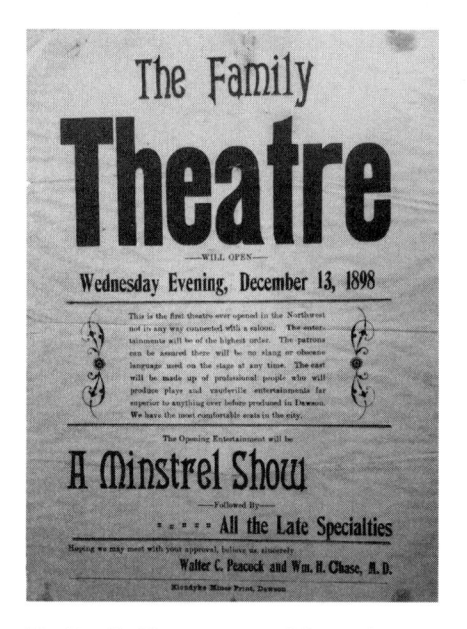

The Family Theatre opened December 13, 1898, but it did not offer the kind of entertainment the miners wanted and lasted only a few months. Yukon Archives, P-421.

This theatre originally opened as the Family Theatre in 1898, but it quickly became the Criterion, then ceased operating as a dance hall and theatre altogether by the summer of 1899.
National Museum of Canada/Library and Archives Canada/PA-013516.

was no longer being advertised as a saloon and dance hall but rather as a hotel and club rooms.[52]

Winter arrives early in the Klondike, and when the Yukon River froze, all commercial transportation ceased for the next seven months. Thousands of men were trapped in the North until spring. They had nowhere to go and thus became a large captive audience for the lively theatres to entertain over the coming months. Theatre managers were very creative, constantly dreaming up ideas for new attractions. One of the most popular of these was boxing matches. The manly art was very popular in those early days, and boxing matches were often added to the evening entertainment to attract patrons. Some events were three-round sparring matches, others grudge matches, but they always attracted a crowd.

One of the most interesting bouts was linked to Frank Slavin, a professional boxer from Australia known as the Sydney Cornstalk, who had once challenged the British Commonwealth champion. On one occasion Slavin was drinking in the Monte Carlo saloon when he got into an altercation with Archie Hoffman, a man who styled himself the heavyweight champion of the Pacific coast. Hoffman knocked Slavin to the floor. "My man," said Slavin as he got up, "you can knock me about a saloon when I'm drunk but I'll show you what I can do in a ring when I'm sober."[53] Wilson Mizner and Tex Rickard, who were working behind the bar in the Monte Carlo, saw an opportunity and quickly arranged a match. They set up a ring on the tiny stage of the Monte Carlo and charged $15 and $25 admission to the bout.

It wasn't much of a fight. Slavin entered the ring wearing a pair of white flannel trousers and a long white sweater with rolled-up collar, in contrast to his opponent, who was in boxing trunks and bare chested. It didn't take long; in the first round, Slavin bobbed and weaved a little bit, then with a single swing punched Hoffman in the jaw. Hoffman went down like a sack of potatoes without ever having touched Slavin.[54] The fight was the start of a long career for Rickard, who went on to become one of the biggest fight promoters in America. Mizner later had a colourful career as a *bon vivant* and writer of stage plays and film scripts.

Another of the activities frequently sponsored by the dance halls and theatres were benefit events for charitable causes. These were usually well attended and raised substantial sums of money, but they did not always shine for their virtue. The Fraternal Order of Elks held a benefit concert at the Tivoli Theatre the evening of October 26, 1898. The purpose: to raise money for the order's sick and burial fund. The event was attended by many of the respectable ladies of Dawson. The bill for the evening included everybody who was anybody in the Dawson theatre world. The Oatley Sisters sang, and the Brocee sisters, Myrtle and Florence, danced. Fred Breen delivered one of his monologues to the delight of a receptive crowd, and the Newman children, most notably little Margie, were well received, especially by the ladies in the audience.

Cad Wilson closed the program with selections from her extensive repertoire of dance hall material. The men applauded her performance and wished for more, but the ladies in the audience were scandalized. The *Klondike Nugget* later reported on their reaction:

> Cad's act caused ladies to reach for their wraps and many and severe were the comments at the conclusion. They felt they had been inveigled to a charity benefit under false pretenses ... Cad Wilson made no friends by her acts that night. Her audacity called out applause in the rear of the hall, but the ladies in front hung their heads and the escorts wished they had never brought them ... words were hardly strong enough to express our condemnation of anyone who deliberately and premeditatively insults the better part of an audience.[55]

Special events such as dances and masquerade balls were popular, and on Sundays special "sacred" concerts were offered. But the mainstay of theatre entertainment at the time were the vaudeville and burlesque performances rather than serious drama. Singing, dancing, comedy and a variety of other entertainments were combined in an evening's performance to keep the customers satisfied.

The Silver Screen

One amusement that caught on quickly was moving pictures, the first of which was shown August 30, 1898, in the Combination Music Hall. The *Klondike Nugget* reported on this new feature: "Besides the strong drawing attractions of Mulligan, Maurettus and the host of supporters, they are showing the most modern of Edison's inventions, the 'Projectoscope.' It resembles a stereopticon, in that pictures of objects are projected upon a screen but there the resemblance ceases, for in the Projectoscope the pictures move exactly as in life. The sensational rounds of a prize-fight, bull-fight, naval battle, etc., are reproduced exactly as in life."[56]

Crowds lined up at the door on opening night to witness, among other things, a steam locomotive chug across the screen. One of the miners was so thrilled that he jumped up and shouted: "Run her through again! Run her through again! I ain't seen a locomotive for nigh on ten years."[57]

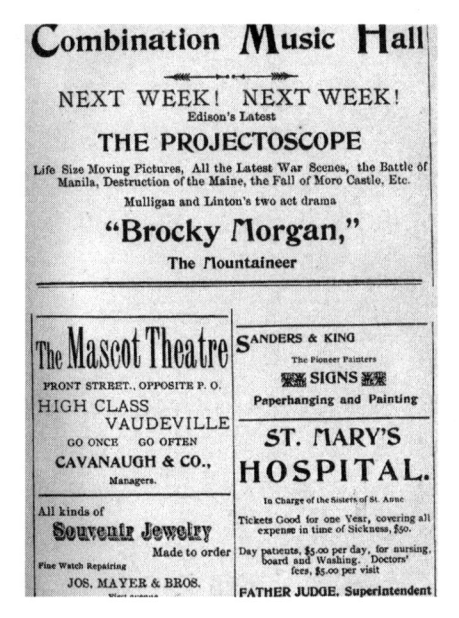

The Combination Music Hall advertised the first moving pictures in Dawson City in September of 1898. *Yukon Sun*, September 1898, Yukon Archives.

A second projector, this one called an Animatoscope, was brought into service on September 14 at the Oatley Sisters' dance hall, offering footage of the Corbett-Courtney boxing match to attract patrons.[58] This film projector was part of the luggage brought by two wealthy American ladies who encamped in a large circus tent across the river from Dawson City. Screenings of such features as fights or the Spanish-American War were viewed merely as "a novelty, nothing to compare with the livelier delight of theatre-in-the-flesh."[59] The Pioneer Hall was rented for the evenings of November 18 and 19 to show films and stereopticon views produced by the Wondroscope Company. Fred Tracy, the singer, took to the stage to accompany certain illustrated songs. His performance was a hit, and Tracy was called back for several encores.[60] The Monte Carlo was the next establishment to offer moving-film presentations, and when they were first shown in late November, they were the featured attraction at the Sunday performances in an "entertaining and instructive program."[61]

On Sunday, December 11, the Monte Carlo again featured entertainment by the Wondroscope Company. The projectionist was Professor Walter Parkes, who narrated a trip from Seattle over the Chilkoot Trail.[62] "The audience was completely carried away by the beautiful and realistic views thrown upon the screen," reported the *Klondike Nugget*.[63] Fred Tracy and little Margie Newman enthralled the audience with their singing, but what captivated viewers the most according to the *Nugget* were the moving pictures that followed. "Every picture was perfect, and when the 'Black Diamond Express' came tearing down right into the audience, the cheering and yelling and stamping of feet could have been heard for two blocks away. The program was not allowed to continue until it was shown again. Mr. Sparkes [Parkes] showed his ability as a moving picture manipulator by reversing the train and bringing it on again at lightning speed."[64]

A month later, Vitascope moving pictures were being advertised as part of the offering at the Tivoli Theatre, which had been wired for electricity and was now under the management of Fred Tracy, who was formerly at the Monte Carlo. The Tivoli electric light system was the source of much praise: "Behind the proscenium arch [was] a switch-board of ten switches making an endless variety of combinations instantly possible in the lighting of the house."[65] Also offered on the playbill: "A clean, wholesome border drama, and after that a variety of single numbers and some new faces … A concert will be given on Sunday night with new numbers and new faces."[66]

The Monte Carlo, meanwhile, continued to offer never-before-seen moving pictures. On February 4, 1899, the theatre crowed that "Professor Park[e]s has not yet exhausted his supply of moving pictures and continues to dig up new films each week."[67] The Sunday night program promised a screening of President McKinley taking the oath of office.[68] Other films shown later in the month included the Corbett-Courtney boxing match, Thomas Edison working in his laboratory, Cuban refugees waiting for rations, and the steamer *Willamette* leaving Seattle for a voyage to Alaska.[69]

Throughout the long, dark winter of 1898–99, the theatres served a huge audience of transient gold seekers who were trapped by circumstance and weather, waiting out the darkness and cold. Many battled illnesses such as pneumonia, scurvy and typhoid. A number of the prospectors had plans to take their gold and leave for the outside in the spring; others would be glad simply to escape the harsh conditions. While some laboured in the goldfields to stockpile their frozen pay dirt in anticipation of recovering the gold during the spring cleanup, many sought refuge in the warmth and companionship in the saloons, dance halls and theatres of Front Street.[70] Amid the singing and dancing, the boxing matches, the sacred concerts and the masquerade balls, Klondikers were captivated by the first stirrings of the nascent movie industry. Yet at this time, moving pictures were a mere novelty amid the live entertainment that sustained the gold-rush town. There would be much more to come.

Dance Hall Girls and Trophy Wives

The women who participated in the gold rush were strictly confined by the social and moral values of their time. Beyond the domestic duties expected of a Victorian-era wife, there were few opportunities for careers open to ladies. Further, society did not feel that a rough-and-ready gold-rush town was any place for a woman. Few women participated in the early stages of the gold rush. It is estimated that during the preliminary phase of development of the Klondike in 1898, there were only a few hundred non-Indigenous women in the territory. When Martha Purdy, a woman from a wealthy American family, accompanied her brother to the Klondike, she was the six hundred and thirty-first woman to have registered at the Northwest Mounted Police post at Tagish, while eighteen thousand men had done so.[71]

Purdy was one of a handful of women shielded behind respectability from some of the worst conditions that confronted women who joined the gold rush. Among her rank were just a few other women—wives of officials, or those who had accompanied their husbands to the mines. Mrs. Purdy classified the women who joined her in the stampede into three categories: "members of the 'oldest profession in the world,' who ever follow armies and gold rushes; dance hall and variety girls, whose business was to entertain and be dancing partners; and a few others, wives with unbounded faith in and love for their mates, or the odd person like myself on a special mission."[72]

Belinda Mulroney, proprietor of the Fairview Hotel, who became one of the most notable entrepreneurs during the frantic gold-rush times, was one who fit into Purdy's latter category. Similar observations were made by Jeremiah Lynch in his book, *Three Years in the Klondike*. "There was no honest occupation for women. Many went professedly as housekeepers to miners who were rich enough to employ one; but it was only another name. A very few found precarious and unremunerative employment in the stores and others drifted into houses kept for dancing, with gambling at faro and roulette as a principal adjunct. Those who could, danced and played; those who could not assisted as *claqueuses*."[73]

Between the two extremes of respectability and depravity lay a small but varied hierarchy of women who were more difficult to classify. One observer noted: "It was a simple matter to classify these two extremes. The women who could not be classified, and therefore at once became interesting, were the women of the dance halls. They were there to make a fortune. Some didn't care how they made it and others were very particular. Many of them were as clean [and] wholesome looking young women as could be found anywhere. A man who danced with them was expected to buy drinks at the bar before and after each dance, and many girls scarcely tasted their drinks."[74]

Historian Robert Coutts broke the dance hall sorority into three broad groups: the legitimate stage actresses and performers; the girls who sang and danced but did not otherwise mingle with customers; and finally the percentage girls, who shared the dance floor for a dollar a turn, or who took a percentage of each drink that they sold. He summed it up: "To their admirers they were 'all classes of beauties from all nations,' but to their detractors, they were more like 'ill-blended paper flowers, badly crumpled' … men who had 'worked, sweat and froze were just damned fools to swap pure gold for such bait.'"[75] A New Zealander described how it worked:

> The dance girls walk and talk on the dance floor side and ask the men to dance. When they have had a dance, the man takes his partner to a bar set in one end of the hall. He shouts for her at a cost of $1.00; she receives a counter or check. They have another dance and another drink and after another little dance, another shout. He is getting a bit wobbly now and blunders through the next dance, a laughing stock for everybody. He pulls his poke (gold sack) out and gives it to the barman to help himself. When the dance is over [he] is helplessly drunk. If he has any pals there, they

may take him home. If he is by himself, he may come to his senses the next day, sad but wiser, I wonder?[76]

Some of these percentage girls were able to accumulate a tidy sum before they left the Klondike. One girl came from her home in Oregon at the invitation of her fiancé, who had already established himself in the Klondike. They had been engaged to be married for a while when the news of the gold strike made headlines in the newspapers. "While he was assembling his outfit, they talked it over, and planned that Joe should send for her when he struck it rich; she would go to Dawson; they would be married there, and after Joe had gold enough, they would return to the States."[77]

Early in 1898, she received his letter telling her he had struck it rich, so she rushed to Dawson "with a light heart and a light purse," but found no trace of him. When her money ran out, she sought work in one of the dance halls, still waiting for Joe. She told her story to another miner, who believed it was fabricated to elicit his sympathy, until one evening while he was talking to some strangers, one of them told him about a foolish girl he had "on a string" back in Oregon. "Last winter," the man said, "sometimes, just to kid her, I wrote her that I's struck it rich and for her to come on up here. And would you believe it, the little fool packed up her grip and came in on the first boat. Now she is making bushels of money down at Dawson and I haven't $10.00."[78]

A few were able to land rich miners. As Jeremiah Lynch noted, "More than a dozen of these same dancing-hall girls are to-day enjoying married happiness in London, Paris, New York and other places. And I make no doubt that they are quite as moral as the traditional Becky Sharpe.[79] I know more than one case where the lady has reformed her dissipated husband, and keeps him in good strong leading-strings, to the edification of everyone who has witnessed a glimpse of the Klondike past. Those who have lived and are not altogether lost make excellent exemplars of virtue."[80] Examples of dance hall girls who married into respectability if not affluence were "Diamond Tooth" Gertie Lovejoy, who married prominent Dawson lawyer Charles Tabor, and soprano Beatrice Lorne, the "Klondike Nightingale," who married Dr. George Smith, a veterinarian and mine broker.[81]

"Today in San Francisco," stated an article in the *St. Louis Post-Dispatch* of April 14, 1901, "there are a dozen mansions presided over by ex-gaiety girls of the frozen north. Their husbands are men who made their pile up there and lost their hearts to the vaudeville fairies." The article lists more than a dozen women who hit the matrimonial jackpot by marrying wealthy Klondike miners.

The one who topped the list was Mrs. Lillian Hall, who had the good fortune to wed James "Arkansaw Jim" Hall. Hall made his fortune from Claim Number 17 on Eldorado Creek. He had been in the Yukon for a decade before the gold rush and had the good fortune to stake the richest claim in the entire Klondike.

Lillian Green was a vaudeville actress originally from San Francisco. She had been performing in Victoria, BC, before making her way down the Yukon River to Dawson City in October 1899, so the story goes, when the boat she was in was caught in the ice floes and wrecked below Fort Selkirk. She made her way to a nearby camp, falling through the ice en route. Standing in front of the campfire, she recounted her perils as she thawed out. In her audience was the wealthy James L. Hall, more than thirty years her senior, who fell for her hard. Hall subsequently went on a drinking spree in Dawson and was arrested and detained by the Mounted Police "for no other reason than to protect him from committing a matrimonial error which

CHAPTER 3

after sober reflection might cause a chain of remorseful regrets."[82] But despite the warning, a couple of days later Reverend Naylor joined the two in marriage.[83]

"My husband is the best nugget in the Klondike," proclaimed the fortunate Mrs. Hall when later visiting her mother in San Francisco. "Before I left Dawson, he gave me $50,000 to put away for myself for a rainy day, and an extra $10,000 to spend amusing myself." Meanwhile, Hall remained in the Yukon, presumably digging up more gold for his beautiful wife to spend. Not surprisingly, the couple were shipwrecked on the shoals of marital discord, and they ended up in court in 1909, with Hall trying to curtail his wife's spending. It didn't work, and in 1918 Hall, at age seventy-four, committed suicide by shooting himself on the ferry *Napa Valley* as it was docking at the Maine Street terminal in Vallejo, California.[84]

James "Arkansaw Jim" Hall, owner of the richest claim on Eldorado Creek, married actress Lillian Green in December 1898. He bought the Palace Grand Theatre for her in 1901 for the cut-rate price of $16,000. Dawson City Museum, 1984.96.11.

Marriage wasn't the only option for women to cash in on the opportunities available to them during the gold rush. On August 18, 1899, less than a year after arriving in Dawson City, Cad Wilson left the Klondike, headed for San Francisco and Chicago. She took with her a sizeable bankroll (newspapers varied widely in the amount they reported, from $20,000 to $150,000), her jewellery and other baubles, as well as a nugget-encrusted waistband given to her by the miners on Eldorado Creek. The belt, which was worth $2,500, was so large that she could wrap it around her waist one and a half times. She placed this gaudy adornment on display in San Francisco after leaving the Klondike. She had done enough, reported the *San Francisco Call*, that she was ready to retire.[85]

The Wicked Side of Dawson: Life of a Soubrette as Told by Herself

The following is a letter published in the *Dawson Daily News*. In an explanatory note introducing the article, the *DDN* stated that this "interesting letter was recently found on the streets of Dawson, having evidently been accidentally dropped by the writer."

Dawson, Y.T., 1900

My dear Mr. V—— What am I doing? I am working and there is no legitimate theatre in this country. They are a sort of combination theatres, consisting usually of a short, impromptu sketch, followed by a series of songs, dances, etc., given by "artists," scraped up from God knows where.

Then comes the "drama"—a name given to burlesques, tragedies, or anything the capricious managers may see fit to put on at the last moment, though usually you are given three days for rehearsing and learning your parts. After all this follows the big dance, in which all the aforesaid artists and dance hall girls engaged for that purpose join.

The show starts at 9 p.m. and ends about 2:30 a.m. and the dance continues all night and day if there is anyone foolish enough to remain, though the time for the musicians to leave is 6 a.m.

Now you may wonder why, in this land of gold, they give so much for a paltry 50 cents or one dollar, the price of admission, but there's the catch! The wise and sturdy old miner will pay his admission and if he walks straight to his place in the pit he may escape. But lo, if he lingers around the bar to take a drink he is almost sure to be led astray by a pair of promising eyes and the first thing the poor chap knows, he finds himself alone with his siren in one of the boxes—you must know the upper part of all these houses are allotted to boxes—and there the fair one proceeds to "blow" him or "take him down the line" to the tune of $1 a drink or $15 a small bottle of wine. Out of this the little soubrette gets 25 or 50 per cent, according to her arrangements with the house. In addition to this they get from $50 to $150 a week.

Salaries are gauges, not according to their ability on the stage, but their cleverness in the boxes. Though there are some engaged for the show, it is optional with them whether they go into the boxes or not, and in justice to a few I must say there are some clever specialty people here.

Strange and incredible as it may sound to you, many of the girls, whose chief ambition apparently is to get men drunk, are comparatively moral and faithful to their husbands or lovers, and the poor chap to whom their eyes promised so much finds himself the next morning with empty pockets and a frightful head—the only souvenir of the beautiful vision his lustful eyes beheld the night before, and considering himself, I suppose, very badly treated and even cheated. Do not think, my dear friend, that I condone this mode of extracting gold from the Klondiker's poke, but the society of any woman must be worth a great deal to these lonely fellows and, so far from blaming the girls, I cannot help but admire the clever way in which they blend pleasure and commerce. But how degrading.

Now in all this jumble I suppose you ask yourself what part I take. Well, I am playing in the dramas at a weekly salary of $——, and am privileged to go home when I finish my show, so can avoid all the dissipation. I keep my eyes open, hoping that something will turn up that will in a way recompense me for the sacrifice I am making by living in this morbid and obnoxious atmosphere.

The plays go very well here, notwithstanding the fact that most of them are very badly done. Keeping such late hours and so much dissipation prevents proper study, and, with the existing state of things, it would not pay a manager to keep a company for plays alone. You cannot increase the price of admission and the salaries, scenery etc., entail an enormous outlay. I do not believe that really artistic acting would be appreciated; certainly it would not pay a legitimate actor to come to this country unless he had other interests.

The shows are for the men and as the wine flows they become less particular as to the kind of amusements they beguile the hours with.

Besides the miners there are men about town who come to have what they call a good time and will spend thousands with but little urging, and will walk up to the boxes like little men without the least bit of coaxing. These are what the girls call "good fellows," be they gentlemen or the personification of all that is uncouth and vulgar.

Here is where we can see the man as he is, and you don't have to scratch the skin to find the gentleman, however they may pose on the outside. In here the veneering only serves to reflect the animal within, and no one has a better opportunity to study man than the little girl who touches the button for another small bottle.[86]

Not All Glitz and Glamour

The sisters Myrtle and Florence Brocee were a song-and-dance duo originally from Lindsay, Ontario. They were teenagers when they first hit the theatre circuit in the Northwest in 1897. Starting in Chicago, they went on to perform their variety act in Indiana, in Butte, Montana, and in Spokane and Seattle, Washington. At Victoria, their theatre troupe had an extended booking at the Trilby Theatre. During her time at the Trilby, Myrtle became involved with a married man, Ivan Malchin, a "swordsman, adventurer and alleged baron." Malchin was living a triple life, however, and absconded to Tacoma with a widow instead of Myrtle, leaving the jilted teenager behind.[87] She later confessed that she had attempted suicide after this fiasco, but she survived. When they heard stories of the Klondike gold rush, the sisters decided to join in. One newspaper reported that "they went north for the avowed intention of marrying a rich Klondiker, but ostensibly left for the purpose of performing in one of the many concert halls in Dawson City."[88]

If Myrtle was planning on landing a rich miner, she was disappointed. Upon arriving in Dawson City on a scow, just before freeze-up in October 1898, the sisters were quickly hired to perform their song-and-dance routine at the Tivoli Theatre.[89] While Myrtle attempted a life beyond reproach, she was exposed to many forms of temptation and low standards of moral behaviour in her line of work. Life in Dawson did not hold the promise that she had hoped for: instead of wealth, she found hardship; instead of honourable suitors, she found tempters on every side. Myrtle became sick and ran low on funds. She hated the theatre life, but what other choice did she have? In despair, she borrowed a pistol from an acquaintance, and on the evening of December 9 in an upstairs room at the Monte Carlo, she put the gun to her head and pulled the trigger. At the inquest that followed, several male witnesses testified that Myrtle had kept her virtue until the end.[90] Her sister, Florence, remained in Dawson until 1904, and then performed in theatres across Canada and the United States for the next twenty-five years.

The lifestyle was also too much for another dance hall girl who worked at the Monte Carlo. Her name was Kittie Straub, formerly from Oregon. Before the gold rush she had come from Juneau to work at Forty Mile, and later at Circle, Alaska. Kittie went by the name Stella Hill and had been living for some time with Charlie Hill, a bartender at the Pioneer saloon. After completing her shift at the Monte Carlo at six o'clock one morning, she went to join her lover at the Pioneer, only to learn that he had left work earlier with another woman. Distraught at his apparent betrayal, she went to the drug store and purchased some strychnine. She then returned to her room at the Monte Carlo, bade some friends goodbye and locked herself in. By the time Charlie arrived to kick down the door, she had consumed the strychnine, and she died a short time later. In a hastily scribbled note to Charlie she had written: "Dear Charlie: I am disgusted with life since you deceived me. I guess you will be sorry when you find me."[91]

Two months later, another dance hall girl, Libby White, was shot to death in a room above the Monte Carlo by the man she had been living with for two months, Dave Evans. White had been working in the dance hall beside the Monte Carlo that had formerly been rented by the Oatley Sisters. Evans was jealous of her promiscuous behaviour, and they had argued repeatedly before he finally killed her. Immediately remorseful of his actions, he then turned the gun on himself and concluded the pact.[92] The Monte Carlo seemed to be a popular place to end it all: in August 1899 a man named Harry Davis shot actress Maude Roselle there, and then himself in another murder-suicide.[93]

Dawson Dies for a Day

Nothing illustrates the importance of the theatre scene to Dawson social life more than an incident in the spring of 1899 that caused the social life of the town to shut down entirely for a day.

At 1:00 on Sunday afternoon of May 28, 1899, two hundred passengers embarked on the steamer *Tyrrell*. It had been chartered by two men named Cooper and O'Brien to take the party down the Yukon River for some merrymaking, beyond the reach of the Mounted Police. A few minutes later the *Bonanza King* departed with 368 more, under the chaperonage of Tom Chisholm, Harry Edwards and Thomas Sparks. Both vessels arrived in Forty Mile three hours later after a pleasant journey downriver. They spent an hour exploring the old townsite before departing for the return voyage to Dawson. A short time later, a cracked cylinder on the engine of the *Tyrrell* brought progress to a halt. Passing by, the *Bonanza King* failed to respond to the signals of the injured steamer, but stopped a short distance upstream to take on more firewood. The captain of the *Tyrrell* dispatched a messenger in a small boat to request assistance from the *Bonanza King*, which returned to the *Tyrrell* and took on fifty-one passengers amid joshing from those on the functioning vessel.

The *Bonanza King* finally pulled away while the orchestra on board played "The Girl I left Behind Me" and "Farewell My Own True Love," and the orchestra on board the *Tyrrell* responded with "We'll Not Go Home Till Morning." The heavily laden *Bonanza King* struggled upstream until its supply of firewood was exhausted, at which point the crew came ashore to forage for more fuel. Much time had expired and many of the revellers, exhausted by the partying, lay sleeping. "Both decks were covered with sleepers lying in all sorts of positions and on all kinds of objects, from the top of a valuable upright piano to a single fourteen-inch board suspended eight feet from the floor. These became the game to three roisterers who, armed with two drums and a harmonica, paraded noisily throughout the ship, waking everybody from their slumber and bringing many to their feet in wild alarm."[94]

But the *Bonanza King* was unable to build enough steam to make upstream progress because of the poor quality of the firewood gathered. A passing steamer, the *Victorian*, pulled ashore in response to the signals from the stranded *Bonanza King*, and for the price of two dollars a head, a hundred of the stranded passengers were soon sailing back to Dawson, arriving at 4:30 in the morning. Meanwhile, the crew of the *Tyrrell* had made the necessary repair and she was on her way again. Now it was the turn of the *Tyrrell* to make fun of the remaining stranded passengers of the *Bonanza King*,

CHAPTER 3

playing tunes such as "Hold the Fort for I Am Coming," "Rescue the Perishing" and "The Rogue's March." Finally, they took on a hundred of the *Bonanza King*'s passengers, and the *Tyrrell* arrived back in Dawson about 9:00 on Monday evening, where they were greeted by thousands of ecstatic Dawsonites, while the band on board played "Home Again" and "My Country, 'Tis of Thee." Finally, having loaded enough firewood, the *Bonanza King* steamed ahead, arriving in Dawson about 2:00 on Tuesday morning.[95]

The *Klondike Nugget* reported the following:

> The excursionists had been away from home a day and a half, but it seemed like a week to them, so crowded with events had been the hours. It was the best natured crowd that ever existed; not a harsh word was spoken and the annoyances were accepted without a grumble. At home the situation was odd. Most of the amusements and resorts and saloons had turned out en masse to the excursion and when Monday dawned without the return of the boats there was hardly a place but was affected. New forces were seen behind the bars, gambling layouts were left unmanned; there were no bands for the theatres and several business houses were not opened at all. Not a little anxiety was felt about town, which increased as the hours grew, the popular theory being that that one or the other of the absent boats had met with a dreadful disaster.[96]

CHAPTER 4

THE BUSY YEARS

1899-1900

An Air of Permanence

The gold-rush stampede that occurred in 1898 finished almost as quickly as it had begun.

In the spring of 1898, after the ice broke up on the upper Yukon River, thousands of adventurers made their way north, struggling over the trails as they surged toward Dawson City. Once the railroad over the White Pass from Skagway was completed to Bennett, there was no practical reason to continue using the Chilkoot Trail. Almost overnight, Dyea, Alaska, was abandoned. Skagway fared better as the railway link guaranteed a continuing economic base.

But while the frenzied stampede to the Klondike was over by the end of the summer of 1898, Dawson City continued to thrive. Gold production in the Klondike continued to rise. In 1896, only 14,513 ounces of gold were recovered in the Yukon; that number increased ninefold to 120,937 ounces the following year, which quadrupled to 483,750 ounces in 1898. It nearly doubled from that in 1899, to 774,000 ounces, finally peaking at a million ounces in 1900, an astounding 7,000 per cent increase over the production prior to the discovery of four years before. In the ensuing century, the individual placer miner would come to be an iconic symbol of the industry driving the economy of the Yukon Territory.

Within a few years, it was apparent that the supply of gold was not about to run out anytime soon. Dawson City began to take on an air of permanence. The 1901 census showed more than twenty-eight thousand people still living in the Yukon Territory (the Yukon became a distinct territory of Canada with the coming into force of the Yukon Act on June 13, 1898).

A telegraph line was constructed in 1899 to connect Dawson with the outside world. The railroad under construction over the White Pass to White Horse (later shortened to Whitehorse) would provide a more reliable and economical means of transporting goods, but it was not complete until 1900, long after the stampede had subsided.

By 1899, the gravels of Bonanza, Eldorado, Hunker and Gold Bottom Creeks were proven entities, rich in placer gold. There was reason to invest, and the miners who had put back-breaking effort into mining for the previous three years were purchasing steam-power equipment to speed up production while reducing labour costs. Soon steam engines could be seen on every claim. The hillsides became denuded of trees, and fuel had to be imported from greater distances to supply the voracious appetites of the countless boilers.

The gold came out of the ground in huge quantities and poured into Dawson in a continuous stream. Services for the mining industry were becoming well established. Sawmills provided lumber, and hardware and mining equipment were imported for sale. There were several machine shops, blacksmiths and boilermakers. Transportation companies blossomed. There were three brickyards, eight warehouses, two planing mills and numerous general merchants, grocers and butchers. Dawson City could boast of five newspapers and two firehalls. These were the heyday years in the Klondike, and its citizens were filled with equal quantities of optimism and pride.

As the spring of 1899 approached, the days lengthened and the restive stirring of throngs who had been held captive for seven months filled the streets, dance halls and saloons. Both men and women impatiently waited for the breakup of the Yukon River so they could go upriver or downriver, or receive long-awaited supplies from the outside. As the temperature rose, miners waited with anticipation for the spring thaw so they could wash the gold that had been stockpiled over the winter by thousands of men burrowing underground.

A Spring Inferno

The anticipation was interrupted by another conflagration. On April 26, a fire started in the apartment of Helen Holden, on the second storey of the Bodega Saloon on Front Street. As smoke billowed from the building, the new fire engine was quickly brought into play to extinguish the flames. It was wheeled down Front Street within five minutes and the hose was extended out to the river for a supply of water, but there was a problem raising steam in the engine.

Without water to extinguish the fire, in minutes the Bodega was engulfed by roaring flames fanned by a steady wind blowing in off the river from the north. Soon the Northern Café was consumed. Next to it, the Tivoli Theatre was taken; flames spread to the rear, and a number of the small cribs occupied by prostitutes began burning fiercely as the women desperately removed their belongings into the street, where they were trampled in the chaos. The minutes

CHAPTER 4

The centre of Dawson City was gutted when flames were fanned by a strong wind blowing off the Yukon River on April 26, 1899. Dawson City Museum, 2000.196.65.

ticked by and the fire expanded in every direction, yet the fire engine could produce nothing more than a few weak pulses of water.

The heat by this time was so intense that the buildings on the opposite side of the street, their backs facing the river, were engulfed: a cigar store, barber shop, market, laundry and bakery. The flames jumped Queen Street and, beginning with the Victoria Saloon, worked their way hungrily south along the block, consuming one building after another. The flames moved north, taking hold in the Board of Trade Saloon, then spread to Clark's Barber Shop and the Dominion Saloon, and still no water was coming forth from the pumper parked on Front Street. Next the fire took hold in the Opera House. Finally, after twenty-five minutes of struggling to make the fire engine operational, the firemen got up a head of steam, and the water flowed from the hoses and held the flames at bay so that only half of the Opera House was consumed by the blaze.

When the inferno expired, the heart of Dawson's business district lay in smoking ruins. The streets were filled with merchandise, much of it ruined by smoke or mishandling. Many men, fuelled by whisky while fighting the fire, staggered amid the rubble. Sam Steele, superintendent of the Mounted Police, ordered all the saloons to close until 7:00 the following morning. One hundred and eleven buildings burned to the ground; another fifteen were demolished to stop the spread of the flames. People poked around in the smoking ruins, looking for anything that might be salvageable, but there was little to be found. The safe housed in the Bank of Commerce was left standing, open, warped and twisted out of shape amid a field of smoking embers. During the fire, the safe had blown open, spewing gold dust. Twenty-dollar gold pieces, watches and jewellery were scattered about in fused masses. A Mounted Police officer was stationed at all times to protect the site until the ashes could be sluiced and the gold and jewellery could be winnowed from the residue of the fire.[1]

The cost of the damage was estimated to be $1 million. The Tivoli Theatre was totally destroyed at a loss of $30,000 to its owners, while Joe Cooper, who was leasing the theatre, lost $15,000 in stage furnishings. The Opera House now lay open as though someone had sawn through the middle and torn down one half, exposing the interior, the damage estimated at $50,000. But before the smoke had died, reconstruction began and continued at a frantic pace. Soon, the sounds of saws and hammers reverberated along the waterfront, and the smell of sawdust mingled with smoke as the buildings "went up like mushrooms amid the ruins."[2]

CHAPTER 4

Losing the Rough Edges

Within two weeks, the Opera House was back in business. "Open Again, Old Stand," proclaimed the newspaper advertisements.[3] The Novelty Theatre, formerly the Tivoli, opened May 22, 1899, just in time for the Queen's birthday celebration, along with other establishments spared from the flames, including the Horseshoe (J. W. Marchbank, manager), Jim Daugherty's New Pavilion on King Street and the Phoenix (risen from the ashes) Dance Hall.[4] The Monte Carlo opened the week of June 7 with a farce based upon the hilarious Forty Mile trip of the steamers *Bonanza King* and *Tyrrell*. The cast included the Drummond Sisters, Cad Wilson, Blanche La Mont, Mulligan and Linton, and Nellie Lamore. The Novelty Theatre was offering some of the brightest acts in Dawson, including Fred Breen, Dick Maurettus, the Newman children, Maude Raymond, the Oatley Sisters, Daisy D'Avara and Freda Maloof.[5]

The Novelty Theatre was in the news when Freda Maloof was brought into court on charges of committing an indecent act in a public place. The reason: belly dancing in public. According to the *Klondike Nugget*,

> Freda, a seductive Greek dancer, whose portraits have graced the shop windows for a week, while her charms of person were simultaneously exhibited at the Novelty Theatre, was before Colonel Steele on Tuesday afternoon on the formal charge of committing an indecent act in a public place. In practical phraseology, objection was taken to her "whirlwind dance" from a moral standpoint.
>
> Freda was the most innocent of looking [sic] damsels as she stood before the soldier-justice, and she was evidently certain that he would succumb to the fascination

of her grace did he but give her an opportunity to exhibit her talents. "I assure you there is nothing wrong about the dance: I will show you how it goes," she said.

"Oh, never mind," quickly interrupted his worship, and he lost no time to calling the first witness to the stand in the person of Constable Owen.

Corporal Wilson conducted the prosecution and in answer to his questions, the constable said he had seen the can-can dance and the houchee-couchee, the Midway Plaisance, and the dancing of Miss Maloof is like the latter. "She doesn't dance with her feet," he said, "but it is done with the muscles of her stomach."

"Indeed, it's not the Midway dance at all, your honor," said Freda seriously; "it is a Mohammedan religious dance. I have danced it all over Turkey and the United States, before ladies and children, and this is the first time I have seen it objected to. If you would only let me show you how it is done judge," and the last remark was accompanied with a threatening tug upwards of the skirts.

But his lordship insisted on denying himself the pleasure, and Constable Dick was next put on the stand. He admitted that he had witnessed the celebrated muscle dance and considered it indecent ... his worship didn't consider that it made any difference if it was "a Mohammedan religious dance," and Freda was fined $25 and costs.[6]

That was not the only ruling that Sam Steele made as the overseer of law in Dawson City. By 1899 Dawson was losing the rough edges of its frontier existence, and this was the first of many actions that would be taken by subsequent administrations to civilize the gold-rush town. After the fire that had destroyed the heart of Dawson, Steele banished the prostitutes of Paradise Alley to swampy land well back from the business section of Dawson, on Fourth Avenue between King and Queen Streets. At one point, consideration was given to the construction of a large building in which they could ply their trade, but that didn't work out. In the end, they settled for two rows of small cribs facing each other along Fourth Avenue.[7]

Another amusement palace opened on July 28. The Amphitheatre, a large tent structure located behind the Regina Hotel offering legitimate drama to its audience, opened that evening with a performance titled *Sentenced to Death*. Corinne B. Gray, the leading lady, was noted for her acting ability as well as her extensive selection of costumes that allowed her to go through six complete changes each evening. Either the community was not yet ready for serious theatre, the location was too far from the Front Street hub, or Miss Gray's talents were not sufficient to attract an audience. The theatre troupe failed to get a full house on opening night, and after that little more was heard of the Amphitheatre.[8]

In addition to the theatre troupe that performed at the Amphitheatre, other professional theatre groups were starting to come into town. Frank Simons arrived in Dawson in a scow with "The Female Extravaganza Company," twenty actresses also known as "Frank Simons' Fairies."[9] Later in the season, A. B. Levie arrived with a new theatrical troupe, including the well-known comedy duo of Jennings and O'Brien.[10]

"There is probably no city of its size in the world," wrote Sam Dunham in a letter, "where there are so many orchestras and bands playing continuously as here, for all the dance halls and theaters, from 8 o'clock every night until 8 o'clock in the morning, are in full sway, with the exception of Saturday night, as they have to close at 12 o'clock then."[11] The newly established *Dawson Daily News* echoed that report when it stated, "Theatres, opera houses, dances, musicales and congenial companionship at the clubs serve to divert and console the exile, especially if he finds his stay is to be longer than he expected."[12]

In June, news started trickling into Dawson that gold had been discovered on the beaches of Nome, Alaska, looking out onto the Bering Sea.[13] Laura Berton, in her book *I Married the Klondike*, reports that eight thousand people left Dawson for Nome in one week in August, but this number is an exaggeration; the number of people who left the Klondike for the goldfields of Nome is likely closer to twenty-five hundred, of whom only fifteen hundred reached the Alaskan town before freeze-up.[14] Among these were several theatrical people. The character of theatre work in Nome differed from that in Dawson. While many well-known Dawson performers made the move, they seemed to perform less legitimate theatre. Vaudeville, amateur productions and minstrel shows, seldom performed in Dawson, were Nome favourites.[15] And while Nome attracted many, gold production in the Klondike continued to rise and the population of the Yukon stabilized, most of it in the Klondike region, with the population of Dawson settling at around forty-five hundred.

The Novelty Theatre closed for good on July 18 after being open for only two months, and the Amphitheatre was a flash in the pan, but the Dawson economy was still robust enough to support a lively theatre scene.[16] In fact, the Monte Carlo had a facelift in midsummer, reopening under the management of Harry Woolrich. The theatre was thoroughly remodelled and redecorated from top to bottom.[17] The poor-quality performances that had nonetheless thrilled audiences a year before were being replaced by more professional theatrical companies in 1899, with more frequent changes in programs and younger, prettier dance hall girls. Dance hall/theatre/

saloon/gambling hall combinations were one of the most remunerative service industries in Dawson. While the Mounted Police kept a close watch on behaviour, there were still few restrictions, and the Klondike was producing plenty of gold to fuel the local economy. The grandest theatre of them all was constructed and opened in the summer of 1899; it was called the Grand Opera House, and it was built by a supreme showman.

"Arizona Charlie" Meadows: King of the Cowboys

At almost six and a half feet tall, "Arizona Charlie" Meadows stood a head above the crowd. His hair flowed down to his shoulders from beneath his broad-brimmed hat. With moustache and a patch of whiskers below his bottom lip, wearing his signature red bandana around his neck and a fringed buckskin jacket, he was a sight from a Wild West show. He looked as if he was always on display.

In fact, Charlie Meadows *was* from a Wild West show. Often called King of the Cowboys, he had travelled around the world as part of one Wild West show after another. He had ridden in Buffalo Bill's world-famous event, and he had rubbed shoulders with the likes of Rudyard Kipling and Will Rogers. He was a persistent rainbow chaser, and he could certainly have been the prototype for the dime-novel hero of the era. It was no surprise that he chose to follow the throng north to the Klondike when gold fever struck in 1897.

Charlie, his wife Mae and an entourage headed north loaded down with food and several tons of supplies and equipment, including Charlie's rifle, a fancy pistol and plenty of whisky. It was one of the largest outfits being taken north the winter of 1897–98. The Meadows party avoided the seedy criminal elements of Skagway by taking their gear to Dyea and over the Chilkoot Trail. Once on the trail to Dawson, it seemed that everything that could go wrong did—flood, disease (his horses all died), shipwreck and freeze-up all impeded his progress to the Klondike—but despite these obstacles he made it to Dawson City by December of 1897.

Meadows was what they called a *plunger*, a person who took a chance at every opportunity. Soon he had shares in many claims in the Klondike. He printed a special vanity newspaper called the *Klondike News*—one edition only—and made $50,000 from that venture alone. But the venture for which Meadows is still remembered today is the building of the Grand Opera House. Always a showman, Meadows preferred entertainment to mining, so he sold off his mining investments and ploughed the proceeds into building the finest theatre in Dawson City. This building went through many name changes—the Grand Opera House, the Palace Grand, the Savoy, the Old Savoy, the Auditorium, the New Theatre, the De Luxe and the Nugget Dance Hall. But the name it is known by today is the Palace Grand.

The theatre was designed by C. H. Albertson, an architect from Portland, Oregon. The facade of the theatre is said to have been

The Grand Opera House, built by "Arizona Charlie" Meadows, was the largest theatre constructed in Dawson City. Now known as the Palace Grand, it was demolished and reconstructed by Parks Canada, opening on July 1, 1962. Dawson City Museum, 1998.22.704.

built from the remains of two abandoned sternwheelers because lumber was in short supply. The building was three storeys high with horseshoe-shaped balconies on the second and third floors that were filled with private boxes for the use of wealthy patrons. In the Grand Opera House, the saloon and gambling hall occupied the front portion of the building, and the theatre, the rear. A bar ran along the right-hand wall of the saloon, behind which, instead of the traditional panels of mirrors, the walls were decorated with large scenic northern views painted by artist Arthur Buel.

The smoke-filled saloon was usually filled with a boisterous crowd of men, "spitting, smoking, swearing, drinking and gambling."[18] The most popular game of the time was faro, along with roulette and poker. Marathon poker games often went on for days, with some that ran up stakes as high as $50,000. This was not the most comfortable environment for respectable women to have to pass through if they wished to attend the theatre, and as the community became more settled and stable, anti-saloon lobbyists would later cause saloons and theatres to be run in separate establishments.

The theatre was a mixture of elegance and frontier—ornate decorative features set against rough timber. When he couldn't find the appropriate theatre seating in time for the opening, for example, Meadows settled for five hundred high-backed kitchen chairs. The paint wasn't entirely dry for the first performance in the new theatre, and the curtains and stage settings didn't work properly at first, but the town filled the building anyway. Included among the throng were people from all strata of society, plus a couple of stray dogs, which were eventually removed from the premises. Despite the uncomfortable seating, Charlie's take for the opening night performance on July 18, 1899, was $12,000.

The performances in Klondike theatres at this time were a mixture of professional performers and rowdy audiences. The *Klondike*

Nugget explained to newcomers that when a theatre patron was pleased with the performance, "his outward expression of appreciation takes the form of a well stimulated malamoot howl."[19] From outside, the casual passerby might conclude that the building was filled with howling huskies, or lunatics.

Members of Frank Simons's theatrical troupe, having arrived in Dawson the previous month, entertained the crowd at the Grand Opera House on opening night. First, a "beauteous fairy queen drawn in a luxurious barge by a pair of swans came on the scene. Alighting gracefully and with all the dignity of royalty, she advanced to the front of the stage … But then, instead of addressing her subjects upon grave and lofty matters of state … she turned toward the audience and regaled them with a rendition of the masterpiece of harmony and sentiment, entitled 'All Coons Look Alike to Me.'"[20] This was followed by a ballet. The audience was captivated by one lithesome dancer, who was so thin that she became almost "invisible except at certain angles."[21] This was followed by Pauline Caine's performance of the serpentine dance, a juggler, a trick bicyclist, and the magic act of Vorhees and Davis.[22]

The Grand Opera House quickly became the centre of Dawson theatre life. Acts varied from melodramas to acrobats, trained dogs, dancing bears, magicians, knife-throwers, tumblers and comedians. The theatre also presented special events such as boxing matches, dramatic readings, chorus lines, benefits, balls and even sacred concerts.

Acting as the master of ceremonies, "Arizona Charlie" typically appeared on stage before the curtain was raised, where, sombrero in hand, he would make a broad sweeping bow and introduce the evening's program. On a slow night, he would liven up the crowd with demonstrations of his prowess with a gun by shooting at a cigarette held in his wife Mae's mouth, or targeting glass balls held between her fingers. That always put life back into

CHAPTER 4

In addition to putting on theatrical productions, the Palace Grand was used for social functions such as this fundraising dinner in 1900. Dawson City Museum, 1962.7.62.

the crowd, until one evening he shot off the end of one of her fingers, and the shooting demonstrations ceased for good. In another presentation titled "The Arizona Scout," Meadows almost drowned in a set of his own design, in which he was to fall into a tank filled with almost three metres of water while on the back of a horse. As the horse fell in, he grabbed for the rail and missed, finding himself in the tank and under the flailing horse. Fortunately, stagehands pulled him to safety.[23] The newspaper account does not report on the horse's status, but a description of the event suggested the tank contained a platform at the bottom that could be raised to stage level for the horse to get out.

In October, Meadows turned the management of the theatre over to George Hillyer, who changed its name from Grand Opera House to the Palace Grand and promised to turn it into a "strictly legitimate house" where ladies would not have to run the gauntlet through the saloon and gambling area. But Dawson was not yet ready for legitimate theatre. The first play, a production of Goethe's *Faust*, although it received positive reviews, was not well attended. Hillyer stumbled through an unprofitable run in October, turning the theatre over to a joint stock company managed by Frank Gardner in November.[24] This proved equally unpopular and unprofitable and quickly folded, leaving the theatre open to rentals for special events. The St. Andrew's Ball and Banquet brought out a full house on November 30. Dawson ladies sponsored a bazaar at the Palace Grand in the days leading up to Christmas, a masquerade ball for New Year's Eve, and a Sunday evening concert played to a full house on January 7.[25]

Up in Flames

At 3:20 p.m. on January 9, 1900, fire broke out in the attic of the Monte Carlo, above Florence Brocee's room. The building was quickly engulfed, but the fire department responded promptly, arriving on the scene with two pumpers within five minutes. Great progress was made with the fire engine until one of the hoses ruptured, and the blaze picked up and spread to the south, consuming all the buildings to the Aurora Saloon at the south end of the block, which was itself spared.[26] Again, the businesspeople on Front Street began rebuilding as soon as the embers had died. Arrangements were made to replace the former Horseshoe with a theatre, and the Monte Carlo would soon be reconstructed. But the Opera House had seen its last performance and never reopened. The fire wiped out its owners financially; Gus Bakke and Ramps Peterson left for downriver, while the third partner, Tom Wilson, died a short time later and was buried in the cemetery above Dawson.[27]

The occupants of the Monte Carlo and the Opera House, many of them members of the theatre companies performing there, escaped with their lives, but not their belongings. Among those living at the Monte Carlo who lost everything were the O'Brien family, Lucy Lovell, Gertie Lovejoy, Rose Blumkin and Jacqueline, as well as Josie Myers, the proprietor of the Monte Carlo. Among the members of the stock company occupying the upper storey of the Opera House were Gussie Lamore, Beatrice Lorne, Mamie Hightower and Alex Pantages. The Board of Trade building (formerly the Horseshoe) situated beside the Monte Carlo to the north was also destroyed. After the fire, the Pavilion, which was well removed from the scene of the blaze, was the only dance hall still operating; consequently, the joint was jumping the following night.

The Orpheum Theatre: New Kid on the Block

Before the fire, the stock company performing at the Opera House was a co-operative enterprise. Paul Boardman was chosen as the stage manager, and Alexander Pantages served as the manager of the theatre in conjunction with a board of trustees that consisted of Theo Eggert, Tom Rooney and Claude Staton. Pantages was a "stocky, tough and robust, self-made man."[28] Later described as "a meek-eyed swarthy son of southern Europe" by the *Dawson Daily News*, he had a square face with intense dark eyes and neat short black hair parted in the middle and combed back on each side.[29] There is some debate about his birthdate and place of origin, although most agree that he was born in Greece. He worked and travelled from a young age before joining the stampede to the Klondike in the early stages of the gold rush. Pantages first became a well-known porter working at the Dawson City Opera House. He spoke half a dozen languages, English as badly as any. He was illiterate but known to be thrifty with his money and had saved up a substantial sum to invest in Dawson show business. He also proved to be one of the more successful theatre managers during the turbulent gold-rush years.

After the Horseshoe was destroyed by fire in January of 1900, it was rebuilt as the Orpheum Theatre. The first theatrical production performed in the new building on February 26, 1900, was *Who's Baby?*

Dawson City Museum, Frederick Atwood fonds.

Pantages ensured that the salaries of his performers were on par with what they had received before the stock company was formed. Surplus revenue would be set aside for contingencies.[30] While Ed O'Brien's company was performing George Bernard Shaw's farce *A Hole in the Wall* at the Monte Carlo, Pantages and his new company were into the second week of *The Circus Girl* at the Opera House. The actress Blossom was featured in *Fanchon the Cricket*, soprano Beatrice Lorne

CHAPTER 4

Once opened, the Orpheum became a mainstay of live theatre in Dawson, and later for the screening of moving pictures. Goetzman photo, Gates collection.

was becoming a crowd favourite and Blanche Cammetta, another singer, was gaining popularity. But all of that came to a skidding halt with the fire on January 9.

There was a mad scramble after the fire to re-establish theatrical entertainment. Charlie Meadows came to an agreement with Ed O'Brien and Dick Davenport from the Monte Carlo troupe to lease the Palace Grand Theatre to them until the end of April.[31] Henceforth, the Monte Carlo did not feature in the theatrical world in Dawson. The performance in the Palace Grand on January 13, which was for families, featured well-known stage names including Conchita, Cecil Marion and Beatrice Lorne. The play titled *Josh Whitcomb* was followed by regular vaudeville acts, concluding with one of O'Brien's popular comedy sketches.[32]

The task for Pantages and the Opera House co-operative stock company was going to take longer. They came to an agreement with property owners George Apple and Ben Levy to build a new house of entertainment where the Horseshoe had once stood. The building was to be the full size of the lot, with two tiers of theatre boxes. The fourteen rooms on the second floor would be rented out as office space. The building would be wired for electrical lighting (no kerosene lamps were allowed), and all the chimneys would be of brick. In addition to the actors, all from the Opera House company, the orchestra would also be conducted by an Opera House transplant, William Brennan.[33] They had a tight construction schedule, and the theatre was to reopen by January 22. That was too ambitious, however, and it was later rescheduled to open February 12. That too was overly optimistic, and the Orpheum Theatre finally opened to an appreciative full house on February 26, 1900.

The evening was heralded as a success; the building was praised, the actors were lauded, and the orchestra, led by Brennan, was judged first rate. According to the *Dawson Daily News*: "It was a typical night of 'wine, women and song,' characteristic of Dawson and its energetic population, and recalled to many a sourdough the palmy days of '97 and '98 ..." The three-act Nat Goodwin comedy *Who's Baby?* was considered, aside from a few technical glitches normal for an opening night, a success from the moment the lights came up until the curtain came down at 2:30 in the morning. The receipts for wine and other "concoctions" exceeded $3,000.[34] But the

CHAPTER 4

same week, the Palace Grand Theatre was dark, as explained in the *News*, because the co-operative plan had proved to be a financial failure for the performers.[35] A month later, however, it was back in business under new management. Maurettus and Hull, Mulligan and Linton and comedian Eddie Dolan were included on the playbill along with slack wire performer Miss Garrett.[36]

Over the following months, the three main theatres, the Orpheum, the Palace Grand and the Pavilion, were engaged in a fierce competition for customers. The Palace Grand and the Orpheum programs now featured a comedy or a dramatic performance as well as the variety acts that patrons had long been accustomed to. The Pavilion operated as a dance hall during the same period. Through the spring and summer, the Palace Grand was the scene of special events—special Sunday evening concerts, symphony concerts, boxing matches, fundraising events for charitable causes (including one event that featured musicians from both the Orpheum and the Pavilion), minstrel shows (featuring local talent) and public meetings. Not to be outdone, the Orpheum came up with similar events, with some notable attention-getters including a circus street parade that reportedly featured a chariot, giraffes, a brass band and camels. Following them was a cage holding "Bug House Ike, the Wild Man," a specimen of manhood from Lousetown. Another cage contained "hootch worms," a third restrained the "Congo It," and two more followed, one containing Arizona lizards and the other two young bears. No parade would be complete without a clown, who, in this case, had a trick donkey. Bringing up the rear were mule and dog teams pulling carts, all to the amusement of the onlookers.[37]

"Lifelike and Real"

Among the special features that both the Orpheum and the Palace Grand offered to their patrons were animated films. From the moment his Armatuograph projector arrived on June 18, 1900, Alex Pantages was offering movies as a regular part of the program at the Orpheum, featuring Tomerlin's moving pictures.[38] He kept amusing his patrons with new selections as the reels arrived on the boats from outside. Late in August, the *Dawson Daily News* announced the arrival of a fresh batch of reels: "These pictures are all new, embracing the most interesting, exciting and up-to-date subjects, including thrilling war scenes, movements of troops, a Spanish bullfight and others. They are cast upon the canvas by the Armatuograph and are so lifelike and real that the originals could not be viewed to any better advantage. During the evening a phonograph of large proportions with a sonorous megaphone attached, discourses the latest selections. None should miss seeing these pictures and hearing the big phonograph, for they are a treat."[39]

Meanwhile, Walter Parkes was back in Dawson at the Palace Grand Theatre giving his illustrated lecture covering a trip to Nome by both the Pacific and Yukon routes. The *News* reported that the hit of the evening was "the moving picture of a scow running the White Horse rapids. This aroused the audience and the picture had to be repeated."[40] While not the first to record the Klondike on moving film—the Edison Company had come to the Klondike in 1899 to film the gold rush (see sidebar)—the footage of the Whitehorse Rapids may have been the first of the Yukon ever shown in Dawson City.[41] Parkes would be in Dawson for some time to capture more Klondike scenes on his camera and occasionally repeat his illustrated lectures.

The Edison Company Films the Klondike Gold Rush

The Weekly Wisconsin published the following story on November 11, 1899:

Workmen are busy in the Edison laboratory in West Orange [New Jersey] developing the most unique collection of moving picture films ever yet exhibited. The pictures were brought back by a party of photographers who were sent to the Klondike by the Edison company, and are intended to be part of the Edison exhibit in the Paris exposition. All of the films which so far have been developed are successes, and the entire series will exhibit the actual life in the Klondike regions as it has never before been illustrated. R. K. Bonine, Mr. Edison's personal representative, and Thomas Crahan were the heads of the photographing party, which started for the Klondike in June, 1898. Mr. Bonine previously had visited the region, and was in charge of the route and selection of the scenes to be photographed. Among the films are scenes in the Klondike all along the route between Skaguay, on the Alaska coast, to Dawson. They also show views of mining and washing of gold. The pictures were taken with a new giant machine arranged by Mr. Edison for the trip. It took pictures nine times the size of ordinary film pictures. To use the larger film it was necessary to reduce the speed of the machine from forty-five to twenty pictures a second. The scenes gained in clearness by the process.[42]

A Busy Season

The Frank Simons theatre troupe, which had a short run at the Palace Grand, packed up and left Dawson for Nome in the middle of July, taking with them the popular family act now billed as O'Brien, Jennings and O'Brien. The O'Briens planned to return to Dawson in the fall if the conditions were favourable. The theatre remained dark for several weeks until the arrival of a new troupe, fresh from Victoria.

The arrival of the steamer *Yukoner* on August 9 was heralded triumphantly. Lashed to the mast on the bow of the vessel by the jubilant crew of the *Yukoner* was a broom, which symbolized the sweeping away of the record for the fastest trip from Whitehorse to Dawson ever recorded to that time.[43] The *Yukoner* carried with her from Whitehorse forty-two members of the Savoy Theatre Company from Victoria, headed by Steve O'Brien (no relation to the family act that had just departed for Nome) and W. R. Jackson. The company consisted of the orchestra and an assortment of entertainers including singers, dancers, comedians, acrobats and actresses, and a young sketch artist named Kathleen "Kate" Rockwell. Rockwell had been a regular on the theatre circuit in the Northwest before coming north with the Savoy Company.[44]

Jackson and O'Brien's Savoy Company signed a fourteen-month lease for the use of the Palace Grand Theatre and renamed the building the Savoy Theatre. Ever since it first opened, the theatre had struggled with its identity. It was clearly the best built and most suited as a theatre of any of the buildings in Dawson, and its owner had aspired to introduce legitimate theatre to Dawson City, but the town still wasn't ready for refined entertainment. Not only did the theatre struggle to draw patrons from the more cultured elements of society, but those people would not fill enough seats to make it profitable. Getting a liquor license would increase profitability but would discourage the more genteel members of society from attending. Thus, to isolate the more offensive aspect of the theatre and make it more respectable, the saloon and gambling areas at the front of the main floor had been partitioned off, creating a corridor from the front entrance into the theatre. When the Savoy Company took possession of the space, they doubled down by obtaining a license to operate a bar on the second floor.[45]

Meanwhile, Alexander Pantages, the manager of the Orpheum, was proving to be the most durable and successful theatre manager in Dawson. The Orpheum opened on August 21 with *The Circus Girl*, starring Blossom and Lucy Lovell. The comedy team of Post and Ashley made an appearance, followed by entertaining songstress Ida Howell, billed as the "dashing serio-comic singer and dancer." Others on the bill included Alf Layne, Fred Breen, Billy Mullen and Mamie Hightower.[46]

The Pavilion, which had continued to operate but with a low profile during the period after the January fire, came under new management in August. Theodore Eggert, the new manager, closed the theatre for renovations, which, he claimed, would make it the finest theatre in Dawson City. It was enlarged, given a face-lift, remodelled and wired for electricity. Improved ventilation and heating were installed to add to the comfort and enjoyment of patrons. The new theatre reopened as the Standard on September 3. All the actors who had performed at the Orpheum the previous week appeared at the Standard in Charles Fawcett's three-act farce, *Tragedy*.

Cad Wilson, who had just arrived back in Dawson from Nome on the steamer *Hannah*, was added to the Standard's program along with Ida Howell.[47] Earlier in June, Wilson had stopped in Dawson for two weeks, in the company of Nellie Holgate, and performed

The Pavilion Theatre reopened on September 3, 1900 as the Standard. Pictured here is the New Year's Eve ball in the Standard on December 31, 1900. Yukon Archives, Clayton Betts Collection, 83/47, #9434.

at the Orpheum Theatre before heading downriver aboard the *Hannah*.[48] Her time in Nome had not panned out, so she was now back in Dawson again, where she continued to perform until at least December. The three theatres, the Savoy, the Standard and the Orpheum, vied for customers over the winter of 1900–01, but business was highly competitive and the clientele was shrinking.

The territorial council put the squeeze on the Dawson theatre world by establishing regulations that prohibited women from soliciting drinks or drinking in the theatre boxes. "Last night the houses were well filled," reported the *Klondike Nugget* of December 6, "but that cannot be taken as a basis for a forecast of the matter, because the houses always draw better on the first and second nights than later in the week, so that it is still an open question as to whether or not legitimate theatrical business, run solely upon its merits, will pay in Dawson, or whether the first gloomy view taken by the managers after the issuance of the order was a correct one."[49] The managers of the Savoy and the Standard were both compliant with the new liquor regulations and also changed their programs to include more legitimate theatrical presentations.

By January 1901, Theodore Eggert had split the management responsibilities at the Standard with Alf Layne, who managed the theatrical side of things while Eggert focused on managing the bar. To make the theatre more appealing to respectable Dawson ladies, they were planning to give family-rated performances and cover over the bar for the evening. "The management will devote its energies to making the Standard a first class, respectable resort," they announced in the *Klondike Nugget*, "sure to be appreciated by a large element of both those who at present patronize theatres and many who do not."[50] The tide had turned, and events and circumstances would come together to foretell the gradual decline of professional theatre in Dawson City. Dawson was changing, its tastes becoming more refined, but it was a slow change.

CHAPTER 5

THE TWILIGHT YEARS

1901-1914

Machines over Men

Nineteen hundred was the peak year of gold production in the Klondike; after that, the richest Klondike ground was worked out, and the amount recovered from the frozen gravels went into a gradual decline. The era of individual miners gave way to highly efficient industrial-scale mining techniques that required capital investments beyond the means of a single miner, no matter how rich he might be.

Men like Arthur Newton Christian Treadgold and Joe Boyle secured concessions to large tracts of land in the valleys of the Klondike River basin. Treadgold and Boyle were men of vision, and while neither was an expert in the science of mining, they both made up for that with their ability to inspire investors and attract money. Boyle secured a concession in the Klondike Valley that stretched from the mouth of the Klondike River all the way to Hunker Creek;

Treadgold's concession gave him control of Bonanza, Eldorado, Hunker and Bear Creeks. Boyle's company set about mining below the mouth of Bear Creek, and in 1905, he oversaw the construction of the first in a fleet of gold dredges. Treadgold got the financial backing of the Guggenheims, who initiated an ambitious program of development in the goldfields starting in 1906. That year heralded the advent of corporate industrial mining in the Klondike. Both Treadgold's and Boyle's companies consolidated the large tracts of placer ground necessary to mine with dredges or to use jets of water to wash gold from the gravels of the hills above by hydraulic means.

A railroad was constructed in 1905 that enabled the cheap transportation of machinery from Dawson City into the goldfields. The replacement of hand labour with steam-powered machinery further accelerated the depopulation of the creeks. The creek bottoms were filled with networks of thawing points, long hollow steel rods that injected steam into the frozen ground to thaw it so the dredges, with their insatiable appetites, could chew up the softened ground and process the gold. A massive ditch and pipeline system reaching more than a hundred kilometres into the Ogilvie Mountains north of Dawson was constructed to transport water for hydraulic mining on the hills above Bonanza Creek.

In the early stages, the construction of these ambitious projects kept hundreds of men employed. During peak periods of activity, there were eighteen hundred men working and a payroll of $300,000 per month. By 1913, Treadgold's brainchild, the Yukon Gold Company, was regularly churning through several million cubic metres of gravel each year. The company had prospecting drills systematically testing the frozen ground for future development. Tens of thousands of cords of wood were burned annually to produce the steam for thawing the ground ahead of the dredges. Thawing the ground represented half the cost of mining with dredges. Water was washing away hillsides at sixteen different hydraulic operations, three-quarters of them on Bonanza and Eldorado Creeks, and nine electrically powered dredges scoured the valley bottoms. Seven of the nine were plowing their way through the gravels of Bonanza and Eldorado Creeks.

The bustling goldfield communities that had thrived at the height of the gold rush began to disappear. Gold Bottom, Gold Run, Sulphur City and Caribou were abandoned by people moving to greener pastures and were replaced by temporary mining camps that serviced the dredges. Grand Forks, the largest of the goldfield centres, which had once thrived at the confluence of Bonanza and Eldorado Creeks, gradually shrank. By 1909, it was a shell of its former self. The town acquired a gap-toothed appearance as buildings were demolished or moved. In 1910, half of what remained went up in smoke when a major fire swept through town. Another fire completed the devastation the following year. By that time, the Yukon Gold Company was constructing Dredge No. 9 a short distance from where the NAT&T CO. store had once stood. When completed, the dredge began undercutting the very ground upon which the town was located. The Gold Hill Hotel, built by Belinda Mulroney at the peak of the gold rush, continued to operate for a few more years. After that, Grand Forks became a ghost town, merely another memory of the glory days of the gold rush.

Although it shrank, Dawson City did not suffer the same fate as Grand Forks. It remained the supply centre and hub for mining in the surrounding goldfields. Between 1901 and 1911, the population declined to three thousand, but the community stabilized. Gone were the outrageous excesses of the Klondike stampede, replaced by a more civilized infrastructure that supported the new order. The federal government brought in architect Thomas W. Fuller, who in 1901 oversaw the construction of several massive federal buildings:

an administrative centre, courthouse, school, post office, telegraph station, and a luxurious mansion to house the commissioner, the federal government's chief executive in the territory.[1] Through the generosity of steel magnate Andrew Carnegie, Dawson built an impressive new library in 1903. Two substantial banks were built, and the Anglican, Catholic and Presbyterian churches filled the streetscape. Dawson was becoming an example of post-Victorian modernity; civilization had arrived in the Klondike.

The remaining theatres, dance halls and saloons in the business district faced declining revenues and falling patronage. The discovery of gold in Nome drew many away from Dawson, while the birth of Fairbanks in 1903 near another goldfield lured even more away from the Klondike. The demographic gradually changed; Dawson became less American and more British, while the imbalance between men and women began to even out. With this came a new social order that dramatically changed the character of the bustling little mining town. Thus, it was not only the economic decline and the falling population that started to squeeze the pleasure palaces of Dawson. Increasing pressure to instill higher moral values as well as government regulations finally forced the issue.

"Shameful Evils": Temperance Takes Hold

In the early days of Dawson, establishing licenses and fines for saloons, gaming houses and brothels helped finance the infrastructure of the community. The Yukon Act in 1898 established a licensing structure. Hotels paid two thousand dollars per year, saloons, twenty-five hundred, and theatres with bars also required a saloon license. Similarly, when Superintendent Sam Steele of the Mounted Police arrived in Dawson, he established the practice of fining "knights of the green cloth" every month, with the hint to leave town. The gambling fraternity came to regard this as a form of licensing and carried on as usual. Some came to court and paid their fines voluntarily, without waiting for a summons. The Mounted Police wanted a crackdown on gambling, yet they recognized that the saloons, dance halls and theatres were an important part of the local economy, and immediate closure would throw people out of work, causing financial hardship for many prominent businessmen. It was a fine balance, but they kept close watch on activities in the saloons and dance halls, even having undercover agents providing vital information on the bad elements that inhabited them.[2]

In the autumn of 1899, after Superintendent Sam Steele had forced the relocation of the doxies of Paradise Alley to Fourth Avenue, forty-three of them were listed by name in a Mounted Police report prepared for Steele's replacement, A. B. Perry. By the spring of 1900, many of them had left for greener pastures in the goldfields of Nome. When Dawson's new public school was built in 1901 across the street from the row of cribs along either side of Fourth Avenue, the remaining prostitutes were forced to move again, this time to the south end of Dawson. But by May 1, it was decreed that all prostitutes within the city limits would be prosecuted, so they moved across the Klondike River to Klondike City, despite the protests of residents there. By October of 1901, only twenty-five remained in Dawson.[3]

Also in 1901, regulations were imposed by the territorial council that no liquor should be served in a dance hall, except from a bar. When that didn't seem to work, the regulation was modified the following year to stipulate that no dancing was to be permitted in any establishment that served liquor. They doubled down on this by adding an additional clause that there should be "no connection between any licensed premises and any dance hall or room in which public dancing is allowed, by means of doors, windows, wickets, elevators, chutes or openings of any kind."[4] Fines would be imposed for dance halls or saloons renting rooms for immoral purposes, and women serving alcohol for a percentage was prohibited. Enforcement of such laws was left to the discretion of the commissioner through his license inspectors. When Frederick Congdon assumed the commissionership in 1903, he used this power as a form of patronage, and those who were sympathetic with his political cause could flout the law with impunity provided that kickbacks were paid to the Congdon machine. This all came to an end in 1904, when Congdon resigned his position as commissioner to seek the Yukon seat in the federal election in December of that year.[5]

The most serious of the vices in early Dawson was seen to be gambling. At the time, it was reported that there were eight gambling halls and two dance halls (with gaming tables) in Dawson, inhabited by 110 gamblers and forty-two dance hall girls.[6] Early in 1900, complaints were sent to Ottawa from church congregations and temperance groups to put an end to the "shameful evils that are a disgrace to our Christian civilization" in the Klondike. Clifford Sifton, the government minister in Ottawa responsible for the administration of the Yukon, sent instructions to Commissioner Ogilvie demanding that the gambling dens be shut down. Ogilvie, feeling that gambling was one of the necessary evils associated with the gold-rush town, first protested Sifton's instructions before he finally relented. On February 27, 1901, he ordered the dance halls and gambling palaces be shut down by Friday, March 15. In response to the public uproar, especially from the proprietors of the businesses affected (arguing financial hardship), Sifton postponed his order of closure to June 1, but his instructions for the reversal did not reach Dawson until the March 15 closure had been put into effect. Dawson was dead calm for a day but reopened for business the following Monday.

In the meantime, Commissioner Ogilvie had resigned, and it was left to his successor, J. H. Ross, to put the second closure into effect. The protests to the second closure date were so loud that Ross came up with a compromise: roulette, faro and craps would be banned, but blackjack and poker would be allowed provided that the dealers were not employed by the house, chips were used, and the games were removed from the barrooms. But this order was rescinded in November, and legal gaming was closed for good in Dawson City.[7] In theory, that meant Dawson was like most comparable Canadian cities, but in reality, that closure did not happen until the patronage of the Congdon administration was brought to a halt in 1904 after his resignation. After that time, entertainment was limited to dry theatres and "temperance dance halls."[8]

A Slow Decline

These changes did not immediately foretell the end of theatre in Dawson. The playhouses were offering more legitimate stage productions throughout the winter of 1901. Early in the new year, the Savoy was offering a series of skits featuring Jim Post and Dick Maurettus, Ashley and Bryant, and Jennie Guichard, followed by variety performances. The orchestra was up to its usual high standard. Meanwhile, the Orpheum was offering *The Ticket-of-Leave Man* starring P. C. Lewis in the leading role, supported by a cast that included Fred Breen and Babe Pyne.

The variety acts at the Orpheum, including performances by May Miner, Lillian Haynes, Gladys Gates and Kate Rockwell, brought prolonged applause. Rockwell had left the Savoy troupe the previous fall and moved in with the Orpheum stock company and its manager, Alex Pantages. The Standard was offering the play

Champagne and Oysters to its discerning clientele, with a strong cast including Alf Layne, Daisy D'Avara, Beatrice Lorne and a new addition to the troupe, George Troxwell. The acts that followed included Eddie Dolan, Beatrice Lorne, Dolly Mitchell, Troxwell and Evans, and the Winchell Sisters. A farce titled *Trouble* ended the evening performance.[9]

The Savoy was packed when, on January 31, 1901, a memorial service was held to mourn the death of Queen Victoria. It continued to offer its Sunday sacred concerts, augmented by the moving pictures of Professor Walter Parkes and his Wondroscope projector, despite an injunction obtained by Alex Pantages for the films to be shown only at the Orpheum Theatre.[10]

The Standard Theatre, formerly the Pavilion, came under the sole ownership of Murray Eads in late March, Eads having bought out the interests of Theodore Eggert and others. Eads had plans to make improvements to the theatre; meanwhile, new vaudeville acts were on their way to Dawson "over the ice." The Standard Theatre was the most active entertainment centre during the following months, offering a steady stream of new productions. The lease for the Savoy Theatre by Jackson and O'Brien ended in early October, and the Savoy Stock Company moved to a new location on Front Street opposite the ritish Yukon Navigation's waterfront building. Presumably, the Orpheum Theatre was renamed the New Savoy while occupied by Jackson and O'Brien's Savoy troupe. In early January the theatre was being managed by Alex Pantages, and many of the regulars from the Orpheum company including Kate Rockwell (the Fashion Plate), Cecil Marion (the Sweet Singer), Dollie Mitchell (the Queen of Song and Dance), John Mulligan (the ventriloquist) and Maurettus and Brown (in an act described as "Too Hard to Beat") also performed on stage.[11]

After the Savoy Company completed its lease, Charlie Meadows put the Old Savoy up for sale. Mining millionaire "Arkansaw Jim"

Hall, owner of Claim Number 17 on Eldorado Creek, the richest claim in the Klondike, bought the theatre from Meadows in October 1901 for roughly $16,000, half paid in cash and half in gold dust from Hall's Eldorado Creek claim. Hall renamed the theatre the Auditorium a few weeks later. It is a reflection of the declining fortunes of Dawson business that an offer had been made on the theatre in the spring of 1901 for $36,000 and the value had been downgraded to half of that in the fall, and the actual sale price failed to meet even that amount.[12] The Standard Theatre faded from the scene in 1902, leaving the Orpheum and the "Old" Savoy, now renamed the Auditorium, to duke it out.

Willie Bittner: The Father of Legitimate Theatre

Shortly after the transaction was completed, the new manager of the theatre, William "Willie" Bittner, arrived on November 1, 1901, aboard the *Emma Nott*, one of the last vessels to reach Dawson before freeze-up. The hefty theatrical manager would eventually become known as the father of legitimate theatre in Dawson.

In the months that followed, Bittner produced a series of theatrical events at the Auditorium. "The run of the play, 'The Land of the Midnight Sun,' this week at the Auditorium," proclaimed the *Yukon Sun*, "is one of the most successful since the opening of the house under the current management. The house is crowded every night, and those who go are more than satisfied that they have gotten the worth of their money."[13] The production was succeeded by *David Harum* the following week (it is interesting to note that at the same time, the Orpheum was advertising the more titillating title, *A Turkish Harem*, against it) and *The Golden Giant* the week after that.[14] But Bittner's legitimate stage productions did not seem

CHAPTER 5

> **Orpheum Theatre**
> ALEX. PANTAGES, Mgr.
> **"A JAY CIRCUS!"**
> By Dick Maurettus.
> **New Specialties!**
> Living Pictures by Kate Rockwell.

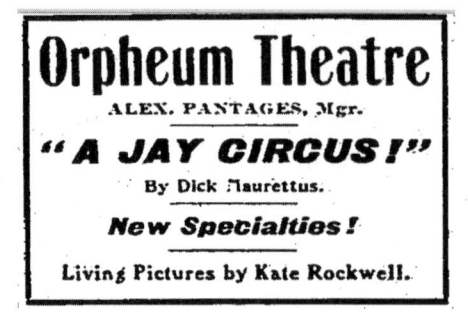

Alex Pantages managed the Orpheum Theatre, and Kate Rockwell produced her standard offering of tableaux, or "living pictures." *Dawson Daily News*, May 10, 1902, Yukon Archives.

to hold the same attraction for patrons. The *Dawson Daily News* reported only "a small though very appreciative audience" attended *The Golden Giant*, and Bittner made sarcastic note of the poor turnout at the front of the stage while the curtains were drawn closed between acts.[15] The *News* contrasted this against the large audience that attended the Orpheum production of the comedy *A Country Circus* the same evening. The Orpheum introduced something that would become a specialty for Kate Rockwell. A dozen artistic statuary groupings, or tableaux, were presented, including *An Affair of Honor, Diana, Night, Morning* and *Song of the Slave*.[16]

Attendance swelled at the Auditorium for the production of *The Girl I Left Behind Me*. Joining Bittner on stage were such thespian regulars as Lucy Lovell, Alf Layne, Ralph Cummings and Ray Southard. However, the surge in attendance was not the rule but the exception. On May 27, 1902, Bittner announced that despite regular patronage during the winter months, he was going to close the theatre. He had surpassed everybody's expectations by attracting a regular clientele to his productions of legitimate theatre, but as the summer months approached, house numbers had dwindled to an alarming level. According to Bittner, "Everybody told me when I came in last fall that during the winter it was dull, but in the spring—oh, my! Now, instead of business picking up, there has been a decided falling off in the last three weeks, especially with my best patrons who occupy the boxes ... I find that I'm in hock—in hock. So, you see, I can't stay here and wait for the dull times after having seen what you call good times."[17]

But despite his predictions of doom, by the beginning of June Bittner had enlisted commitments from enough patrons to confirm another six-week engagement. He would decide at the end of that time if he could afford to continue for another year. Many of the same names would remain in the cast, including Layne, Southard, Cummings and Lovell. The theatrical community threw its support behind the effort to save Bittner's company. On June 15, a Sunday benefit concert attracted a full house and featured a variety of acts, including Mr. and Mrs. Bittner, Noel the female impersonator, Madge Melville, Rooney and Forrester (with a rollicking sketch), Dunn the whistler, plus Ray Southard and singer Carrie Winchell. As a novelty act, "Professor" Placell played several phonograph records on a huge player with a pair of large resonators.

In early July, buoyed by the positive community response, Bittner announced that he would undertake theatre renovations for the next five weeks. The stage would be deepened by six metres and the space over it heightened to accommodate the scenery changes. Seating at the back would be raised to afford a better view of the stage, the lower tier of boxes would be removed and the upper ones would have added privacy.[18] New faces would be added when the theatre reopened. Three days after the early July announcement, Bittner left Dawson aboard the steamer *La France*.[19] Before a month had passed, he returned with new actors and actresses in tow and with plans to open the theatre with a performance within a few days.

During Bittner's absence, Jim Hall had spent money to make improvements to the Auditorium. The boxes were now more presentable, the stairway was widened and a second staircase was built and carpeting laid. The stairs no longer squeaked. The tickets for the first night's performance quickly sold out.

But Willie Bittner's dream of bringing legitimate theatre to Dawson City was undermined by a shrinking economy and declining population. He would leave Dawson City the following year, never to return. "The withdrawal of Bittner from the Yukon closes an interesting chapter in the theatrical history of the place," reported the *Dawson Daily News* in October of 1903. Although he had succeeded financially at first, declining receipts caused Bittner to join forces with the Lillian Hall and Newman theatrical companies the summer of 1903.[20] The rotund actor departed Dawson aboard the tiny vessel *Thistle*. "When he went on the starboard side," reported the *News*, there was a list to that side of the ship. When he went to the other side, there was a port list."[21] Bittner was one of many actors who were abandoning Dawson City for greener pastures and full houses. Theo Eggert and his wife accompanied Bittner on the *Thistle*, while Mike Hooley, another member of his production company, departed aboard the *Dawson*.

The Exodus

They weren't the only ones leaving Dawson. According to Ellis Lucia, in his book *Klondike Kate*, Kate Rockwell left Dawson in the spring of the year before and set up a moving-picture theatre in Victoria. We know, however, that she was still in Dawson City in July 1902, performing at the Orpheum.[22] She arrived in Victoria aboard the steamer *Charmer* from Vancouver on November 24, 1902.[23] Within days, she was performing at the Delmonico Theatre.[24] By February of 1903, she had leased the Orpheum Theatre at 67 Yates

Street in Victoria.[25] In an interview, she told long-time Yukoner Victoria Faulkner:

> I had the first moving picture in Victoria, a silent machine called a Biograph. The entertainment consisted of one act vaudeville and the Biograph machine. Admittance was 10¢ and 15¢ and there have been times when I have seen only two people as audience. We also had items of illustrated song. The illustrated song was a soloist usually who [sang] sentimental songs to the accompaniment of colored lantern slides.
>
> We advertised an afternoon matinee too. But it was my money which supported it. I pawned my diamonds for $350 with Mr. Aronson the pawnbroker, borrowed it with my diamonds as security, and then bought out Johnson and Tracey, who had operated the theatre, the purchase including the Biograph machine, the benches and some wide curtains on the stage and side curtains. Johnson and Tracey had started it but did not care for it; what they were doing I do not know, perhaps drinking, anyway they were not looking after it, so I bought them out. I saw that the Biograph had a future, but it was very hard to convince anyone else.[26]

In Lucia's account, Pantages was furious with Rockwell for this. It is not known when he arrived in Victoria, but starting in April 1903 and continuing through the summer, he was listed as the proprietor and manager of the theatre, which often featured moving pictures as well as names familiar to the stage in Dawson.[27] Rockwell appeared at the theatre as a performer during the autumn and winter of 1903.[28]

By February 1904, now under the management of George W. Boyd, the Orpheum Theatre in Victoria had been completely remodelled and renamed Le Petit Crystal. Kate Rockwell, meanwhile, appeared at the Empire Theatre in Tacoma, Washington, performing her serpentine dance.[29] That did not last long, however; the siren call of the Klondike was too strong. By March, she was on her way back to Dawson City, where she continued to perform her serpentine dance at the Auditorium while also employed as one of nearly forty dance hall girls, later described in the *Dawson Daily News* as "frequenters" ... "engaged in immoral practices and in enticing men to frequent said places."[30]

Rockwell left Dawson for good on September 14, giving the Alcazar Theatre in Seattle, which was managed by her mother, as her forwarding address. With her was Lotus Rockwell, long suspected to be her "illegitimate" daughter with Pantages. Rockwell hit the road when she arrived outside. In 1904, the *Daily News* reported that Alex Pantages was operating a "ten cent family show house" in Seattle.[31] It was the beginning of a career that would make him millions.

Farewell to Little Margie

By 1904, there had been a major exodus of talent from Dawson's local theatres. Most notable among these entertainers was little Margie Newman. Over the years, she had frequently been singled out in newspaper reports for her stage performances, singing, dancing and dramatic work. In September of 1902, Margie and her mother departed the Yukon on the steamer *Tyrrell*. While outside, she gained stage experience, presumably in Oakland, California, and then in Portland, Oregon, before returning to the Yukon in the spring of 1903. She came in with the acting troupe assembled by

Lillian Hall, the actress who had married wealthy miner Jim Hall, owner of the Auditorium Theatre.

Lillian Hall had been in the United States during the winter and arrived in Dawson, followed in mid-June 1903 by the actors of the Hall Theatre Company, with ambitions of putting on a summer season of legitimate theatrical performances. "I wouldn't take a year's salary in exchange for the trip," reported actor Henry Wilson, a member of the company, "even if we did get stuck on four sandbars. It was the greatest outing I have had in years."[32]

On June 17, Margie Newman arrived in Dawson with her mother on the steamer *Canadian*. In addition to Margie Newman and Mr. Wilson, the company featured the talents of Frank Fanning, Bessie Chandon (Lillian Hall's sister), Chris Moran, Jack McDonald, Frank Montgomery and Miss Franklyn Gale. The opening of the season was well received with the play *The Christian*, in which Lillian Hall played the leading role and Margie Newman appeared as Liza. The *Dawson Daily News* described the performance as "acceptably presented," and "the most serious drama given in Dawson."[33] Performances of *Camille*, *Turned Up* and *Human Hearts*, which played to a full house July 20, followed, but full houses were few and far between.

The 1903 theatrical season wrapped up at the end of August with a mixed bill that included selected scenes from *Camille*, *The Christian* and *A Bachelor's Romance*.[34] Lillian Hall was losing money at the rate of five hundred dollars per week, which she could not sustain. In fact, for only three weeks during the summer was the company out of the red. She was making plans to take the theatrical group to Nome to perform until they left for outside later in the fall. "There is little doubt that the departure of the company will be cause of keen regret," stated the *Yukon Sun*. "While the public is sympathetic about patronizing a playhouse, it generally likes to feel that

The Lillian M. Hall. Stock Co. performs the first act's "Supper Scene" in the play *Camille* at the Auditorium during the week of July 6 to 12, 1903. Dawson City Museum, 1984.96.14.

there is some place to go on occasion."[35] That wasn't enough to keep the theatricians gainfully employed. In the end, the plans to go to Nome fell through and the company was disbanded, so the performers were free to leave before the onset of winter. Lillian Hall remained in Dawson for a while to attend to various properties that she still held there.

Most of the Lillian Hall troupe then departed for the outside, but Margie Newman remained behind. In September, she was featured with Lottie Oatley between acts in a performance of the *Mirror Dance*.[36] Her father took up the management of the Auditorium Theatre, and Margie was reunited with her brothers. In addition to dramatic performances, they put on a vaudeville program and Sunday concerts and participated in fundraising events.

They reopened the Auditorium Theatre when the weather became warm enough in the spring of 1904, but the Newman family's Dawson run was at an end. Their final performance came in early June before a packed house; little Margie was the object of the community's praise. Margie was applauded for having "contributed more to the entertainment of Dawson people in larger measure than any other of her profession."[37]

"When children were scarce in the camp," eulogized the *Dawson Daily News* in a tribute to Margie, "and many a heart-hungry miner was hugging in his bosom the pictures of his dear ones at home, 'Little' Margie, the child actress, made their acquaintance and became a great deal more than the mere child actress, singing and dancing for their amusement. Her acquaintances on the creeks probably became wider than that of any single individual in the country, while in Dawson, she was known to every man, woman and child."[38]

Little Margie had grown up with Dawson City, and she embodied the spirit of the gold rush. Her performances in the early days were long remembered in the hearts of many homesick miners, but by 1904 the gold rush had subsided and the population diminished. Her departure symbolized, in a sad way, the decline of the gold-rush town, and everybody knew it.

On June 14, 1904, the Newman family stepped aboard the steamer *Monarch* and headed downriver for the Tanana country in Alaska.[39] The plan was for her to return to the outside in the fall, where she would attend finishing school and receive professional theatrical training for a career on the stage. The following year, the newspaper noted that Miss Newman had passed through Dawson from the Tanana district en route to the outside, where she was to receive medical treatment. She died in Portland, Oregon, on July 5,

1906, of "exothropic goitre, with heart complications, hastened by extreme [summer] heat."[40] The little gold-rush heartthrob was dead at the age of sixteen, and a promising future on the stage would never come to be.

The Hewett Family: A Quest for Closure

From this time on, professional theatre in Dawson became an occasional occurrence. Every summer, talented performers and theatrical companies would pass through town on a circuit that included stops at Juneau, Skagway, Whitehorse and Fairbanks, performing for a few nights or weeks at the Auditorium Theatre before moving on. One of these, the Hewett family theatrical troupe, made a regular seasonal appearance for several years, the first being in Dawson City in the summer of 1905.[41] The family presented a variety act that included stage plays like *Little Lord Fauntleroy*, a magic act, singing and projection of novelty silent films. Newspaper accounts of the entertainment, which was said to be clean, wholesome and clever, reported that the performances were popular and well attended by Dawsonites.

Mr. Hewett, in his Prince Albert coat, was the stereotypical disciple of the stage and was said to "quote Shakespeare by the yard."[42] He demonstrated his magic skills with several illusions and tricks of sleight of hand. He called daughter Edwina onto the stage and performed an illusion in which she appeared to float above the stage with no visible means of support. In another magic trick, Edwina entered a box on one side of the stage and exited from another box on the opposite side.[43]

Because her brother was too young to perform on stage, Edwina was enlisted to take the lead role in *Little Lord Fauntleroy*. After that she returned to the stage in a buckskin cowgirl outfit to sing *Tony, Tony, Tony Boy, Come and Be My Pony Boy*. Her powerful voice reached every corner and crevice of the cavernous theatre.[44] The programs were varied each night. One evening little Edwina starred in the opening sketch, titled *Bessie's Burglar*. She was as sweet as she was clever, and the newspaper was quick to add, "the whole tenor of the piece is moral and edifying."

Mrs. Hewett flexed her psychic powers when, on stage with her back to the crowd, she called out the objects that her husband had borrowed from members of the audience.[45] Mr. Hewett further tantalized and amused the patrons when he produced a string of ribbons from his bare hands, then changed the ribbons to handkerchiefs, then to an American flag, which transformed into the Union Jack along with a shower of flowers. Frank Hewett, the master magician, also arranged performances in various communities in the goldfields. "The miners of the Klondike were the finest fellows I ever met," reported Hewett in 1905, and he vowed to repeat the tour the following year (he did).[46]

But there was a deeper motivation for the Hewett family to tour the North. Frank Hewett's sister, Dr. Edith Chambers, was the first woman to graduate from the Minneapolis School of Dentistry, and she had a practice in Dawson for a brief period after she arrived in 1900. She was described as a bright and cultured woman, one who had determined to live her life her way regardless of the customs of the day.

In 1901, having an adventurous spirit, Edith decided to embark on a journey. Rumours abounded about the motivation behind her trip, but in fact she planned to write a book about her travels. Her intention was to trek alone by horseback to the Tanana district. That was the last time that anyone saw her alive. She might have succeeded in her travels if her supply of food had not been vandalized by marauding bears. Daily entries in her diary, which was found at her last campsite, indicate her plight and impending doom from slow starvation, but also show that Edith was alert and aware of her circumstances until the bitter end. Remains of her outfit were found at the head of the Goodpaster River about thirty-five kilometres from Central, Alaska, by a member of the American Signal Corps.[47]

There were suggestions that the story of Frank Hewett's missing sister was nothing more than a publicity stunt, but the earnestness of his quest was later borne out by those with whom he searched and corresponded. When the remains of his sister were not found in 1905, Hewett and his family performed in Dawson again in 1906. When they reached Fairbanks, he made his way to the last camp in the Tanana region of Alaska where she was known to have stayed. There, in September 1906, he collected the scattered remains of her clothing and other items which were later identified with certainty by various Dawson residents to be hers. The second day at her final camp, he found enough of her scattered bones that he could take them back to Seattle for a proper burial.[48]

Hewett had accomplished the mission he had set out on, but the subarctic held enough of an attraction for him and his family that they returned to perform in the Yukon and Alaskan interior for a third season in 1907, and again in 1908, with the added attraction of popular songs accompanied by stereopticon slides and moving pictures.[49] After that, they disappeared from the stage in Dawson City.

Marjorie Rambeau: Stranded in Dawson

Other theatre companies and attractions made brief appearances at the Auditorium Theatre between 1903 and 1910. Solo artists performed there and benefit concerts were held. The Orpheum stock company performed there in 1907, and *Clark's Moving Pictures* appeared on the screen in 1908. In 1909 the Frawley Theatre Troupe performed in the Auditorium, as did the Clarke Taylor Stock Company and the Musical Clays, while the Dante-Durwood Company made a showing at the Arctic Brotherhood Hall. In 1910, the Howard Stock Company made an appearance on the boards at the Auditorium.[50]

However, most notable during this period was the Thorne-Southard Company, which performed on the stage at the Auditorium in the summer of 1906 during a tour that included Ketchikan, Juneau, Skagway and Whitehorse.[51] The company folded during its Dawson engagement and most of the actors left town quickly after the dissolution. But the premier act, a young stage wonder named Marjorie Rambeau (she was only seventeen, or even sixteen or fifteen by some reports) accompanied by her mother, remained for almost a year and gave substance to the amateur dramatic society that had been active for several years.

"I used to go about the various mining camps, dressed in boys' clothes," recalled Rambeau about her time during the gold rush to Nome a few years earlier (she was only about ten years old at that time), "with my hair cropped close, playing my banjo for all I was worth ... sometimes ... the men would shake gold dust into my cap. Nobody suspected that I wasn't a boy."[52]

In post-gold rush Dawson, theatre no longer consisted of "uninhibited productions characterized by risqué themes and double entendres."[53] Gambling had been shut down, and the former saloon at the front of the Auditorium had been partitioned off into storerooms. But the building was still capable of presenting formidable stage performances.

Rambeau starred in *Merely Mary Ann*, a play that had enjoyed previous success in London and New York.[54] On opening night,

By 1908, Dawson had become a settled and established community. The Orpheum was the only theatre remaining on Front Street. Gates collection.

many Dawson socialites attended, including Yukon commissioner William McInnes and a large stag party that occupied the biggest box in the house.[55] Among those joining her on stage were Dick Thorne and Ray Southard, the principals of the troupe, and a young Roscoe "Fatty" Arbuckle. *Merely Mary Ann* was followed a week later by *Captain Racket*, and then the comedy *Two Married Men*.[56] After that, the theatre company fell apart and most of them departed in July, leaving Marjorie and her mother stranded in the Klondike capital. Dawsonites were quick to offer their support to put on a benefit performance of *The Maid of Croissey*, which locals had staged the year before as an amateur production. This time Rambeau performed the lead role.

The event was a success. The cast performed before a full house that again included Commissioner McInnes. The *Dawson Daily News* reported of Marjorie, "The cleverness with which she deals with this part gives the stronger light and shadow of the plot, the intrigue of which falls chiefly to her to intensify."[57]

Either the event did not raise enough money to enable the stranded mother and daughter to leave Dawson, or they liked the gig.[58] Throughout the fall and winter, Marjorie Rambeau kept busy establishing a drama school, giving private instruction in elocution and directing amateur performers in plays such as *Carrots* and *The Young Mrs. Winthrop* in September.[59] The newspaper opined that if the attendance at the September performances was good, the Rambeaus would take that as an indication of encouragement to "remain all winter and put on occasional first class drama with local assistance."[60] It worked, and Marjorie stayed. *When We Were Twenty One* hit the boards November 20 and 21, followed in February 1907 by *A Texas Steer*, in which Rambeau played the role of Bossy.[61] The *Daily News* later announced that this was her farewell performance. The community prevailed upon her to remain in Dawson until breakup later in the spring, but she

Marjorie Rambeau, a child prodigy, performed in the Auditorium Theatre through the winter of 1906-07. She and her mother left Dawson before the Yukon River ice broke up in the spring of 1907. Dawson City Museum, Frederick Atwood fonds.

and her mother hit the snowy trail south at the beginning of April. An offer to play with an Ogden stock company and the departure of Sam Magnum, the leading man in Marjorie's winter performances, tipped the scales in favour of leaving.[62]

Rambeau's knowledge of geography and politics and her memories of the period later became inadvertently or purposely vague. In an interview with gossip columnist Hedda Hopper in 1959, she said that the "governor general," who was "appointed by the president of the United States," enticed her and her mother to stay in Canada by offering them food and accommodation for a year and a half. Her arrival and departure dates are well documented; she stayed in Dawson City for less than ten months. "I stood outside the little house [where she lived while in Dawson] with the sod roof and wept. 'Good-by little cabin,' I kept saying thru my tears. Robert Service was among the friends who gathered to see me off; he wrote the poem 'Good-by Little Cabin' from my words."[63] That was a remarkable feat; Robert Service did not arrive in Dawson City until a year after Rambeau had left!

The men of the Klondike? "Rough and tough they were," her mother recalled in a 1916 interview, "fighters all and not used to women folk. They had notches cut in their pistol butts and they had some evil ways."[64] New Year's Day in Dawson was notorious for the heavy drinking, she related in another interview, so they locked the doors and shuttered the windows of their little cabin, ignoring the pleas of the party-goers to join them in revelry.[65] But the New Year's costume dance in Dawson lasted until four o'clock in the morning, according to the *Dawson Daily News* of January 1, 1907, and Marjorie and her mother were there.[66] The people of Dawson remembered her time in Dawson City—perhaps more clearly than she did.

Amateur Theatre

Amateur theatre, which had been unsuccessful when attempted four years earlier by Mertie Houck, again made its entrance onto the Dawson stage in 1902. The Dawson Amateur Operatic Society produced a three-day run of Gilbert and Sullivan's HMS *Pinafore* on March 13, 14 and 15, starring Fred Atwood as First Lord of the Admiralty.[67] The production was well reviewed, and the society had plans to follow up with a production of Gilbert and Sullivan's *The Mikado* in May.

Amateur theatre became an important contribution to the Dawson social calendar, involving prominent citizens such as lawyers, doctors, businessmen and their wives. Entire families were involved, both on stage and behind the scenes. The most enthusiastic of these amateurs was Fred Atwood, who contributed in various ways to theatre events throughout his time in Dawson. Frederick Nelson Atwood Jr. was in born in Boston (Suffolk), Massachusetts, on December 4, 1867. His father was a decorative painter of some prominence and Fred Jr. followed in his footsteps, training at several art schools in the eastern United States and specializing in fresco and decorative arts for the theatre.

In 1897, Atwood outfitted himself for the Klondike and headed to Skagway on the ss *Seattle*. He crossed over the Chilkoot Pass, arriving in Dawson City in 1898. After several years of disappointment on the creeks, Atwood resumed his former work in the decorative arts. Following a trip outside to purchase decorating supplies, he returned to Dawson City in 1901 along with his young wife, Mary. He established a business partnership with photographer George Cantwell in which he painted signs, designed and painted theatre sets, hung wallpaper and did other interior decorating work.

CHAPTER 5

Atwood was lauded as a talented performer and athlete. He was associated with numerous productions at the Auditorium Theatre and was a prominent member of the Arctic Brotherhood, a fraternal order formed during the gold rush. He remained in Dawson City until 1912, when he and his family relocated to Seattle. There he embarked on a new business venture with several former Yukoners—the Hippodrome Amusement Company.[68]

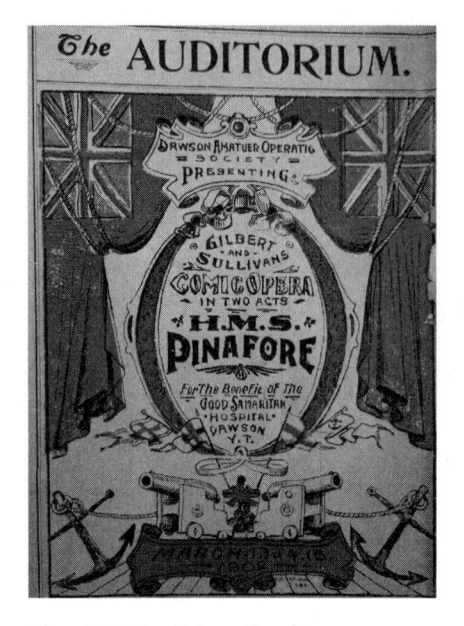

After 1901, the Palace Grand, now renamed the Auditorium Theatre, was the scene of many amateur productions such as HMS *Pinafore*, a fundraiser that opened for three nights on March 13, 1902. Dawson City Museum, Frederick Atwood fonds.

Two or three times a year special plays were staged in Dawson, interspersed with occasional concerts and minstrel shows. Many of these events, which were held in the Auditorium Theatre or the Arctic Brotherhood Hall, raised money for charitable causes.[69] But some of these productions proved less than successful in their charitable intent. In June of 1902 the Dawson Amateur Operatic Society spent $3,158.50 to produce a charitable donation of $459.39. "Doubtless they [the people of Dawson] would donate their money to aid the hospitals directly if found necessary," wrote the *Yukon Sun*, "as willingly as they would patronize any performance, thus diverting the whole proceeds into channels that enlist—or should enlist—before all things else—public sympathy."[70] The primary goal of the society was to put on entertainment, and making charitable donations was secondary.

For a town that, by the end of the first decade in the twentieth century, had shrunk to a quarter of its former population, Dawson still had plenty of talent. But this was still amateur entertainment, and the performers seemed to take their roles less seriously than a professional troupe would have. Marjorie Rambeau later recalled that she and her mother had patrolled backstage during the production of *A Texas Steer* to ensure that the decanters and bottles used as props were emptied of Dutch Courage, but to no effect. By the end of the play, cast members were missing their cues and forgetting their lines. According to Rambeau, "When the scene came in which the capitol steps were shown in the background [backdrop], one of the young men walked to the backdrop and started to climb it. The drop swung back, his feet flew up, and he landed with a crash."[71]

W. S. Dill witnessed the same debacle, which turned a drama into a comedy, and described it in more colourful detail:

> It was a dark and stormy night and cold. The mercury had shrunk to the point where it had to stand on its tiptoes to see fifty. There was no fire in the Orpheum, where a company of amateurs strode about the stage, and declaimed at one another with an earnestness that precluded all suggestion of humour. They looked like a family of performing bears, in fur coats and caps and Dolge boots.
>
> This was the dress rehearsal.
>
> The prompter, who was the busiest member of the cast, seemed to be the only person who entertained any uneasiness as to the success of the production. The

others complimented one another with the sublimest sort of optimism.

"For God's sake, have plenty of Scotch in the banquet scene," implored the King. "This pretending to drink looks so beastly amateurish."

"Rather!" agreed the other gentlemen.

On the following night, however, ... most of the male members of the cast had anticipated the banquet scene before coming to the theatre.

The temperature was more than warm—it was hot, and the house was sold to the roof. ... The heat, the glare, the queer swimming haze of faces, and more than all the familiar stage trappings were responsible for a few minor mishaps during the first act. The Queen, entering a hitherto untried doorway and intending to precipitate herself into her lover's arms, was jerked somewhat violently backward when the door closed upon her train and several of the stage retainers broke into the scene to lift her to her feet. ...

Also, the lady-in-waiting, conforming to the fixed habit of rehearsing without props, extended an empty hand to the wounded warrior, urging him to, "Der-rink up, der-rink up from this golden goblet, sir, and may its potent contents infuse you with new life!"

Whereupon the gasping warrior, his head bowed upon his arm, thrashed wildly for the cup and breathed in a hoarse whisper, intended only for the stage, "The Scotch ... in God's name, where's the Scotch?"

The second act went very well, beginning with the banquet scene and ending when the King (frantically beckoned off the stage), left his weeping lady awaiting the entrance of the First Messenger.

This was the fellow's maiden speech. Save for passing goblets at the banquet, he had never been on the stage before.

"*Weep no more, Madame, your liver loves!*"

The third act went with a snap. A perceptible spontaneity replaced the laboured nervousness that temperament and the lines had produced. Even the diction of the characters lost its forced pomposity, and Burns [one of the actors], who in dismissing a hireling had previously proclaimed, "Away varlet, out of my presence, forthwith," improved upon his lines by crying, "Get the H— out of here or I'll knock your silly block off!"

The last act was set in the reception hall of a Ducal Palace; gilt chairs and canvas pillars of marble and a dais and such. The back drop was magnificent, carrying the idea of a columned distance into a bower of roses near the sea. To left, a canvas fountain played. To right, a marble stairway mounted to Paradaisical [*sic*] heights above.

Now, the Second Courtier had played his big scene with the flagons in the second act. He didn't appear in the end until just about the fall of the curtain. Unfortunately, however, it was the wrong curtain.

Of course, in strange surroundings anyone is likely to become confused, to take a wrong turning; and that's what happened to the Courtier. When he essayed to retire, he observed the stairs for the first time and feeling pretty exhausted by the evening's production, decided that climbing the floor above, was as good a method of exit as any.

Douglas Fairbanks, or the Human Fly might have succeeded, but the Courtier failed. After clawing frequently at those swaying steps, he made a resolute plunge that

CHAPTER 5

Amateur theatre became an important contribution to the Dawson City social calendar, involving prominent citizens including lawyers, doctors, businessmen and their wives. Entire families were involved, both on stage and behind the scenes. The amateur production of Gilbert and Sullivan's operetta *Patience* opened on April 24, 1905. Dawson City Museum, Frederick Atwood fonds.

resulted in dragging the backdrop to the floor—a disturbing circumstance which ruined the King's final line.

But it was a weak line, anyhow!

But public appreciation was long and noisy. The principals had at least eight curtain calls and both bouquets of flowers were presented to the leading lady.

You haven't forgotten those perpetual bouquets? There were, in early days, no flowers in Dawson, so the management of the Orpheum numbered two bunches of artificial blossoms among their props and these were presented, inevitably, to the leads of all companies. After the performance, they were returned to the house.[72]

Between 1902 and 1910, a number of amateur productions graced the stages of the Auditorium Theatre and the Arctic Brotherhood Hall: *Ermine, The Island of Kokomolo, The Chimes of Normandy, Pygmalion and Galatea, Patience, Prince of Liars, Confusion* and *The Heir to Hoorah*, to name a few.[73] These were sometimes supplemented by the screening of moving pictures. The Auditorium struggled to serve a purpose when it was not being used for dramatic performances or variety shows. At various times, the grand old building was rented for visiting lecturers or political rallies, or used as a polling station on election day. The Orpheum continued to offer professional performances on a sporadic basis, but by 1910 it was shifting into the cinematic business. By that time, the transformation from live theatre to cinema was complete.

Robert Service: A Master Class in Human Nature

Though the professionals of the stage had abandoned Dawson a decade after the gold rush, one individual came to Dawson during that later time who would shape the mystique of the gold rush more than anybody else. He was an unassuming bank clerk named Robert W. Service.

Born on January 16, 1874, in Preston, Lancashire, but raised in Scotland, Service left school at the age of thirteen and went to work in a Scottish bank until he immigrated to Canada when he was twenty-two years old. He wandered widely along the west coast for the next seven years before settling down as a bank clerk with the Canadian Bank of Commerce, first in Victoria, then in Kamloops, BC. In 1904 he was told that he was being transferred to the branch in Whitehorse. The posting came with a $50-a-month living allowance, free accommodation and a $200 disbursement with which

CHAPTER 5

to purchase the clothing he would require to live in the tiny, frozen northern village. Little more than a small cluster of wooden buildings at the time, Whitehorse served as the point where passengers and goods were transferred from the White Pass and Yukon Route Railroad, which had been completed in 1900, to the sturdy sternwheel riverboats that carried their loads to Dawson.

Robert Service lived in the Yukon for only a few years, but the poems he wrote during that time have set the Yukon firmly in the public consciousness for more than a century. Gates collection.

The average term of service for employees posted to Whitehorse was rather short, but Service adapted readily to this remote little community. When not working in the bank he would take long walks in the countryside, soaking in the beauty of the wilderness; at other times he listened to others tell stories, from which he absorbed Klondike lore and tales of survival. Service had a knack for the language; he could turn a good phrase and mastered metre and rhyme. He combined that with his innate sense of irony and his gentle wit. Though he had submitted the occasional verse for publication (one of his contributions was published in the *Whitehorse Star* in 1902 before he was posted there by the bank), it was in Whitehorse that he took a serious turn to creating verse in his spare time.[74] Inspired by the stark beauty of the North, enchanted by tales of the gold rush and with a keen eye for human nature, he poured out what he saw and heard onto page after page.

On one occasion, he later wrote in his autobiography, he was composing "The Shooting of Dan McGrew" late at night at his wicket in the bank when he was almost shot and killed by an alarmed night watchman (though in his later years he admitted that this story was a fabrication).[75] A month later, he penned "The Cremation of Sam McGee." He continued to write amusing rhymes until he had accumulated enough to send them off, along with a cheque, to a printer in Toronto to have copies typeset and bound as gifts to give to friends. Titled *Songs of a Sourdough*, it contained "The Shooting of Dan McGrew," "The Cremation of Sam McGee" and other poems such as "The Spell of the Yukon" and "The Call of the Wild." They would become classics enjoyed by generations of readers. While critics and academics would dismiss them as trivial, the public loved them, and they would make Service world famous and the best-selling poet of the twentieth century.

Instead of receiving the volumes he had ordered, however, Service received in the mail a contract from the publisher, offering him a royalty for every book of verse they sold. In 1907 *Songs of a Sourdough* became an instant best-seller. Within a year, tourists were flocking to the bank where the mild-mannered clerk worked to meet the famous poet, while locals looked on with a combination of bemusement and awe.

After spending three years posted in Whitehorse, Service took a mandatory three-month furlough in Vancouver, after which he was transferred to the branch of the Canadian Bank of Commerce in Dawson City. He returned to Whitehorse in March of 1908, and by April he was on his way to Dawson. He worked at the Dawson City branch of the Canadian Bank of Commerce, prominently built on the waterfront side of Front Street at the foot of Queen Street. He roomed with the other bank employees in the company bunkhouse, a two-storey log building in the government reserve at the south end of town.

In this busy accommodation, it was hard for Service to set to his task of composition, so he would go to bed early in the evening and rise again at midnight to work alone on his poems. In this fashion, he crafted his second book of verse. Dawson City became his muse, and the poems flowed easily from his pen. "If he studied anything," wrote Service biographer Enid Mallory, "it was people. He was always on the outside looking in, trying to figure out what made people tick and then applying the knowledge to his writing."[76] Dawson became a master class in human nature where he found "humor, courage, pathos and tragedy, the epic struggle with the elements, the obsession with gold, fear of the grizzly or the loup-garou (werewolf), loneliness that could make a man crazy, and the grim reality of scurvy and starvation."[77]

Robert Service did not have to fabricate fictional plots for his poems because the truth was more interesting than fiction. Here's a good example: the *Dawson Daily News* contained an article about an English bank clerk newly arrived in Dawson City who was treated to a tasty ice worm cocktail by his new friends at the M&N Saloon on Front Street. To be initiated as a sourdough, he was told, he would have to drink this concoction. A drink was poured and into it was dropped a long pale ice worm. In truth, it was nothing more than a piece of spaghetti with ink dotted on to create the impression that it had eyes. The Englishman was later reported to have dashed to the drugstore for a "stomach pacifier." The account, which Service had undoubtedly heard from his bank colleagues or had even read in the newspaper, eventually became one of his more popular rhymes, "The Ballad of the Ice Worm Cocktail," which demonstrates that the truth can be more inspirational, and more interesting, than fiction.[78]

Service sent his latest collection of poems to his publisher, and when they balked at the ribald nature of his work, he threatened to find another publisher. They compromised: Service agreed to take out one especially raunchy poem about the Tenderloin, and Briggs, the publisher, agreed to increase his royalty to 15 per cent. In 1909, *Ballads of a Cheechako* also became a best-seller.

Service now had two best-selling books, and the royalties began to inflate his bank account. In the fall of 1909, he was offered the position of relieving manager of the Whitehorse branch, but he could not entertain the thought of leaving Dawson City. When he realized that his income from his book royalties was five times that of his salary at the bank, he decided to abandon the security of banking for the challenge of writing. His last day of work was November 15, 1909, and he moved into a tiny two-room log cabin on Eighth Avenue, high up on the hillside overlooking Dawson. There, he set about his next challenge: to write a novel about the gold rush.

For eight months, he laboured over the creation of an epic tale of romance in the Klondike, which he titled *The Trail of '98*. In the spring of 1910, he decided to take the manuscript to the publishers in person. He first went to Toronto, then New York, where his publisher insisted that he revise the ending to conform to the strict moral standards of the day. *The Trail of '98* also became a best-seller, not only in Canada but internationally. Despite the fears of his friends and neighbours back in Dawson that the novel painted a picture of the Klondike capital as being a city of sin, Dawsonites bought the book in record-breaking numbers. Service ultimately found the affectations of New York distasteful and too far removed from "the blunt, raw honesty of the Yukon," and was soon on the move again.[79]

CHAPTER 5

Stricken by wanderlust, he visited New Orleans and then Cuba before a joyful reunion with his family, who were now living on a farm east of Edmonton, Alberta. In the spring of 1911, he made his departure for the Yukon. But rather than take the conventional trip by train over the White Pass trail, he chose a more difficult path down the Mackenzie River and over the Richardson Mountains to the Porcupine River, which he followed to its confluence with the mighty Yukon. From there, it was a comparably easy paddlewheel boat ride upriver to Dawson. The trip through the wilderness of the Northwest Territories had been physically challenging for Service, who arrived back in Dawson a lean figure "in an ebony thicket of three weeks' growth, nose broiled to lobstered, hands a Mongolian shade, trousers shredded, feet partly missing, and with those parts which remained full of thistles, thorns and fish bones. ... I can count the sections in my backbone, with my finger tip," he quipped when interviewed by the *Dawson Daily News*, "feeling them from the front."[80] The thinner version was happy to be back in Dawson City after his arduous trek through the Northwest Territories. He settled back into his little cabin on Eighth Avenue and set to work on his third book of verse, which would be titled *Rhymes of a Rolling Stone*.

Whether Service could see the future of the gold-rush town closing in on itself or whether he was gripped by his perpetual wanderlust, his Dawson days were numbered. He boarded a steamer the morning of June 29, 1912, ostensibly for a business trip to the coast. The bard of the Yukon, reported the *Dawson Daily News*, expected to return before long.[81] In truth, he had turned his back on the North and he never returned. With him he carried the draft for his third book of poems. He arrived in Vancouver ten days later and lost no time in retiring to the Olympic Mountains on Puget Sound to put the finishing touches on these latest poems.[82] Included among them was the prophetic verse "Goodbye Little Cabin," which expresses a sad farewell to Dawson and the little cabin in which he wrote his novel *The Trail of '98*.

A short time later, he was in Toronto to meet with his publisher, then in New York briefly before departing for the Balkans as a war correspondent. *Rhymes of a Rolling Stone* was in bookstores by the beginning of December. It too would become a best-seller. By that time his fame was diversifying. His poem "The Ballad of the Brand" from his book *Ballads of a Cheechako* had been adapted to the silver screen, and by June of 1912 it was being shown in theatres under the title of *The Brand*.[83] It would not be the last film adaptation of Service's work.

A decade after the gold rush, Dawson City had been transformed into an approximation of post-Victorian gentility. Gone were the bustling crowds, the carnival atmosphere and the rough edges, though the gambling, drinking and carousing hadn't been entirely abolished. Dawson had settled into respectability with more families and more of the social amenities associated with the settled British communities spread out across Canada. The population was declining, and by the end of the first decade of the twentieth century the Yukon would be a quarter of what it had been a decade before. Live professional theatre, with a variety of entertainers with a variety of talents, had been displaced in large part by amateur theatre. In this new reality, moving pictures became a staple ingredient in any evening's entertainment.

Projecting a New Image: Cinema Comes to Dawson City

The 1906 summer season at the Orpheum Theatre kicked off with a fancy dress ball on May 14. The up-to-date orchestra performed

CHAPTER 5

By 1906, travelling theatre groups were visiting Dawson City during the summer. Moving pictures were now included in their programs. Dawson City Museum, Frederick Atwood fonds.

under the careful guidance of its conductors, Freimuth and Fawcett. The celebrants were entertained on the screen by the latest Edison Biograph moving pictures, featuring boxing matches with Champion Jim Jeffries, Jimmy Britt, Battling Nelson, "Kid" Lavigne and others. The films were reported to be a show in themselves.[84] In September, the film offering at the Orpheum included such titles as *The Unlucky Burglars* and *The Bigamist*.[85] Orpheum proprietors McDonald and Nelson announced that the film features would be changed weekly. The Auditorium Theatre was also open for business, showing the Britt-Nelson fight and the 1902 eruption of Mount Pelée (in Martinique) in June.

The following year, 1907, the Orpheum continued to augment its live entertainment with moving films. Six films were featured on each bill along with live entertainment. When the Hewett family arrived in Dawson, they supplemented their magic show with "the very latest moving pictures." The Auditorium was packed for the program the evening of June 12, when the audience was entertained with the film comedy titled *The Drunken Mattress*. In it, an old woman hired to mend a mattress went away to get a drink of chocolate. When she was gone an intoxicated gentleman fell into the mattress and went to sleep in the hay. The old woman returned, and sewed the mattress tight. She unknowingly sewed him in the tick, and then started off with him. The mattress sat upright, rolled, jumped, kicked, turned somersaults, and did everything imaginable, and she had to wrestle with it like a demon. When it was put on the bed the climax came when the old woman and her husband were kicked out of the bed by the man in the mattress.[86]

Over the following years, the Orpheum and the Auditorium and the Arctic Brotherhood Hall battled for the patronage of Dawsonites by offering moving pictures. In 1909, the Arctic Brotherhood Hall featured a two-hour matinee targeting children. In March of 1910, it announced the arrival of a new selection of moving pictures.[87]

In October of 1910, Ben Levy, the owner of the Orpheum, moved the competition up a notch, announcing the arrival of a new projector and many new films, and also the news that it would be opening for the winter with new selections of films every week. Levy started billing the titles of the films in his advertisements in the newspaper. One of the first titles was *Frankenstein*.[88] Levy upped his game even more by announcing major renovations to the Orpheum in February 1911: "The balcony has been extended around the entire three walls circling from one side of the stage to the other. The new boxes are open, and one is particularly large, and is mate to the historic green room," stated the *Dawson Daily News*.[89] In the same article in the *News*, Levy cast a wide net, stating that the theatre was catering to all classes of customers, especially family patronage. A year after Levy converted the Orpheum to a movie theatre, a new competitor entered the arena: the Family Theatre in the Dawson Amateur Athletic Association (DAAA) building.

The D-Three-A

The DAAA building was originally built by public subscription in the fall of 1902. Construction began on September 17, and the first shareholders' meeting was held in the building, which went up in record time three weeks later. The official opening took place in November, by which time it was already in use by the public. The main entrance was through the impressive facade on Queen Street, inside which were a ticket booth to the left and a handsomely decorated reception or club room to the right. On the second floor was a large gymnasium with ceilings high enough to afford the construction of a running track on a mezzanine that encircled the walls. There were dressing rooms with Turkish and shower baths. A large ice arena for

The Dawson Amateur Athletic Association building, or DAAA, was built in 1902 and included an ice rink, gymnasium and social rooms. Gates collection.

The Renzonis and Reginas Playing Hocky at the D.A.A.A Rink, Dawson Y. T. Apr. 1910.

In the winter, the ice rink in the DAAA was used for hockey and curling. Yukon Archives, 82_219_119.

curling, skating and hockey, thirty-five metres in length and twenty-five metres in width, was attached to the rear of the main building. There was space for seating on both sides of the rink as well as in a gallery above that encircled the entire space. From the beginning, the building was a popular and well-used feature of Dawson social and sporting life.

In May 1908, under the management of Walter Creamer, a swimming pool twenty metres long by eight metres wide was added to the building. Proclaimed to be one of the finest resorts north of San Francisco, the new natatorium was officially opened June 13.[90] The pool was constructed in the floor of the ice arena; the ground was excavated by blasting in order to prevent the permafrost from

CHAPTER 5

In 1908, Walter Creamer added a swimming pool to the ice arena in the DAAA building. In the fall, the pool was covered over, but hockey and curling continued during the winter. Yukon Archives, 82_219_5.

melting. The pool was heated by injecting boiling water into it from the steam plant that heated the building. Platforms, a diving board, trapeze rings, chutes, a slide and a skylight overhead gave the interior of the space a welcoming feeling. Afternoons were set aside for ladies' use, and once a week the pool was reserved for toddlers. In the winter, the pool was drained of water and covered over, and the arena was again used for winter sports.

Creamer was a creative entrepreneur, eager to keep the DAAA a profitable concern, so in 1911, after seeing Levy's upgrades to the Orpheum, he decided to make another change: he converted the second-floor gymnasium into a theatre. A large stage and dressing

In 1911, the gymnasium on the second floor of the DAAA was turned into the Family Theatre for plays, moving pictures and other events. Note that a conventional piano is visible to the left of the stage. The American Photoplayer piano came later. Gates collection.

rooms were built at the south end. The stage was enclosed by a proscenium arch and had attractive backdrops and several fine curtains, the main one being a magnificent green colour. The running track was converted into horseshoe-shaped balcony with seating on three sides, each said to have an excellent view of the stage.

Hanging from the ceiling in the centre of the room was a resplendent chandelier with many brilliant globes. The theatre was designed both to show films and to stage live performances. The feature on opening night, October 26, 1911, was the amateur theatre production of *Captain Racket*. Hundreds watched the fine new

> **MOVING PICTURE SHOW TONIGHT**
> Commencing 8:30 p. m.
> **NEW FILMS**
> ALL GOOD CLEAN PICTURES. NO OBJECTIONABLE FEATURES.
> Tomorrow night entire change of program will be given.
> **Bring Your Families**
> **ORPHEUM THEATER**
> FRONT STREET
> GENERAL ADMISSION 25c

By 1910, the Arctic Brotherhood Hall and the Orpheum Theatre were both screening moving pictures. *Dawson Daily News*, October 18, 1910, p. 4, Yukon Archives.

curtains rise at 9:00 sharp to the music of John Dines's five-piece orchestra.[91]

Henceforth, the DAAA and the Orpheum vied for the reputation of being family entertainment. Early in 1912, to compete for clientele, Ben Levy offered free admission to the Orpheum's early-evening show to children accompanied by an adult. By the following summer, Levy had placed the day-to-day management of the Orpheum in the hands of two men named Edwards and Victor. This was preparatory to selling the theatre to Olaf Olsen in August of 1912. Levy's big stake in the Klondike was his rich Claim Number 27A on Eldorado Creek, but he also made money from his Front Street establishment, turning over a quarter of a million dollars in one year during the height of the gold rush. Levy and his wife, who had joined him in Dawson in 1898, were moving to Los Angeles, where he had one business property and was planning to build a second.

"Apple Jimmy" Oglow operated a confectionery store and gift shop in the front of the Orpheum Theatre for thirty years. Dawson City Museum, 1984.187.10.

Edwards and Victor continued to manage the Orpheum under the new owner, and James "Apple Jimmy" Oglow operated his confectionery and novelty shop in the theatre's main-floor storefront. The new theatre proprietors soon made more improvements, adding a sloping floor and folding seats for better viewing and more comfort.[92] The movie houses were constantly improving their facilities to attract more business, and they weren't afraid of gimmicks to draw patrons to their films. In September 1912, Victor and Edwards featured the film *Seven Capital Sins*. "The play is said by some to be almost equal in dramatic intensity to the great 'Passion Play,'" announced an article in the *Dawson Daily News*. "The films are hand colored throughout. All scenery and every garment and other factor is colored, thus adding greatly to the beauty of the film. Augmented musical accompaniments have been provided. In order to have more fitting strains for certain touching sketches, an organ will be used. Miss Lucille MacKay will play the organ and Miss Grace Hodgkin the piano. The extra pictures, completing the bill for the evening, are 'The Longshoreman,' and 'Hydraulic Mining in New South Wales.'"[93]

American Photoplayer: All the Bells and Whistles

Live musical accompaniment was a standard element in the era of silent films, with the pianist often mentioned in advertisements as an added feature, perhaps to draw patrons to a show coloured with the musical stylings of their favourite accompanist. To draw in more customers, even this was subject to gimmickry. Perhaps the flashiest and most outrageous attempt to upgrade the musical accompaniment was the American Photoplayer, a musical device purpose made for movie theatres. It literally came with all the bells and whistles.

Walter Creamer (now called Barnum Creamer in the newspaper, a reference to showman P. T. Barnum) proudly announced the arrival of his new "motion picture orchestra piano," the first ever brought into the Yukon. The newspaper account bubbled with enthusiasm:

> This instrument is truly wonderful. It has been the sensation of the picture show conventions wherever exhibited. It was put on the market last December. It can be played by hand as an ordinary piano, or automatically by means of paper rolls. The new instrument is a combination of piano, flute, mandolin, violin, organ, bass drum, snare drum, cymbal,

triangle, tremolo stop, tom-tom, tambourine, horse trot, telephone bell and fire gong.

There is absolutely no limit to the musical possibilities of this instrument.

The different musical divisions can be played in solo or in concert[;] any section can be cut off or used in any combination desired.

The longer a musician works with it the more skillful he becomes. It will be operated tonight by Prof. Carpenter.[94]

The Coming Darkness: Dawson Cinema before the Great War

By 1913, the theatre business in Dawson had settled into a routine, with the Orpheum and the DAAA Family Theatre remaining as the main competition for Dawson patrons. Advertisements appeared in every issue of the *Dawson Daily News*, usually on the lower half of page four, on opposing corners. The films were changed twice a week and were listed by title, with remarks regarding content (drama, western, comedy, newsreels, and so on). The ads sometimes identified the film studio that had made the films and occasionally the director, but not the actors. They also identified the name of the featured live accompanist as this was of some interest to local theatre-goers. Sometimes another performer would be added to the playbill, singing songs or playing an instrument to fill in between films, but the live performances were secondary.

There was enough interest in moving pictures by this time that Billy Mullen, a local resident who had performed in the Orpheum Theatre with Mamie Hightower, Fred Breen and Lucy Lovell a dozen years earlier, threw his hat into the ring. In December 1913 Mullen leased the Auditorium Theatre, renamed it the New Theatre and invested $5,000 of his own money to remodel and refurnish the aging building. Miss Grace Hopkins was hired to accompany the films and the advertisements proclaimed that the theatre would be heated with hot air from a large furnace.[95] Mullen continued to offer films at the New Theatre through the remainder of December and into January of 1914, but the challenge of competing with two well-established opponents in a small market and the cost of heating the massive building in the dead of winter were more than he could overcome. On January 26, he placed a small announcement in the newspaper stating that, due to the delay in the arrival of new films, there would be no new shows until they reached Dawson.[96] By February Mullen's venture had disappeared from Dawson's cinematic scene.

Mullen's venture had failed, but the Auditorium Theatre reopened on July 25, 1914, under new management, showing only "First-Class Feature Films" accompanied by Miss Zella Goodman, who also offered vocal performances between films.[97] There was a resurgence of theatre choices in early August that harkened back to the glory days of the gold rush. The Shriners and their wives visited Dawson City from the Gizeh Temple in Victoria, and the Klondike capital was bustling during the week they were in town. Tours of the goldfields were arranged for the male guests, including a visit to the Bear Creek headquarters of the Canadian Klondyke Mining Company, where Joe Boyle hosted a luncheon for them. Meanwhile, their wives were treated to an afternoon tea at the home of Mrs. Gus Johnson, the wife of a Dawson businessman.

On the evening of August 3, the town had film offerings to choose from at various theatres. The Auditorium was showing the dramas *Heroes One and All* and *For His Child's Sake* plus two comedy reels. Frank Unger the contortionist, late of the Sells Bothers' Circus, put on a display of physical configurations and Zella Goodman appeared for the last time that week.[98]

Meanwhile, at the Family Theatre in the DAAA building, Miss Hazel Hartshorn sang, and Danny Green demonstrated buck-and-wing dancing. Half the balcony was filled with Shriners. The films were *A Would-be Shriner* (comedy), *Willie Becomes an Artist* (comedy), *The Fighting Lieutenant* (drama), *Fancy Poultry* (instructive) and *Two Gay Dogs* (comedy). Professor Carpenter was at the keyboard to provide accompaniment.[99]

Not to be outdone, the Orpheum presented a film of Professor G. Hepburn Wilson demonstrating how to dance the Argentinian Tango. Other pictures included *Murray the Masher* (comedy) and *The Country Boy* (Pathé drama), and the Pathé weekly newsreel, chosen to appeal to the conventioneers, featured the "Nobles of the Mystic Shrine leaving Seattle, Wash., on the longest of their long pilgrimages—14,000 miles in Pacific Waters, ending in Manilla."[100]

The following evening, the theatre entertainment was eclipsed by news that fundamentally altered the future of the Yukon. British patriotism was stirred when, just as the performance was ending at the Family Theatre, an extra edition copy of the *Dawson Daily News* reached Walter Creamer, the manager. News that the British fleet had sunk six German ships was read out to the audience while Creamer projected a slide of King George V on the screen. On the piano, Mr. Carpenter struck the introductory chords to "Rule Britannia," and the audience rose in a body and sang "until the house shook." That was followed by "God Save the King." When the picture of Queen Mary was projected on the screen, the crowd sang "The Maple Leaf Forever."[101]

Meanwhile, Yukon Territory commissioner George Black and his wife Martha were over at the Auditorium on the same night, and the theatre was packed to capacity. Commissioner Black was handed a cable from the secretary of state in Ottawa saying that Britain was in a state of war against Germany. He went to the stage and, after a dramatic pause, read the cable with great emotion. In silence, men and women looked at each other, aghast, while trying to comprehend what he had said. His wife Martha, in her book *My Seventy Years*, later recalled the scene.

> In the centre of the house, about twenty scarlet coated Royal Northwest Mounted Policemen occupied seats. Two of the men were former members of one of your crack regiments, the Coldstream Guards—brothers well over six feet in height. They looked at each other, whispered to other members of the force with them, rose to their feet and commenced singing "God Save the King." The effect was electrical. With one move the audience was on its feet, and never in the world, I dare say, was the national anthem sung with greater fervor, or more depth of feeling than that night in the mining city just on the edge of the Arctic.[102]

As people filled the streets of Dawson that evening, the crowd was abuzz with conversation about what this meant. Canada was now at war, and Dawson City would never be the same.

CHAPTER 6

MOVIE NIGHT IN DAWSON

1915-1979

Answering the Call

If Dawson City had been on a decline, then the Great War (which later came to be known as World War 1) accelerated the descent. During the four years of conflict, 1914 to 1918, more than a thousand Yukon men and a small number of women volunteered to serve their "king and country." Although the ties to the British Empire were loosening, Canada was still not an independent nation at this point. Most Yukoners who stepped forward at the beginning of the war to enlist, even those born in Canada, identified themselves not as Canadians, but as British.

For the duration of the war, in addition to contributing a high percentage of its population as volunteers, every level of Yukon society contributed to the war effort—by making donations to charitable war-related causes, participating in fundraising events and preparing care packages to send to the "boys" overseas. Yukoners were proud of the fact that during the war they contributed more per capita to the war effort than any other part of the country.[1]

But it came at a price. The Yukon hemorrhaged men at a precipitous rate, dramatically reducing the workforce. After the war, only a small proportion of these individuals, slightly more than 10 per cent, returned to the North. Consequently, most mining operations had to curtail their activity, reducing employment and cash flow, much of which had already been diverted to the war effort. Nor was gold mining considered to be an essential war industry. Finding materials for operation and maintenance of mining equipment became ever more of a challenge during the war years, and the large dredging companies struggled to remain solvent.

Dawson's precarious situation and its future were both impacted profoundly when, in March of 1918, it was announced that federal spending in the Yukon was to be greatly reduced, and government positions, including that of commissioner, were to be abolished. For a while it appeared that the Yukon would lose representative government, but in the end the territorial council was reduced in size but not eliminated. Then, in late October of 1918, the Canadian Pacific ss *Princess Sophia* hit Vanderbilt Reef during a fierce storm and eventually sank. Every passenger aboard the *Sophia*, 367 souls in total, perished, many of them prominent Dawson businesspeople and their families.[2] It was a blow to the economic balance of the Klondike capital from which it never recovered.[3]

Three Theatres in Competition

Shortly after war was declared in 1914, the Auditorium Theatre closed its doors, leaving only the Orpheum and the DAAA Family Theatre

During the Great War (1914-18), the Family Theatre became the venue for many patriotic fundraising events. Children often played an important role in these events. Dawson City Museum, 1995.345.1.13.

to entertain Dawsonites. The following spring, under the proprietorship of Harry McHenry and Charley Drake, the Auditorium was given a facelift. Carpeting or linoleum with cork underlay was placed on the floors to reduce noise. The walls were "finished and tinted," and new fire escapes were added to the second and third floors. A special projection booth was constructed, lined with metal for protection against the highly flammable films. "In case of fire the door to the operating [projection] room can be closed," announced the *Dawson News*, "and metal shutters will close over other apertures."[4]

When the Auditorium reopened for business, the Orpheum closed temporarily, reopening in August under the management of Ed Victor.[5] The Auditorium closed again August 20 of 1915 but reopened October 2, while the Orpheum closed a week later. The

CHAPTER 6

The DAAA baseball team poses in front of the entrance to the Family Theatre on June 9, 1915. Showing in the theatre at the time was the 1913 silent short film *The Legend of Lovers Leap*. Dawson City Museum, 2006.15.4.

Auditorium continued to operate in competition with the Family Theatre through the Christmas season. The evening of December 22, Moose Night at the Auditorium replaced the usual screening of films and was heralded as a successful event.[6] The following night the movies returned with the three-reel drama *The Reward of Thrift* and a Hearst-Selig *War Weekly* newsreel as the feature, while the Family Theatre countered with *Exoneration* (in two acts), *Bunny's Birthday* and the comedy *The Chicken Inspector*.[7]

While the DAAA Family Theatre continued as usual, offering a variety of recreational facilities to the public in addition to movies, the Auditorium Theatre closed for business beginning January 1, 1916, presumably because of the cost of heating during the cold weather. It reopened in early spring under the management of two young men in their early twenties, Tip Oneel and Hal Noziglia, this time under the banner of the De Luxe Theatre.[8] Mrs. Oneel provided musical accompaniment to the films. "In addition to high class picture plays and the best music," proclaimed the *Dawson News*, "they will present the latest song hits and other specialties from outside."[9] The tenure of the De Luxe Theatre was short-lived, however, and it ceased advertising movies after June 8.

Another attempt was made to resurrect the Auditorium Theatre on November 2, 1917, under the management of Mrs. Vining, a well-known old-time Dawsonite. The film shown that evening for an admission fee of fifty cents (one dollar for reserved seating) was the Famous Players production of *The Seven Sisters* starring Marguerite Clark, "the darling of the screen, and Mary Pickford's greatest rival."[10] Mrs. Iseman accompanied the film on piano. The theatre was reported as "perfectly comfortable," hinting that winter had descended upon the gold-rush city.[11] The cost of heating the theatre at this time of year would have been a substantial drain on Mrs. Vining's pocketbook.

Not to be outdone, Walter Creamer responded by placing not one, but two advertisements on the same page as the advertisement for the Auditorium. One of them, three columns wide, announced the screening of *The Dawn of Tomorrow* with the name of the star, Mary Pickford, in bold letters. Also on the billing for the evening for regular patrons was episode eight of the serial *The Strange Case of Mary Page*.[12]

Mrs. Vining couldn't compete. The expense of heating the grand old theatre plus stiff competition from an established rival quickly put her out of business. The Auditorium advertised movie screenings sporadically through November, but by the beginning of December, there were no more movies being shown in Dawson City's largest theatre.[13]

The seesaw opening and closing of the Orpheum and the Auditorium ceased for a few years, leaving the Family Theatre in the DAAA as the only show in town. But in April of 1921, under the auspices of the Fraternal Order of Eagles, the Orpheum Theatre was renamed the Jewel and opened temporarily to offer "a mixed showing of moving pictures and Vaudeville stunts." The stunts referred to included magic, Russian toe dancing and "Scotch fancy steps." Since the Yukon River was still closed to transportation at this time of year, the vaudeville entertainment was most certainly of the local variety. Shows were advertised sporadically through April, the last one being on April 28, after which Walter Creamer's Family Theatre was again the sole survivor.[14]

End of the Line: The Silent Film Era Draws to an End

Because of its remoteness and seasonal isolation, Dawson City was at the end of the film distribution chain. The cost of shipping films to Dawson City was high, and like many other goods, once they reached the Klondike, they were too expensive to ship outside again. Thus, these films, dog-eared and worn out from heavy use, arrived in Dawson two to three years (or more) after they were first released, a fact that would not have impacted the local market but would make it obvious to summer tourists that Dawson had become a social isolate and cultural backwater. A good example of this delay was *His Madonna*, which was already five years old when it was screened in Dawson in April 1917.[15] Newsreels were somewhat timelier in their arrival in town, but they too were often months or even years old when they appeared on the silver screen in Dawson. Transportation of the films was by ship, train and river steamer in the summer, or by perilously slow horse-drawn sled in the winter. The latter trip, from Whitehorse to Dawson, could take several days. They didn't always arrive on time, and the proprietors would be forced to dig into the selection of films relegated to storage and show movies that had already been presented in Dawson before. Under such circumstances, they would be billed as "back by popular demand."

Occasional film events of local interest were noticed in the *Dawson News*. In April 1916 word reached the newspaper that C. C. Gaisford of the Silver Fox Company was planning a return trip to the North. Included in the moving pictures he filmed in 1915 were steamers, mining scenes, the commissioner's residence, a baseball game and Mrs. George Black pinning a rose on her husband, the commissioner of the territory.[16]

In 1917 Jack Suttles, a placer miner from the Mayo area who volunteered with the George Black contingent to fight "the Hun" overseas, wrote to the ladies of the Imperial Order, Daughters of the Empire (IODE) that he was sending reels of film footage showing the Yukon volunteers at reveille, training in the trenches, bayonet drill, dinner parade and the Yukon men on route march.[17] The films were screened in Dawson to a cheering and patriotic audience in the Family Theatre on January 17. "Klondikers who packed the D.A.A.A. to the last inch of capacity last evening cheered to the echo the pictures of the 'Yukon Huskies,' as they marched past in the movies," reported the *News*. "While the Yukon boys were being reviewed the entire stage and the front row were filled with the kiddies from the public school, who sang with fervent spirit 'Good Luck to the Boys of the Yukon,' 'O Canada,' 'Rule Britannia' and 'Soldiers of the King.'"[18]

August 1, 1917, was the first time a movie advertisement that included a graphic illustration was inserted in the *Dawson News*.[19]

The following summer, advertisements appeared in the *News* heralding the pending showing of the D. W. Griffith 1915 classic film *Birth of a Nation*. The screening was to coincide with the Discovery Day holiday; by the time it reached Dawson, the film was three years old. The 1916 Griffith follow-up, *Intolerance*, was screened on alternate days.[20] Again in 1919, although the war was over, the ladies of the Martha Munger Black chapter of the IODE screened slides of Yukon volunteers in England, training to go to France. Many well-known Dawson men were shown.[21]

Aside from such noted events, few films portraying Yukon scenes were shown in Dawson theatres. Local patrons were more interested in subjects depicting what was happening outside, including a brief reference in 1921 to Mrs. J. Harmon Caskey, wife of a former staff member of the *Dawson Daily News*. Mrs. Caskey appeared in the cast of the movie *Half Breed*, starring Douglas Fairbanks, which was released in July of 1916. *Half Breed* was subsequently screened in Dawson City in August 1920.[22] Controversy stirred a few years later in the spring of 1927 when word reached Dawson that a film crew was coming to the Yukon to capture footage of the gold-rush trail for a screen adaptation of Robert Service's novel, *The Trail of '98*. In an editorial titled "Why Not Dawson?" the *News* bemoaned the fact that the film crew would go as far as Whitehorse, but would not come to Dawson. While Whitehorse had a legitimate link to the gold-rush trail, the *News* argued that "if the picture is to depict an accurate local[e], Dawson should certainly not be overlooked."[23]

While the *News* was griping about the fact that Dawson was to be ignored, an advance party from Metro-Goldwyn-Mayer was already in Whitehorse looking for locations to film.[24] A film crew consisting of Frank Messenger and Bob Newhard arrived in Whitehorse later in the summer, and from there they set out to capture scenes along the Yukon River, including Five Finger Rapid—but not Dawson City. Awaiting an opportunity to film a raft running through Miles Canyon and Whitehorse Rapids, they were held up by smoke and then rain.[25] Finally, on September 13 the sun broke through, and the film crew set about capturing a sequence showing five men negotiating the rapids on a raft constructed by White Pass dock foreman Bert Peterson.[26] When the film was released, there was one brief glimpse of Dawson City in which a fleet of rafts is approaching the town on the river.

The DAAA survived the turmoil of the Great War era and its aftermath and established a virtual monopoly in the Dawson market through most of the 1920s. Walter Creamer, suffering from declining health, sold the business to Fred Elliott in the summer of 1921 before departing for the United States, where he later passed away. The business was closed for one day for an overhaul before reopening under Elliott's management.

Olaf Olsen, who had owned the Orpheum Theatre for a dozen years, died in 1925. The Orpheum continued to rent out business space to "Apple Jimmy" Oglow, who operated his confectionery stand throughout the 1920s. Finally, in late October 1930 the Orpheum reopened as a movie theatre. Len Wickman, the new proprietor, had renovated the interior with fresh paint and wallpaper as well as furnishings. The first film screened in the newly revived theatre was *Wings*, starring Clara Bow, Charles "Buddy" Rogers and an up-and-coming actor named Gary Cooper. Set during the First World War, *Wings* was the first and only silent film to be awarded the Academy Award for best picture. According to the *News*, "the soft, steady, noiseless light of the high-power Mazda lamp used for projection, made every scene stand out on the screen with a most satisfying vivid brilliancy, intensifying an unusually interesting story, wonderfully and marvelously told in picture."[27]

The noiseless projector touted for the silent films was soon replaced with new equipment designed for the newest innovation in film technology, the "talkie." In early August of 1931, Wickman treated Dawson to the first talkie, a film titled *Dancing Sweeties*, a Warner Brothers production starring Grant Withers and Sue Carol. Dawsonites were drawn to the new attraction in droves. *Dancing Sweeties* played to capacity crowds during its two-evening run before being shipped back outside. With that, if a little later than elsewhere, the silent era was over in Dawson City.[28]

Ghost Town

By the end of the 1920s, the gold-rush town had declined dramatically from its glory days of thirty years before. The only place that seemed to be growing was the hospital, which housed an increasing number of aging sourdoughs. Government House, which had housed the commissioner, had been closed since Commissioner Black had left for overseas in 1916. The residence was not occupied again until 1951, except during the brief visit of the Governor General, Lord Byng, in 1922.[29] The war had taken its toll, especially on the youth and vitality of the community. On top of all that was the sinking of the *Princess Sophia* on Vanderbilt Reef, between Skagway and Juneau, on October 25, 1918. Laura Berton described the transition in her book *I Married the Klondike*.

> At first glance, Dawson looked exactly as it had on the day I first saw it from the decks of the riverboat—the same grey-roofed buildings, the same helter-skelter of cabins. But on second glance there was no doubt at all that we were living

in a decaying town. The population had now sunk to eight hundred, though there were buildings enough for ten times that number. Dozens of houses were standing empty, dozens more lots were vacant, dozens more buildings were slowly falling to pieces ... The north end of town had become a desert of boarded-up cabins. For Dawson had shrunk in towards its core.[30]

Many of the quaint and now old-fashioned Victorian social practices continued, but because of a smaller population the class distinctions were blurred. Dawson's citizens clung to old conventions as if their lives depended upon them. The robust economy based upon gold had shrivelled up; the big dredging companies staggered along under a heavy burden of mismanagement and red ink until many of them were brought together in 1929 as the Yukon Consolidated Gold Corporation (YCGC). But by that time, gold production had shrunk to one third of the total mineral production for the territory.[31]

Just as the Great Depression descended upon the world, Dawson City was spared the worst of its effects. The price of gold doubled in 1933, and under the management of Warren H. S. McFarland the YCGC expanded its operation, enlarging its fleet of dredges that busily extracted gold from the frozen gravels for years to come. The local economy, though not robust, was at least stable during the worst years of the unemployment that plagued the rest of the nation. At its peak in the late 1930s, the YCGC employed nearly eight hundred workers during the busy summer season—although working seven days a week, the men seldom found the opportunity to visit Dawson or take in a movie.

CHAPTER 6

Into the River

After the Orpheum introduced sound movies, it continued to compete with the Family Theatre for the tiny Dawson market. The Family Theatre still offered three-year-old silent movies on a sporadic basis, while the Orpheum countered with talkies like *All Quiet on the Western Front*, starring Lew Ayres, and *The Virginian*, starring Gary Cooper. The rivalry between the two theatres continued through the early months of 1932; by the following summer, the Family Theatre was still offering silent films but alternating with tourist dances. However, the era of silent films was at an end, and in late July Fred Elliott threw in the towel. On July 28, he disposed of several tons of silent films in the traditional way—by hauling them to the waterfront and throwing them in the river. "We are only keeping up with the times," said Elliott. "My patrons want the 'talkies,' so we are going to have them."[32]

As a final exclamation point to that announcement, he made a cleanup of the remaining films stored in the building, hauled them down to the waterfront and set them ablaze. "Pictures formerly worth thousands of dollars went up in smoke in a very few minutes," reported the *Dawson News*. "The heat was so intense that a person was unable to get within seventy-five feet of the fire." Elliott, meanwhile, had been making alterations to the theatre to prepare for social events during the winter. He had been holding back a selection of silent films that had not yet been screened in Dawson and was planning to present them on special occasions; he was also planning to install "all talkie" equipment by 1933.[33] Instead, he decided to give up the movie business entirely and returned to mining on Hunker Creek.[34]

The new owner of the DAAA building, Eric Troberg, purchased the sound equipment in the Orpheum Theatre from Len Wickman, and in early April 1933 he announced that the equipment would be installed and operating within a few days under the management of his brother Walter. The projection room was also rebuilt and made both fireproof and soundproof. The newly renovated Family Theatre was back in business on April 8 with a selection of films, all talkies, featuring Gary Cooper and Carol Lombard in *I Take This Woman*.[35]

"Apple Jimmy" Oglow

The Orpheum was once again out of the movie business, but it was not an empty shell. The front of the building continued to be leased to the colourful James "Apple Jimmy" Oglow. His business, Jimmy's Place, had become a fixture on the Dawson waterfront over the years. Born in Greece, Oglow had come to the Klondike during the gold rush and never left. From the very beginning, he specialized in selling fresh fruit. It is said that he acquired his nickname when, one spring after the Yukon River ice had broken up, he received a large order of apples on the first steamer into Dawson. After a long winter without the delights of fresh fruit, Dawsonites quickly purchased the lot from him on the wharf at premium prices, earning him a tidy sum and his eternal moniker.

In 1909, Oglow was running two fruit and candy stores on King Street in partnership with George Sarantis, but their business dissolved, and by 1910 he had struck out on his own. He was well known for the signature fruit basket from which he sold his wares in the early days. "Why, man," he once said, "that little old sourdough basket is the mascot of my life. She's produced $50,000 if she's produced a cent."[36]

In the summer, his shop, prominently situated on Front Street, became one of the feature attractions for visitors disembarking from

CHAPTER 6

Will Rogers and Wiley Post visited Dawson City in August 1935. Rogers wanted "Apple Jimmy" Oglow to come to Hollywood, but Rogers and Post were killed in a plane crash a few days later. Jimmy Oglow (left), Will Rogers (centre) with unidentified man. Gates collection.

the steamers, and he too was one of the featured characters. He certainly caught the eye of one famous visitor. Will Rogers, the beloved film star and humourist, and aviator Wiley Post landed in Dawson City on August 9, 1935, en route to Alaska. During their stopover, Rogers made friends with Apple Jimmy. Taken by Jimmy's colourful personality, the film star offered to bring Jimmy back to Hollywood with them on their return trip. But Rogers and Post were killed when their plane crashed near Point Barrow, Alaska, a few days after leaving Dawson, and Apple Jimmy's opportunity for film celebrity was dashed.[37]

In October of the following year, D. R. Mackenzie announced that the Orpheum Theatre would once again be open to the public. The movie hall had again been completely overhauled with a sloping floor, new cushioned theatre seats, the latest projectors and a "high fidelity wide-range sound system." For seventy-five cents (school children fifty cents), patrons could watch the latest newsreels, features, comedies and cartoons from such studios as MGM, RKO, United Artists, Republic, Reliance, Fox, Paramount, Warner Brothers and more. The Family Theatre and the Orpheum set up a vigorous campaign of competitive advertisements, each filling two columns in the lower corners of page four in the *News*. As usual, the latest films in Dawson would have been old news anywhere else. By the following year, the two movie houses were showing film gems often two or three years old, although some features such as *Reunion*, featuring the Dionne Quintuplets, was viewed within a year of release.

In October of 1936, the Orpheum Theatre was reopened, with a sloping floor, new cushioned theatre seats, the latest projectors and a high fidelity wide-range sound system. *Dawson Daily News*, October 22, 1936, p. 4, Yukon Archives.

The Last Theatre Standing

The competition between the two theatres ended abruptly on December 30, 1937, when the DAAA building was destroyed by fire. Fires related to celluloid film had occurred over the years but previously had been contained, causing limited damage.[38] Eric Troberg and his son Ralph were awakened by the smell of smoke. Ralph went to investigate and discovered the fire. Both father and son escaped without injury, but by morning the building was a total loss. The heat was so intense that the paint on nearby buildings was blistering, but the fire department was able to contain the fire to the one building. The theatre had been undergoing renovations, having recently installed new projection equipment and high-quality theatre chairs. Other construction materials awaiting installation were also consumed by the flames.[39] In the years that followed, the Orpheum remained the only movie theatre in Dawson.

In 1939, the Orpheum was nearly destroyed when the old M&N Saloon, located on the corner of Front Street and King, and the adjacent Yukonia Hotel were destroyed in a fire that started on March 16.[40] Jimmy Oglow announced that he was going to retire after this fire, but a year later, he was still in business when another fire burned the Orpheum to the ground.[41] The film on the evening of May 22, 1940, concluded just after ten o'clock, and everything was normal when the manager did his rounds of the building after closing. The alarm was raised just before midnight and the fire department, which was located across the street, was able to respond quickly. The heat from the flames was so intense that the White Pass freight buildings across the street began to smoke until the fire department doused them with water. Destruction of the adjoining buildings to the south of the theatre was contemplated, and dynamite was brought in to blow a gap between the flames and the adjacent structures, but with a steady stream of water from the fire department's pumper, that proved unnecessary.[42]

Arson was suspected, as several similar fires had occurred in a short span of time, but nothing was ever proven.[43] Apple Jimmy had recovered from the first fire, but the second disaster left him

The DAAA and the Family Theatre were destroyed by fire on December 30, 1937. The structure was never rebuilt. Dawson City Museum, 1984.113.6.

penniless; he never reopened his business. Over the next year, he suffered declining health, and passed away May 10, 1941. He was buried in the Hillside Cemetery a few days later. One of the pallbearers at his funeral was Harry Gleaves, who had been Oglow's landlord for many years.[44] Gone was one of Dawson's most colourful gold-rush characters; gone were Apple Jimmy's dreams of Hollywood fame; long past were the halcyon years of the gold rush and the excitement on Front Street where so many theatres had stood. Only one ghostly reminder remained: "Arizona Charlie" Meadows's magnificent old Palace Grand, now a derelict shell, a block away on King Street.[45]

Before the ashes had cooled, Harry Gleaves set out to rebuild his theatre. New theatre equipment was ordered from outside and lumber arrived on site in late June. Good results were reported from this effort. By early July 1940, the Orpheum site was a bustle of activity, with foundation work underway. By the middle of the month, Gleaves expected the roof to go on very shortly, after which the new seats and projection and sound equipment would be installed. Gleaves was optimistic that within a few days, the new Orpheum Theatre would again be open to the public.[46]

Three weeks after the fire, enterprising "miners" began harvesting gold from the ashes of the burnt-out theatre. Dirt and ash from the lot where the old Orpheum Theatre had stood were hauled across the street to where sluice boxes were set up at the foot of King Street.[47] Toward the end of July, former Dawson entertainer Kate Rockwell (now married to local miner Johnny Matson) was given a sample of dirt by Gleaves, gathered from beneath where the stage she performed upon in the old days had once stood. In a matter of a few minutes she had panned twenty dollars of gold out of the pay dirt as a souvenir from a bygone era.[48]

While all this was going on, two local entrepreneurs, Curly Russell and Nick Sutovich, acquired the Eagles Hall (formerly the Arctic Brotherhood Hall), converted it into the Palomar Theatre and Dance Hall, and started showing films. This continued over the summer while construction on the Orpheum progressed.

A thousand barrels of sawdust had been poured into the walls of the Orpheum to provide insulation from the extreme cold, and the walls and ceiling were covered with Donnaconna, a popular interior panel finish from that era. The seating for 160 patrons, which was installed on a sloping floor, was staggered to improve customer viewing of the screen. According to one patron from Keno City, the new theatre was "a real picture palace."[49] Despite that good review, the new single-storey Orpheum Theatre was a pale reflection of the glorious old gold-rush building, with simpler lines and a plain facade. It opened September 19 with a three-day screening of *The Prisoner of Zenda*, starring Ronald Colman, Mary Astor, Raymond Massey, David Niven and Douglas Fairbanks.[50] Within days, the Palomar

The Orpheum Theatre reconstructed after the fire in 1940 was a pale shadow of the original building. Dawson City Museum, 2010.34.93.

was no longer showing films, and *The Lone Ranger* serial that had started at the Palomar continued in the Orpheum. The Palomar thereafter became a recreational hall, offering dances on an irregular basis through the following months.

World War II and Beyond

The Second World War, which had been raging overseas since September of the previous year, was having a negative effect on the local economy. The YCGC was having difficulty finding the necessary labour and supplies to keep its dredge operation afloat. The workforce, which had peaked at eight hundred before the war, was reduced to less than two hundred as the war advanced. In 1941, labour strife befell the company. The working conditions were unforgiving and the facilities in the dredge camp were appallingly inadequate. The food was unsatisfactory, and the company was accused by its employees of being a "gut-robber." Higher wages outside stirred discontent, and in the summer of 1941, the employees walked off the job and into Dawson. The dredges lay silent for nine days. But there were bigger things brewing. Events would soon change the course of history for the Klondike capital once and for all, and the gold-rush city would almost succumb to the changes.[51]

On December 7, 1941, Japanese forces staged a surprise attack upon the United States fleet anchored in Pearl Harbor at Honolulu, Hawaii, and twenty vessels, including eight battleships, were destroyed or damaged. The following day, US president Franklin Roosevelt asked Congress to declare war on Japan. Suddenly Alaska had strategic importance, and in February 1942, to secure the supply of materiel to the largest state against Japanese attack, the United States began making plans to construct an all-weather road to Alaska. Construction commenced on March 9, 1942, and the link with Alaska was officially opened nine months later. The necessity of the road became more urgent when the Japanese invaded the American islands of Kiska and Attu in the Aleutian Island chain in June 1942. As construction progressed, Whitehorse, not Dawson City, became the hub of Yukon operations. And as Whitehorse expanded, Dawson shrank even more.

Before the war, Whitehorse, with a population of a few hundred, had been a transfer point between rail and water links to Dawson City and Mayo. At its wartime peak, the little village reached ten thousand inhabitants, and the centre of power shifted to the southern end of the territory. Although the YCGC returned to full operation again after the war, rising labour and material costs and a fixed gold price conspired to squeeze the profitability of the company. The final insult to Dawson came when the territorial capital was moved to Whitehorse in 1953. But Dawson never expired entirely, and the population remained stable at eight hundred souls. To many, the derelict buildings that reflected the once-proud status of Dawson City as the Paris of the North became a millstone. Demolition of the old buildings was viewed by Dawsonites as a move toward the future, and not many wanted to dwell in the past.

The Orpheum continued to operate after the war under the steady management of Harry Gleaves until 1954, when it was purchased by Charles Gray, to be operated by him and his wife.[52] The Grays eventually sold it to Len Miller, who in turn transferred it to Ben Warnsby and Mike Stutter in April 1962. Fred and Palma Berger took over the business four years later and continued to operate the theatre for thirteen more years.[53]

But in the 1970s, Dawson started receiving canned television, which had a negative impact upon business. Fred Berger decided to show movies only during the summer, and the theatre continued to be viable until May 2, 1979, when the worst flood in a century inundated the building and most of Dawson City. Berger reported that they were able to catch fish inside the building after the water had receded.[54] The insurance settlement was not enough to pay for new seats in the theatre, let alone cover the cost of rebuilding. By that time, Dawson City was receiving live television broadcasts, and in the early 1980s, the town subsidized distribution of satellite broadcasts, including movies on the Home Box Office channel. It was no longer viable to operate a theatre in Dawson. The Orpheum stood derelict until it was purchased from the Bergers in 2002 by Dave Robertson, a businessman who had the building demolished a short time later.

Many Dawson residents reflected with sadness and fondness on the disappearance of this Dawson City landmark. It had provided jobs for many young people during the 1950s, '60s and '70s.

One former resident remembered it from the 1950s. "It was the only entertainment in the long winter months, and Harry Gleaves was the jolly owner, always asking at the end of the movie, 'How did you like it?'" In particular, she remembered the matinee the Saturday before Christmas when Chuck and Tommy Gray put on free cartoons for the kids, followed by a visit from Santa Claus with his jolly "Ho, ho, ho!"[55] Many residents recalled how much they looked forward to seeing a movie at the Orpheum, especially before television came to town. "It was so large when I was a kid," remarked one resident during the demolition. "Was it really that small?"[56]

The Orpheum was one of the few places to socialize without people having to go to one of the bars in Dawson. As the years passed, the memories increasingly faded into history. The story of theatres in Dawson City was almost complete.

CHAPTER 7

THE KLONDIKE

AND

HOLLYWOOD

By the 1940s, the glory days of Dawson City and the Klondike gold rush were a dwindling memory, summed up by the decaying buildings scattered throughout town. The aging men who had mucked for gold in the early days were now bent and aching, and they were more likely to while away the hours reminiscing about the early days in the bar in the Royal Alexandra Hotel on Front Street or sitting on benches in the sun in front of the Occidental Hotel on Third Avenue. Post-World War II, the old buildings were seen by many residents as a blight on the shrinking community, reminders of the past, and citizens were inclined to demolish them.[1] Nineteen forty-five saw the disappearance of the Green Tree, Yukon and Fairview Hotels, and the ferry tower that had been so prominent on the Dawson waterfront for more than forty years was also razed.

Not until the 1950s did the community begin to recognize the historical significance of the gold-rush legacy. The Klondike Visitors

Association was formed to encourage tourism; the Historic Sites and Monuments Board of Canada recognized the national historical significance of the town and the Department of Indian Affairs and Northern Development, which included national parks and historic sites as its responsibility, began acquiring property in Dawson City to commemorate the gold rush for all Canadians.

Among these buildings was the old Auditorium Theatre, which was demolished and then rebuilt. In 1962 the newly reconstructed theatre, once again christened the Palace Grand, was opened for the off-Broadway production of the stage play *Foxy*. Bert Lahr, the Lion from the movie *The Wizard of Oz*, had the starring role. It was all part of the Dawson Festival, a heavily subsidized event sponsored by the federal government that took place that year to celebrate the gold rush and launch what would become a thriving tourism industry. Once again, each summer the stage of the Palace Grand echoed with the sounds of live theatre and became the centrepiece of the community. The Palace Grand provided the venue for a spring breakup drama festival and for the Gaslight Follies, a summer season variety show aimed at the tourist market that continued each summer into the twenty-first century.

What Happened to the Gold-Rush Legends?

Looking back in time, we see that many of the gold-rush era entertainers left without much of an imprint, while other people had stellar careers in Hollywood. Cad Wilson left Dawson on August 17, 1899, with a heavy purse and her famous gold nugget-studded belt.[2] Arriving in Portland, she and three others took a box in the Fredericksburg Music Hall, from where Cad sang along with the performers. She was finally induced to join them on stage, where, adorned with her famous gold-nugget belt, she performed "Just a Little Lingerie." During the song, she raised her skirt "much higher than necessary" to expose a diamond encrusted garter on her left thigh. For an hour amid repeated encores she belted out one catchy song after another.

She performed in San Francisco in the fall of 1899, then returned to Dawson, where she performed for a couple of weeks before heading to Nome for the summer of 1900. She returned to Dawson later in the summer to perform at the Standard Theatre and remained there for the winter before departing for the south. She disappeared from the theatre scene in later years. One thing is abundantly clear: Cad Wilson was the most popular, even notorious, performer ever to have set foot on a stage in Dawson City during the glory days. But her notoriety paled quickly when she left the Yukon.

George T. Snow, the first theatre man in the Yukon Valley, got into mining when he arrived in Dawson but had to leave the North because of his health in 1898. After a couple of years in Seattle he returned to Juneau in 1900, finally leaving the North for good with his wife, Anna, in 1910. When he died in 1925, he left behind the vestiges of his historical work: unfinished manuscripts and crudely written accounts sent to him by fellow pioneers.

Swiftwater Bill Gates's antics became real-life theatre bordering on comedy, sometimes farce, sometimes tragedy. He married—and abandoned—several wives, at one time being married to two women at once. He moved to Nome and other mining districts, seemingly blessed with good fortune and attracting headlines in the newspapers wherever he went. By 1915, he added another credit to his reputation, that of deadbeat dad. When in Seattle that year, preparing to sail to Peru for more adventure, he was arrested at the insistence of one ex-mother-in-law. This time the charge was child abandonment.[3] Bill eventually made it to Peru, where he lived out his remaining years, still looking for gold, until he was murdered on February 21, 1937.

Joe Boyle spent a brief time in Dawson during the summer of 1897. While there, he instigated boxing matches with his partner, former Australian heavyweight champion Frank Slavin, to attract patronage at the Monte Carlo. Boyle, ever the heroic figure, left Dawson during freeze-up with a small party in October 1897. The group made its way south over the blizzard-cloaked coastal mountains on the Dalton Trail. Boyle's courageous leadership during the trek was instrumental to their survival, so when they reached Seattle they bought him a watch in appreciation.[4] Boyle went on to gain control of one of the biggest dredging companies in the Klondike goldfields, earning the title of King of the Klondike. He once sponsored a Dawson hockey team's trip to Ottawa to challenge for the Stanley Cup.[5] They lost the series, but the contest became legendary. During World War I, he volunteered to go to Russia to help reorganize the Russian train system. His exploits over the next two years are worthy of a blockbuster movie. He was awarded medals by Britain, France, Russia and Romania. In the latter country he became a national hero, and a close personal friend (some say lover) of Queen Marie.[6]

The Oatley Sisters, who established one of the first concert halls in the Klondike, remained active in Klondike theatre, Lottie more so than Polly. Lottie was wooed by and eventually wed Jim Daugherty, the successful miner and owner of the Pavilion, but the marriage didn't last. Lottie left Dawson for Fairbanks in the summer of 1904, and by January of the following year, "the former Mrs. James Daugherty," was once again doing business under her maiden name. She later married gentleman gambler Vernon Dunwood Casley, and for several years they operated a hotel in Prince Rupert, BC. When she passed away in Los Angeles in April 1961 at age eighty-three, she had been operating a forty-room apartment building that catered to film actors and actresses, but after World War II she refused to replace the tenants who moved out with new ones. Her sister, Polly, had predeceased her by forty years, her husband by nineteen years, and her only child, Charlotte, by seventeen.

Mae Isabel Lovejoy, popularly known as "Diamond Tooth" Gertie, became a legend. In the early days the Dawson newspapers covered the theatre circuit with a close eye, yet she is not mentioned in any theatrical advertisements or reviews of the stage attractions. Gertie lost $2,000 worth of personal belongings in the Monte Carlo fire of January 1899, barely escaping with her life. She was obviously doing well, but there is no explanation of precisely what she was doing for a living.

Lovejoy was seen entering the Phoenix Dance Hall on the evening of April 6, 1899, on the arm of US Consul James McCook. They shared a bottle of wine, after which McCook embarked on the most notorious binge of the gold rush.[7] Lovejoy eventually married Charles W. C. Tabor, Dawson City's most prominent lawyer, in Portland, Oregon, on November 7, 1901. In her book, Laura Berton described Gertie in her later years, attending one of socialite Martha Black's evening social functions, as "a demure little woman, quite pretty and very self-effacing. She had little to say, but when she did speak, the famous diamond could be seen glittering between the two front teeth."[8]

Her husband died in the fire of the Yukonia Hotel in Dawson in February 1917 while she was spending the winter outside the Yukon. Three years later, in East Oakland County, California, Isabel Tabor married Stephen C. Hart, a hotel steward, of San Francisco. The documents list Hart as being thirty-five years of age, and Isabel being thirty-two. In truth, she was eleven years older than Hart.

Isabel was married to Stephen until his death thirty-five years later. She became a Christian Scientist in 1926 and a practitioner in 1928. She remained so until she died in San Mateo, California, in 1957. In recent times, she remains one of the most well-known figures from the gold rush, mainly because her name is perpetuated on Dawson City's gambling casino. And that seems to be the story of her life—often misrepresented, misunderstood and mythologized.

Beatrice Lorne, who was born Beatrice Heley in Scotland in 1866, emigrated to Australia as a child with her family, where she became an opera singer on the Australian stage. Billed as the Australian Nightingale, and later as the Klondike Nightingale, she performed in Dawson theatres for a number of years before marrying George Smith, a veterinarian and mining broker, in June of 1901. She continued to appear in theatrical events in Dawson after her marriage and regularly appeared in benefit concerts under her stage name, sometimes accompanied by her daughter from her first marriage, Constance, who joined her in Dawson after she wed Smith.

Like Gertie Lovejoy, Beatrice found it hard to gain social acceptance in the strait-laced Victorian community that Dawson had become, but she was valued by Dawsonites for her vocal talents. When a righteous Methodist objected to her singing in church, her husband George punched him in the nose. The community sided with the Smiths, and the judge, clearly siding with George as well, fined him a mere one dollar when the assault was brought to court.[9] Nearly thirty years later, at the commemoration of the Yukon stained-glass window in the Canadian Memorial Chapel in Vancouver, it was a silver-haired Mrs. Smith whose voice rang out as clear and vibrant as it had during the gold rush. Beatrice Lorne passed away in Vancouver on September 26, 1945.[10]

"Arizona Charlie" Meadows left Dawson City on the *Nora*, one of the last river steamers to depart Dawson in the fall of 1901, and never returned to the Yukon. He was attracted to an adventure on Tiburon, an island in the Gulf of Mexico where, it was said, Montezuma's treasure, a hoard of gold coins, had been hidden. The venture came to nothing, and Meadows settled on a farm near Yuma, Arizona, where he remained for the rest of his years. He established a newspaper and became active in politics. Meadows died on December 9, 1932, at the age of seventy-three.[11]

From the Klondike to Hollywood

Marjorie Rambeau went on to an illustrious career on stage and in film. She performed with the likes of Roscoe Arbuckle (from her Dawson days), Spencer Tracy, Jean Harlow, Loretta Young, Ronald Reagan, James Cagney and John Wayne. She appeared in several films with Clark Gable. She was Annie Gibson in the film *Strictly Personal* (1933), which was cowritten by another Klondike veteran, Wilson Mizner. Over the years she was recognized for her work. She was twice nominated for an Academy Award as best supporting actress in *Primrose Path* (1940) and *Torch Song* (1953). In 1955 she was awarded the National Board of Review Award for Best Supporting Actress for her roles in *A Man Called Peter* and *The View from Pompey's Head*.[12] She has a star on the Hollywood Walk of Fame at 6336 Hollywood Boulevard. Her most admirable accomplishment may have been her comeback from a serious automobile accident in 1945 in which she was nearly killed. She struggled through numerous operations for three years to learn to walk again, graduating from wheelchair to walker to crutches and finally a cane. When she returned to the studio to film John M. Stahl's film *The Walls of Jericho* in 1948, the cast and crew applauded her arrival. She passed away on July 7, 1970, just a few days shy of her eighty-first birthday.[13]

CHAPTER 7

Rambeau frequently appeared on screen in Dawson City, and not without being recognized. In 1934 she appeared at the DAAA Family Theatre in *Silence*, a 1931 production, along with Clive Brook, Peggy Shannon and Charles Starrett.[14] In 1937 the *Dawson News* noted that a "Dawson Girl" appears in the 1934 production of *Grand Canary*, also starring Warner Baxter and Madge Evans. She also appeared in the 1940 Warner Brothers production of *East of the River*, with John Garfield and Brenda Marshall, shown at the Orpheum in Dawson in 1944.[15] Other appearances on a Dawson screen by Rambeau include the 1939 Darryl F. Zanuck production of *The Rains Came* (Twentieth Century Fox), also starring Myrna Loy and Tyrone Power.[16]

After leaving Dawson City, Marjorie Rambeau went on to a spectacular career in Hollywood. She starred opposite some of the great screen actors of the era: Spencer Tracy, Jean Harlow, Loretta Young, Ronald Reagan, James Cagney, John Wayne and Clark Gable. Gates collection.

Ned Sparks was a renowned character actor in silent movies and talkies. Known by gossip columnists as the "moan about town," he was recognized for his ability to crack a joke without cracking a smile. As a publicity stunt, he once had his face insured by Lloyd's of London for $100,000 in case he should ever be photographed smiling in public, something that would damage his film persona. He was born in St. Thomas, Ontario (and frequently spent the summers there in later years), and told of how he ran off to the Klondike in 1898, as a lad of sixteen years, where, lacking any talent for mining, he performed on the Klondike stages. "Why dig for gold," he is quoted as having said, "when I could sing for it?" His career spanned thirty years, and during that time he appeared in nearly a hundred films. He retired a wealthy man,[17] but he left no footprint of his time in the Klondike.

Rickard, Mizner and Grauman

Tex Rickard, who organized pugilistic grudge matches between Joe Boyle and his partner Frank Slavin, went on to great success as one of the biggest boxing promoters of the twentieth century. Among his accomplishments, he founded the New York Rangers hockey team and oversaw the rebuilding of Madison Square Garden. He was something of a showman, sometimes likened to P. T. Barnum.

Rickard's partner in crime for some of his Klondike capers was Wilson Mizner, who helped orchestrate the Boyle-Slavin boxing matches. While in the Klondike, Mizner pulled off confidence games on the unsuspecting, and he once robbed a Dawson store for chocolates to give to his girlfriend. Never one to attempt honest labour, he moved on to Nome, where he is said to have managed a gambling house and casino. His exploits over the years became legendary. Mizner had a short-lived marriage to a New York heiress and a failed real estate venture in Florida with his brother Addison. He eventually ended up in Hollywood where he wrote screenplays for movies, the best known of which was *20,000 Years in Sing Sing*. His addiction to opium and his innate laziness compromised his screenwriting career. He was the co-owner and manager of the famed Brown Derby restaurant in Los Angeles, but in later years he became more well

CHAPTER 7

known for the things he said. When one of the fighters he managed was murdered, he quipped, "Tell 'em to start counting ten over him and he'll get up." He once described the Hollywood scene as a trip through a sewer in a glass-bottomed boat.[18]

While in Dawson, Mizner devised a scheme that allowed both him and a destitute young paperboy named Sid Grauman to turn a quick profit. Grauman obtained possession of a consignment of two thousand newspapers from the United States. He was going to sell these at a dollar apiece to the news-starved citizens of Dawson, and leave Dawson with his profits. When Mizner got wind of this, he came up with a plan. Mizner would pay Grauman $25 for his first sale, provided that Grauman would hold off selling his newspapers for an hour. Mizner then charged admission to a warehouse he had rented, where he read the news stories to two hundred eager listeners.[19]

Tex Rickard went on from Dawson City to become the biggest fight promoter of the twentieth century. He was the founder of the New York Rangers hockey team and the builder of the third edition of Madison Square Garden. Gates collection.

During his two years in Dawson, Grauman claimed to have befriended Jack London and Robert Service (both impossible). He eventually parlayed the $2,000 from the newspaper caper into $6,000 but never explained how he accomplished this (there is no historical footprint to substantiate his account of his time in the Klondike). It is said that he lost this money gambling en route to San Francisco, but we know that he took on a job as a "ticket taker, errand boy and janitor at the Cinemagraph Theatre" in San Francisco. It is also said that this was where he saw his first moving pictures, although it is not inconceivable that this occurred in Dawson City. He and his father managed theatres in San Francisco for several years, offering a combination of vaudeville entertainment and moving pictures for a ten-cent admission price.[20] Within weeks of the earthquake that devastated San Francisco in 1906, the Graumans were operating a theatre again in a tent structure called the National.[21]

Arbuckle, Grauman and Chaplin

According to one account, while attending a beer garden in San Jose one evening, Grauman saw a "rotund singing waiter" perform. Impressed by the waiter's talent, Grauman stole him away to perform in his Bijou Theatre. That waiter was Roscoe "Fatty" Arbuckle. Arbuckle stipulated that the gig come with one free dinner each day. Grauman complied, but with a stipulation of his own: that the meal be consumed in the show window of a nearby Greek restaurant. Passersby were entranced by the man who consumed five full meals at a single sitting, all done in comic fashion. The arrangement proved good publicity for both the restaurant and for Grauman's theatre.[22]

Another version of Arbuckle's Grauman connection has him employed, in 1904, as a singing waiter at the Portola Restaurant owned by Sid's father, David. One evening the elder Grauman introduced Arbuckle to another theatre impresario with a Klondike connection, Alexander Pantages, and Pantages hired him to tour his west coast theatres.[23] One can only speculate on which of these accounts is the more accurate and wonder whether, over the years,

CHAPTER 7

Roscoe "Fatty" Arbuckle appeared on the stage of the Auditorium Theatre the summer of 1906, and later became one of Hollywood's first mega-stars with a million-dollar contract. Gates collection.

these men had ever compared notes about their respective adventures in the Klondike. As the years passed, almost everybody who had participated in the gold rush incorporated elements of the gold-rush saga into their personal narratives. Many claimed to have known Jack London and rubbed shoulders with Robert Service.

Biographers make little or no reference to Roscoe Arbuckle's northern theatre tour in 1906. After his brief appearance in Dawson City with Marjorie Rambeau, he continued to perform on the vaudeville circuit, becoming a featured act. He was also a talented singer. At one point, he met the famed opera star Enrico Caruso. It is reported that Caruso heard him sing and was impressed. In one account, Caruso is said to have told Arbuckle he could have been the second best opera singer in the world.[24] In another version, he was said to have told Arbuckle that with study and training, he might become a good second-rate singer.[25]

In 1909, Arbuckle appeared in his first moving picture. He continued to do so until by 1913 he had appeared in a series of Mack Sennett *Keystone Cop* comedies and become a star. The following year, he was paid $1,000 a week by Paramount Pictures plus a healthy share of the profits from his films. He was so successful that in 1918, Paramount offered him a $3 million, three-year screen contract, which was enormous for the time. But his star was soon to fall. In 1921, he was charged with the rape and accidental killing of an aspiring young actress named Virginia Rappe. After three trials, he was eventually acquitted, but the notoriety of the case ruined his career. On June 28, 1933, just when Arbuckle was making a comeback, he died in his sleep. He was only forty-six years old.

In 1911, Grauman met a comedy duo on their first tour in America: Charlie Chaplin and Stan Laurel. Grauman was immediately taken by Chaplin's immense talent and offered him work on the growing Grauman theatre chain. That arrangement didn't work out, but in later years Grauman put on splashy premieres for Chaplin's films *The Gold Rush* and *The Circus*.[26]

Grauman had opened several lavish movie theatres in Los Angeles, including the Egyptian, the Million Dollar and the Chinese. He was a master of publicity, and many major cinematic productions were premiered in his theatres during the 1920s and '30s. Each was accompanied by a prologue—an extravagant live production employing a full orchestra, ornate stage sets and large cast.

Alexander Pantages managed the Orpheum Theatre in Dawson City before going on to control a chain of theatres across the western half of the continent. Gates collection.

CHAPTER 7

Charlie Chaplin's movie *The Gold Rush*, inspired by the Klondike and perhaps even by Grauman's skillful storytelling, opened in Grauman's Egyptian Theatre on June 26, 1925. The film was heavily promoted during the days leading up to the opening night. For the first time, Grauman insisted that his regular "first-nighters" be in their seats by 8:20 p.m. When the celebrities began to arrive at 8:30, they were announced over a public address system. Among those who attended were the elite of Hollywood personages: Chaplin was there, as were Douglas Fairbanks and Mary Pickford. Sam Goldwyn and his wife strode up the red carpet, followed by Louis B. Mayer. Other Hollywood luminaries made their appearance: Marion Davies, William S. Hart, Cecil B. DeMille, Hoot Gibson, Mae Murray and Rudolph Valentino. Comic screen stars Buster Keaton and Roscoe Arbuckle (who had been in Dawson City nineteen years earlier) were there too.[27]

The press pointed out that Sid Grauman had a Klondike connection to this production. He drew upon his personal experiences in Dawson City to design the elaborate stage setting of the Monte Carlo dance hall for the prologue, in which one hundred people performed on the stage. The prologue, titled *Charlie Chaplin's Dream*, was reported to be at least as interesting for the nearly two thousand patrons as the film itself. It included an ice-skating ballet, "Eskimos," the balloon dancer Lillian Powell and a finale. As for the movie, it is said that Grauman's penchant for storytelling inspired some of Chaplin's best sight gags in it.[28] The movie is considered by many to be Chaplin's best work, and the one for which he most wanted to be remembered.

The Last of the Silents

The works of Robert Service continued to appear on screen during the 1920s. *The Law of the Yukon*, based upon Service's poem of the same name, was released in 1920. Directed by Charles Miller and starring June Elvidge and Edward Earle, it was set in a saloon in the Yukon and includes a healthy dose of romance.

A more ambitious film was the 1928 release of *The Trail of '98*, based upon Robert Service's first novel, for which a film crew had been sent to the Yukon the year before. To add to the realism but to keep the costs down, rather than in the Yukon, many scenes depicting the frozen North were filmed at an elevation of thirty-six hundred metres above sea level on the Continental Divide in Colorado. The crew and cast were subjected to freezing conditions and snowstorms with winds reaching 115 kilometres per hour. The sequence of the stampeders climbing "the Chilkoot" had to be taken twelve times, and many of the extras "were forced to abandon the attempt, just as in the days of '98 when hundreds found this trail their Waterloo."[29] Some actors were buried in avalanches, some suffered from frostbite and exposure, and some even suffered carbon monoxide poisoning. One of the character actors was heard to confess, "I wouldn't have missed the trip for anything—but next time they won't get me any further from Hollywood than Griffith Park."[30]

Adding to the realism of the film, director Clarence Brown had gleaned factual accounts of the Chilkoot from two hundred people who had participated in the Klondike stampede, and he had obtained photostatic copies of newspapers from the era that described the conditions on the trail. To further the effect, he hired a handful of former sourdoughs and dance hall girls among the ten thousand extras to give authenticity to the Dawson City scenes.

The film opened to much acclaim and was proclaimed an immense hit when it premiered in the Astor Theatre in New York in March 1928.[31] Sid Grauman secured the rights to open the film in Los Angeles in early May in his Chinese Theatre.[32] The opening was covered live on radio. A large spotlight projecting a shaft of light into the sky was said to be visible for 160 kilometres. A dance hall and bar were the backdrop for Grauman's usual prologue, starring Bob Blackner (the cowboy tenor), the Rangers (harmony octet), Jimmy Ray (the dancing waiter), Chaz Chase (international comedy star) and Chief Caupolican (famous Italian baritone). As the prologue concluded, half of the dance hall wheeled to the left and half to the right to reveal the wide "Fantom" screen, a new innovation that slowly moved forward to the front of the stage.[33]

The film heralded the end of the silent era in motion pictures. After the last night of *The Trail of '98* at the Chinese, the theatre was closed until August 3 to make preparations for the transition to talkies and the first screening of the new MGM sound motion picture *White Shadows in the South Seas*.[34]

A copy of the film *The Trail of '98* was carried to Nice, France, by MGM film producer Irving Thalberg and his bride, Norma Shearer, to present to Robert Service in person. Service was reported to be "loud in his praise of the faithful manner in which his story had been adhered to and the realism with which it had been portrayed."[35]

The Trail of '98 opened at the Tivoli Theatre in London on August 21, heralded as the most important film ever shown there except for *Ben Hur*. Special note was given to the reality of the avalanche scene on the Chilkoot and the treacherous waters of Whitehorse Rapids.[36] Profusely illustrated programs and opera glasses were available at an extra cost.

If the work of Robert Service was popular for converting into movies with a Yukon theme, the writing of Jack London topped the list. His work has been adapted to the silver screen and television nearly 250 times.[37] Of these productions, sixty or more reflect his Klondike experiences. His brief stay in the Yukon during the winter of 1897–98 fired his imagination and fuelled his career for years to come, yet he died in 1916 still a young man, just forty years of age. Although his fame as an author had spread around the world by that time, he did not live long enough to see his book *The Call of the Wild* translated onto the screen.

The version of the movie *The Call of the Wild* produced in 1923 was the only one created as a silent film. The next version of the film was not released until a dozen years later, when it premiered at both Loew's State and Grauman's Chinese Theatres on July 24, 1935. Clark Gable, Loretta Young and Jack Oakie starred in the film, but if viewers watch closely, they will see Sid Grauman in a cameo appearance in one scene, dealing cards with a familiarity gained from his days in the Klondike nearly forty years before. By the time of its release, the days of the extravagant prologues and gala openings were past. The Chinese Theatre had switched to a policy that dispensed with reserved seating and instead offered two afternoon and two evening shows on a general admission basis. Nevertheless, the film was a powerful draw, and attendance records were being broken along the entire west coast.[38]

Like Sid Grauman, Robert Service made a brief and uncredited cameo appearance at the beginning of the 1942 film adapted from Rex Beach's book *The Spoilers*. It was during the Second World War, and the Service family had relocated to North America, lodging in Los Angeles each winter for the duration of the conflict. He was approached by film producer Frank Lloyd to make an appearance in the forthcoming film starring Marlene Dietrich and John Wayne. It was a short exchange between Service and Dietrich as he sat composing poetry in a booth in a saloon. Cherry Malotte (Dietrich) approaches Service, made up to look twenty years younger, and his twenty-three words were recorded for posterity:

> Cherry: Hello Mr. Service; writing a poem about me?
> Service: Not this time, Cherry. It's about a lady known as Lou.
> Cherry: Is there a man in her life?
> Service: Yes, He's called Dan McGrew. He's a bad actor, he gets shot.
> Cherry: Sounds exciting. The shooting of Dan McGrew.

Dietrich walks away, and Service's brief appearance in the film is over. Service recalls labouring over his lines, but never to his satisfaction. He was not destined to become a film star, but he was thrilled to work with Dietrich.

"Klondike Kate" and Hollywood

In January of 1942, Kate Rockwell Matson rolled into Hollywood to consult on the making of a movie based upon her life story. "When this century was just beginning," wrote columnist Frederick C. Othman, "she was one of the dancing girls in the Savoy Theater, at Dawson, where the boys played roulette between acts. Out front was a 'barker,' name of Frank Gardner. He took one look at the beauty from the States and he yelled: 'Here she comes now—Klondike Kate, the Rocky mountain buck-and-wing dancer!' 'And,' she said [in 1942] between puffs on one of her home-made cigarettes, 'I have been Klondike Kate ever since.'"[39]

The story, though colourful, isn't exactly true. Rockwell did not acquire the name Klondike Kate until thirty years after the gold rush. Indeed, the use of the appellation can be traced back to the era of the gold rush, appearing in newspapers as early as November 1897, but it did not apply to Kate Rockwell specifically at the time. At first, its usage was associated with ladies and events of questionable reputation. But in 1915 author Harry Leon Wilson published the novel *Ruggles of Red Gap*, which includes a character named Klondike Kate; the book became a best-seller and was quickly adapted for the stage. Actress Leonore Harris played the role of Klondike Kate in the Manhattan stage production in the fall of 1915, and Edna Phillips Holmes starred in the same role in the screen version released by Essanay Films in 1917. *Ruggles of Red Gap* was remade in 1923 in a Paramount production with Lois Wilson playing Kate in this version. Kate seems to disappear as a character in the 1935 talkie remake of the film, starring Charles Laughton.

During the 1920s, references were made to "Klondike Kate" Ryan, who lived in Whitehorse, but the woman in question never set foot in the Klondike and appears to have acquired the moniker only after leaving the Yukon.[40] It wasn't until 1929 that Rockwell embraced the name with a passion and made it her own. In that year, Rockwell's former paramour, Alex Pantages, now hugely successful and wealthy, was accused of raping a young woman named Eunice Pringle. Rockwell was brought to Los Angeles as a potential witness for the prosecution, and within a short time the newspapers had branded her as the Klondike Queen, the Flame of the Yukon and Klondike Kate in big banner headlines.[41] Rockwell adopted the latter name, and for the rest of her life she promoted herself as "Klondike Kate."

Decades later her fellow sourdoughs, many of whom remembered Rockwell from the early days, embraced the title as well. From this point on, she appears regularly in newspaper accounts: when she attended social functions, when she travelled north to

CHAPTER 7

Dawson City, when she married Johnny Matson, a Klondike miner who knew her from the gold-rush days, and finally, when she was embraced by Hollywood.[42] In her biography, written late in her life by Ellis Lucia, the claims about her being the premier attraction of the theatre circuit in Dawson City are overstated, but she was there and she did participate in the hard life of the theatres and dance halls. In fact, she was close enough to the epicentre to be considered the real thing. That was enough to earn her the title of Queen of the Klondike.

Cashing in on her notoriety, Kate travelled to Hollywood in May of 1934 to solicit interest in the making of a film based upon her life. She sold her idea to film agent Harry Weber, who had been her vaudeville manager after she left the Klondike many years before. Willard Mack and Edward Paulton set to work scripting the story, with Mack's ex-wife and former sourdough Marjorie Rambeau to play the role of Kate in the movie. Kate left Hollywood with a contract in hand and on May 31 headed north to see her husband, Johnny Matson, who was mining in the Yukon. She planned to return to Hollywood in the fall to serve as "technical advisor" to the scriptwriters.[43]

In the end the film never happened, but eight years later Rockwell was back in Hollywood collaborating with Columbia Pictures, which bought the rights to her story. The afternoon of January 22, 1942, she sat in an office at Columbia Studios giving a demonstration of how to roll your own cigarettes. She pulled out a package of Bull Durham tobacco and tapped a little onto a cigarette paper that she held in one hand while simultaneously tugging with her teeth at the drawstring on the bag of tobacco in her other hand. She did the same thing at the movie studio, giving instructions to actresses Jinx Falkenburg, Shirley Patterson and Evelyn Keyes. Falkenburg was reported to have been a quick learner.

Kate Rockwell showing Hollywood starlets how to roll their own cigarettes, January 22, 1942. From left to right: Shirley Patterson, Jinx Falkenburg, Rockwell and Evelyn Keyes. Gates collection.

"There's hardly a man, woman or child who hasn't heard of the colourful Klondike Kate, so her personally supervised story should have a ready-made audience," stated American movie columnist Louella Parsons when she heard of Kate's impending visit to Los Angeles.[44] Parsons interviewed Rockwell when the latter arrived in Tinseltown. Kate demonstrated the fine art of rolling a cigarette and also gave Parsons a lesson in geography, pointing out that Dawson City was in Canada, as were the Mounted Police.[45]

Being a veteran of the gold rush, Kate was a stickler for authenticity. The Hollywood dance hall girls weren't anything like the real version, she was quick to note. "We danced like ladies—square dances and waltzes and things like that," she said, "and our costumes were not the low-cut sort you see now. On stage we wore tights.

CHAPTER 7

A dance hall in Dawson City during the gold rush days. According to Kate Rockwell, "We danced like ladies—square dances and waltzes and things like that—and our costumes were not the low-cut sort you see now." J. B. Tyrrell collection, Fisher Library, University of Toronto.

Dance hall girls in those days wore high-necked shirtwaists, high button shoes and skirts down to the ground as well as wrist-length sleeves."[46]

Rockwell took pains to clarify that the Klondike wasn't like the wild west. "People get funny ideas," she said. "They think those days were wild and woolly for a fact. It was wild country all right, but the Mounties didn't let much go wrong. As for the girls, I never heard a girl in a dance hall tell a vulgar story, swear, or curse … The scenes you saw in Dawson's dance halls weren't any wilder than what you see in some of the taxi-dance places today."[47]

But Hollywood and reality seldom overlap. The story that Columbia finally settled on was entirely fictional. "I don't recognize anything in it that happened to me," she said in October of 1943 during the filming of the picture. Ann Savage, the actress selected to play Kate in the movie, did not wear lighted candles in her hair in the film, like Rockwell claimed to have done on New Year's Eve of 1900.[48] The film was never screened in Dawson City.

Home-Grown Talent

Dawson City also produced some home-grown talents that later made their way to Hollywood. Mrs. J. Harmon Caskey, who had a reputation as an excellent contralto and performed occasionally at social gatherings and more formal events, appeared in a silent picture starring Douglas Fairbanks in 1916.[49]

William Desmond Taylor, originally born William Cunningham Deane-Tanner in Ireland of Irish-English gentry, moved to America and married into an established New York family in 1901. Known as a philanderer and heavy drinker, he abandoned his wife in 1908 and ended up as timekeeper for the Yukon Gold Company in Dawson City. There, he was considered a "gentleman of the world," conversant in a wide variety of subjects and a delightful guest at social occasions. He was known to attend big social functions wearing white tie and tails, which were unusual in Dawson, and he became known as "the Dude of Dawson City," a remarkable feat on the salary of a clerk.[50] He eventually moved on, ending up in Los Angeles, and in 1913 made his first appearance as an actor in a silent movie. He directed his first film the following year and subsequently directed more than fifty films. Among those actors whose films he directed were Mary Pickford, Wallace Reid, Dustin Farnum and Mary Miles Minter. He was murdered in his Hollywood home in February of 1922, a crime that captured headlines even as far away as Dawson City, and one that was never solved.[51]

CHAPTER 7

DAWSON DAILY NEWS

KLONDIKER CENTER OF MURDER SENSATION

MOVIE MYSTERIES OUTDONE IN TRAGIC DEATH OF YUKONER—NOTED STARS INVOLVED

William Desmond Taylor, who was a timekeeper for the Yukon Gold Company when he was in Dawson City, went on to become a prominent actor and moving picture director—until he was murdered in 1922. *Dawson Daily News,* February 9, 1922, p. 1, Yukon Archives.

Another Klondike resident who made his mark in Hollywood was Pete Huley. He immigrated to Canada from Austria in 1912 and in 1914 he came to the Klondike. Unsuccessful at finding his fortune in gold, he moved to Hollywood in 1923. There, under contract to Columbia Studios, he was said to have secured small parts in films starring Laurel and Hardy, Buster Keaton and Ben Turpin.[52] It was reported that he was once fired from a Harold Lloyd film because he was stealing all the laughs from the film star. He bore a remarkable resemblance to film great Charlie Chaplin, and it was also rumoured that Columbia Studios and Chaplin were going to take him to court for imitating Chaplin until they discovered that Pete had originated the now-famous Chaplin Shuffle.[53] With his thick Austrian accent, his career was killed by the talkies, and Pete moved to Fairbanks, Alaska, before returning to the Klondike in 1932. He worked in the Yukon for the rest of his career and died in Vancouver in 1973.[54]

One Klondike venturer who made a living showing movies but stayed in the North was William David Gross. Born in Russia in 1879 into a family of tailors, Gross immigrated to the United States with his parents as a child. He apprenticed as a tailor in Seattle as a teenager and got a job as a travelling agent for a firm that sold tailoring supplies. When the Klondike fever hit Seattle, he persuaded his suppliers to provide him with a stock of northern apparel and headed for Dawson City. He got only as far as Dyea, at the head of the trail leading over the Chilkoot Pass, before selling out his stock. He returned to Seattle to resupply and eventually ended up in Dawson City, where in 1902 he was operating a shop as a merchant tailor on Front Street between Queen and Princess Streets. Although there is no direct evidence to indicate that Gross was in the moving picture business in Dawson, he subsequently operated in other gold-rush communities where, among his other ventures, he operated theatres. Over the years, he established a chain of theatres along the Alaska Panhandle, operating it as a family business. That business evolved into Gross-Alaska Enterprises, Ltd., which is still in business today, in 2022.[55]

The final Yukoner who went on to Hollywood glory was born in the Yukon on November 23, 1902, but just about everything else about his early years in the North is hazy. The true nature of Victor Jory's time in the Yukon has been clouded by conflicting press reports over the years. An article in the *Syracuse Herald* in 1932, for example, alludes to Jory being born "in a gold rush, up in Dawson City, Alaska."[56]

Depending upon which version you believe, he was born in a roadhouse at Little Salmon, or one on Bonanza Creek. His mother appears to have run the Sixty Roadhouse on Bonanza Creek.

Mrs. Jory left Dawson with her child by stagecoach on March 30, 1904, but returned a short time later. Over the next six years, she continued to reside in the Klondike.

Victor Jory was a well-known character actor who during his long career was typically cast as the villain. He appeared on stage and in numerous films, including the Oscar-winning films *Gone with the Wind* and *The Miracle Worker*. He was Lamont Cranston in the radio program *The Shadow* and a police lieutenant in the syndicated television series *Manhunt*. His name and face were instantly recognizable to millions. Jory's name is even immortalized with a star on the Hollywood Walk of Fame.

In March of 2007, John Steins, the mayor of Dawson City, made a trip to Hollywood accompanied by a film crew to reconnect the actor to his northern birthplace. He even posed at Jory's star on Hollywood Boulevard with Jory's grandson, also named Victor. Sponsored by the Yukon Film Commission, Steins was on a journey of discovery for a Dawson-born man who had a remarkable fifty-year career in films.[57]

The Klondike Gold Rush's Impact on Hollywood

The reader might ask: What impact did the gold rush have on Hollywood? Both were born in the same era. The first moving pictures were being screened in Dawson City in the early days of the gold rush, though more as a curiosity than as a main attraction. Even then, they were popular with customers. Film crews were dispatched to the Klondike to capture some of the features of the gold rush, though only a few of these films survive today. They were more documentary in nature and depicted the mining activities as they were taking place. One such film has survived showing Front Street in Dawson. From the earliest days of film, the Klondike has been mythologized. An early Biograph film depicting can-can dancing in the Klondike is a good example. The film was probably made in a New Jersey studio rather than in Dawson City, as there is no evidence that the can-can made its way onto the stages of Dawson City theatres. Similarly, a stereopticon view of a confrontation in a "Klondike" card game was obviously staged, and not taken in the Klondike.

The Klondike gold rush was a unique event in world history. Reaching Dawson City required overcoming numerous obstacles: rain and snow and extreme cold, avalanches, blizzards, wild animals, raging rapids, wild water in the lakes of the upper Yukon River, and building a boat to complete the journey. Thousands completed it, and it was a memorable story of survival. The Klondike experience was a badge of pride that thousands would wear for the rest of their lives, even if they hadn't struck it rich.

Author Pierre Berton compared the Klondike experience to men returning from war, "wise beyond their years. In the span of the gold rush, they learned more about their fellows, and more about themselves than many mortals absorb in three score years and ten …" The experience had

> taught all these men that they were capable of a kind of achievement they had never dreamed possible. It was this, perhaps more than anything else, that set them apart from their fellows. In the years that followed, they tended to run their lives as if they were scaling a perpetual Chilkoot, secure in the knowledge that any obstacle, real or imagined, can be conquered by a determined man. For each had come to realize that the great stampede, with all its searchings and its yearnings, with all its bitter surprises, its thorny

impediments, and its unexpected fulfilments, was, in a way, a rough approximation to life itself.[58]

The Klondike gold rush was an epic event that required no exaggeration to become legend. The experiences of the stampeders were more memorable than any novel that could be written about it. It was this experience that the stampeders took home with them and repeated over and over for the rest of their lives. Then there were the heroes and colourful characters. Swiftwater Bill, Klondike Joe Boyle, "Diamond Tooth" Gertie Lovejoy and "Klondike Kate" Rockwell are examples of the individuals who contributed to the mythology. They were building blocks of the foundation upon which the Klondike legend was built.

The events that took place during the gold rush were captured in books published soon after. Most notable among these was Tappan Adney's volume *The Klondike Stampede*. Especially in its early stages, the Klondike gold rush was widely publicized in the newspapers of the day, with articles written by journalists travelling to the Yukon and in the thousands of letters sent home and reproduced in the pages of the local dailies. These reports were made even more real with the aid of photography. The stampede to the Klondike was photographed more times by more people than any other gold rush in history. Klondike views were sold as stereoviews and later on postcards. These iconic images were displayed prominently in magazines, newspapers and journals of the period. They were placed in family albums passed down from one generation to the next.

The Klondike gold rush was featured in numerous and generally unreliable travel guides. Handbooks were produced explaining how to build a log cabin and find gold. Countless diaries were kept and letters were written to friends and families because the chroniclers realized they were part of something special. These diaries and letters tell more of the real conditions of the Klondike than anything written in later years.

Memoirs of Klondike stampeders, especially those written long after the event, were textured with very pliable cloth. But that didn't matter. The Klondike experience was a collective one, and if any individual did not see or experience certain events, many others did. These stampeders were granted permission by their peers to tell these stories as if they were their own. In a similar vein, dime novels with few shreds of reality in them added to the Klondike mystique. These were cranked out by the dozens to exploit the interest many readers had in the Klondike, usually by authors who had never stepped foot in the Yukon.

The works of Jack London, Rex Beach and Robert Service did much to shape the public perception of the Klondike at the time and continued to do so in the decades that followed. London's portrayal of the North was of a "pitiless, ice-bound landscape where any sign of life was an affront."[59] This portrayal lingers in the public consciousness today. London's writing, though accurate, was based on his personal experience in the North; he arrived in October of 1897, survived a brutal Arctic winter, and left, crippled by scurvy, in the spring of 1898. He never saw the endless hours of daylight and the bustling streets filled with humanity that was Dawson in the summer of 1898.

Robert Service arrived in the backwash of the gold rush, when the legend was starting to evolve, and he immortalized them in his classic verses. Sam McGee and Dan McGrew, the makings of Service's imagination, have become linked forever with the gold rush. The Klondike was firmly embedded in the popular consciousness by 1910, making it an ideal theme for film adaptation.

The gold rush to the Yukon consisted largely of Americans, and for many of them, the event was an American one. At the time, the

Klondike was viewed as an extension of American manifest destiny, which was one of the reasons the Canadian government sent so many Mounted Police to watch over the hordes of Yankees. To beef up its sovereignty and add to the Canadian presence, Canada dispatched the Yukon Field Force, a company of two hundred regular militia. The misconception that the Klondike was in America is still held by many today; it is an image that has been reinforced by film celebrities in their personal narratives and by motion-picture companies in their gold rush-themed films ever since. Marjorie Rambeau and Victor Jory both Americanized their connections to the Klondike, blurring the Canadian presence, to appeal to an American audience.

Hollywood's Impact on the Klondike

The question of what impact Hollywood had on the Klondike gold rush is more difficult to answer. If the journalists, photographers and authors at the turn of the twentieth century set the Klondike gold rush in the popular mindset, moving pictures served to amplify the Klondike as a lasting, though distorted, representation of the North. The Klondike became a durable setting in which a movie could be crafted. Beyond that, the Klondike and the gold rush have often been kneaded and remoulded beyond recognition as Hollywood's creation.

The film *Klondike Kate* starring Ann Savage had, as Kate Rockwell had lamented, little resemblance to the reality of the Klondike. Chaplin's film *The Gold Rush*, considered to be a classic film from the silent era, has much going for it, but the setting is stereotypical, almost laughable. It is, after all, a comedy.

THE KLONDIKE AND HOLLYWOOD

Many of the films about the gold rush are nothing more than westerns, with the places and events moved farther north. Perhaps the worst and most embarrassing might be *The Far Country*, starring James Stewart, Walter Brennan and Ruth Roman. Filmed in Jasper National Park in Alberta, the movie had Stewart frequently recrossing the Columbia Icefield, which is a poor stand-in for the Chilkoot Pass. The plot is typical of the Hollywood boilerplate: untamed frontier subdued by individual heroes armed with six-guns. One early silent film, however, stands out as an example that attempted to capture the true setting. That was the adaptation of Robert Service's novel *The Trail of '98*, described earlier in this chapter.

Over the past century, hundreds of Klondike-themed films have been made, from B movies to high-budget productions. The stories by Jack London, Robert Service and Rex Beach have proven to be of particularly durable inspiration. Historian Frank Norris listed nearly two hundred when he scrutinized the impact of Hollywood films on the popular image of the North.[60] Sixty of those productions were based on London books and short stories about the Klondike. *The Call of the Wild* has been recast thirteen times by various filmmakers; *White Fang*, twelve. *To Build a Fire* was adapted to film seven times, while *Burning Daylight* was interpreted six times. Robert Service has received less attention by filmmakers, but his works still inspired a respectable number of productions. Of the twenty-six titles listed on one website, eighteen could be linked to his Klondike poems, most notably *The Shooting of Dan McGrew*.[61] The Rex Beach novel *The Spoilers*, which is set in Alaska just after the peak of the Klondike gold rush, was first produced in 1914 followed by one reissue (1916) and four remakes over the following four decades (1923, 1930, 1942 and 1955).

Television has fared no better than movies when considered for historical accuracy. The television series *Klondike*, which was based upon Pierre Berton's book of the same name, was set in Skagway, Alaska, eight hundred kilometres away from the real Klondike, after Berton pointed out that they didn't have lawlessness or gunfights in Dawson City during the gold rush. Berton was hired as a technical consultant for the series, but historical accuracy was sacrificed on the altar of expediency. The series was filmed in California to save money, so the vegetation is oak and pine instead of spruce and aspen. It was too expensive to have muddy streets ($7,000 per episode), so that was out. They couldn't have twenty-four hours of daylight—"nobody's going to believe that."[62] Cigars and pipes, though typical of the era, were out in deference to one of the program's sponsors, a cigarette company. Beards and moustaches were out too, because "the viewers will think it's a comedy."[63]

Canadian film critics could have drawn attention to factual inconsistencies and outright lies, but they didn't; the job of the movie reviewer was to plug such movies, not to pan them, because they were usually heavily advertised in newspapers.

The Klondike gold rush is one of the defining moments in the history of the North, documented by many writers in newspapers, magazines and books, but it has been the overwhelming impact of films that has shaped an indelible though fractured image of the North in the public mind for the past hundred years. Taken together, they have kept the word *Klondike* in the public vocabulary. It conjures up images of a cold, dark, forbidding place, a place of guns and violence, betrayal and murder. But if you want to get a true sense of what the Klondike was really like, you will have to look elsewhere than to Hollywood to find it. As Pierre Berton observed decades ago, "It never occurred to us, or at least not to very many of us, that an entire culture, our own, was being held up to the world to view through a distorted lens."[64] But to point this out will not make you popular.

It is interesting and rather regrettable that none of the films recovered from permafrost in Dawson City in 1978 contained a single frame depicting the land in which they were buried. World news coverage, yes. Hollywood productions, yes. But nothing about the Yukon.

CHAPTER 8

RECOVERY, RESTORATION AND INSPIRATION

By the summer of 1979, the importance of the cache of silent movies uncovered the year before had been realized, and the mysteries surrounding the provenance of this extraordinary find had been resolved.

After the visit of Sam Kula from the National Film, Television and Sound Archives in late July of 1978, Kathy Jones, the director of the Dawson City Museum, went into action. She was a member of the Nutty Club, which in the absence of a regular newspaper produced the *Klondike Korner*, a mimeographed newsletter that was distributed widely to subscribers every second week.[1] In the edition issued August 3, 1978, she placed a small article describing the discovery of the films behind Diamond Tooth Gerties.

While cleaning up the site of the old skating rink, City crews uncovered some old 35mm silent movies—film made of cellulose nitrate, use of which was discontinued prior to 1950 due to its high inflammability. Parks Canada's curator Mike Gates sent samples to the National Film Archives in Ottawa, resulting in Director Sam Kula visiting Dawson. After viewing the site, he gave the Museum Society a small grant to hire students to complete the excavation. The skating rink was erected on the site of the original Dawson Amateur Athletic Association building, which housed a movie theatre until it was destroyed by fire in 1938.

This film may be remnants of newsreels and other movies from a period when copies of films were not necessarily filed in archives. The Museum Society would be interested in hearing from anyone who has knowledge of why the films were stored or left there.[2]

Such requests to readers seldom receive a response, but this one hit pay dirt. Two weeks later, a letter arrived in the mail from a former employee of the Canadian Bank of Commerce.[3] His name was Clifford Thomson, and this is what he wrote:

Dear Editor;

I read with interest your article in your bulletin of August 3rd in regards to the finding of the old films in the skating rink. As I am responsible for placing them in the old swimming pool area, I will give you a summary of just what happened and how they happened to be there.

From 1928 to 1932 I was employed by the Canadian Bank of Commerce in Dawson City and the bank were

CHAPTER 8

agents for the film distributors and film makers in California. The old DAAA Theatre stood in front of the ice arena and adjoined it and when I arrived in Dawson in 1928 there was a swimming tank in the centre of the ice arena. I was appointed Treasurer of the Hockey Association and soon found out that after the flooding of the ice arena and the swimming tank, we were faced with a big bulge in the ice where the swimming tank was located. I, and other members of the Hockey Association decided there was only one thing to do and that was to fill in the swimming tank and in the summer of 1929, we took the wooden top off the tank and proceeded to fill the tank with earth.

For many years it was the custom to ship films into Dawson City but they deemed it too expensive to bother returning them. After Mr. Fred Elliott was through showing the films, they were turned over to the Bank and we stored them in the Carnegie Library building. If they needed a film for reshowing, they would draw from this source. The library was filling up to capacity and we wrote the film people about the fact and they instructed us to destroy hundreds of film [sic]. It was left up to our discretion as to how we would destroy the films and after some thought we decided that [because] they were highly flammable we should not burn them. We also contemplated throwing them into the Yukon River but even in those days we were aware of pollution. It occured [sic] to me they would make excellent fill for the old swimming hole in the ice arena, so with the help of Daniel Coates team of horses and vehicle, we trucked them into the arena and dumped them in to the swimming hole. I felt sure that they would never be found and they would integrate into rubbish and dirt as they were well covered with earth. It must have been the containers that preserved them and it is remarkable that after fifty years they would be found in good condition.

This is the answer to your mystery and if there is any further information you require, do not hesitate to ask.

Yours very truly

Clifford T. Thomson

With his one-page response, Thomson had cleared up the mystery of how the film came to be buried. An article from the *Dawson News* confirmed the details: "The boys decided that the old swimming tank was a hindrance to the making of good ice and work has already been started on it to fill it in."[4] The article also notes that Thomson was the secretary-treasurer of the organization, and that Dan Coates, the teamster, was president at the time. It has not been determined how deep the films were buried, but some lay near the surface. In later years, pieces of film would emerge from the dirt, and mischievous young children would set the film on fire. *The Dawson News* sent out at least one appeal for parents to caution their children to leave the film alone.[5]

Assuming that usable film could be salvaged from the ground, a contract for $2,500 was given to the Dawson City Museum by the Public Archives of Canada to uncover and retrieve the nitrate films from the site of the new recreation centre. Dozens of boxes containing film had already been transported from the burial site to the root cellar at the Bear Creek industrial complex. Now the museum could continue the unearthing and transporting process, examine the films or frames of film on which images had survived, prepare an inventory and ship the salvageable film to Ottawa.[6] Some of the film was unravelled, while other lengths remained tightly wound on badly rusted metal reels. Nobody had an inkling at this time if anything of significance had survived on any of these reels.

CHAPTER 8

Meanwhile, work continued at the construction site, exposing more films, which were scooped up by the excavation contactors along with soil and hauled to a dump site at the north end of Dawson. The museum had already hired several students to begin the sorting and cataloguing process; they were dispatched to the dump site to recover what reels they could from the excavated material. Stanley Richardson, the city manager, gave permission to the museum to post students at the excavation site to continue removing anything further that might be exposed. The films removed from permafrost deeper in the ground came out still frozen, but became wet when they thawed. Even as this work was progressing, souvenir hunters and residents were also taking reels away, most notably Wendell "Windy" Farr, an old-time Dawson resident with a reputation as a scavenger and hoarder.

The number of reels of film kept growing, and with it, the size of the Ottawa contract. Initially there were approximately two hundred reels stored in the root cellar at Bear Creek. By August 9 that number had increased to three hundred, and the reels kept emerging from the frozen ground. Meanwhile, the contract payment increased from the initial $2,500 to $8,000.

After the films had been salvaged, two buildings in the Bear Creek industrial complex owned by Parks Canada became the hub of activity during the next phase. The films stored in the root cellar were carried two hundred metres to a former acetylene plant for processing. Where the root cellar was dark, frigid and claustrophobic, the acetylene plant was bathed in natural light. A small table was placed in a room next to a row of large defunct electrolysis tanks. Any sound was magnified within this space and echoed off the metallic walls. There was no electricity and the building was unheated. The films on the rust-crusted reels were placed on a rewind spool, and as the content on each film was compiled in a list, the film was wound by hand onto a plastic core held in a split reel mounted on a second spool. The films and plastic cores were subsequently returned to the root cellar.

Throughout this process, I exchanged a flurry of phone calls and teletype messages with Ottawa clarifying the safest procedure for handling and examining the reels. As the film was transferred, each reel was numbered in sequence and the title and other information about the film was catalogued. The first reel examined was part two of the 1915 film *The Quest*, starring Joseph Singleton and Robyn Adair.

Day by day, the reels of celluloid were examined and the list of titles grew to include newsreels, comedies, serials and feature films. Dozens of titles grew to hundreds, and by the time all the films were catalogued and the initial list was complete, 437 titles had been recorded. The remaining seventy reels were too badly deteriorated to inspect in Dawson and were left for specialists in Sam Kula's shop to unravel. When the films had all been examined and the compilation completed, Kathy Jones sent a copy to Kula. On September 28, the Public Archives of Canada issued a press release announcing the recovery of the films. The announcement captured the interest of the media. Within days, major papers across Canada and around the globe announced the discovery with headlines such as "Yukon permafrost yields a nugget in old movie cache" (*Vancouver Sun*), "Yukon frost saved silver screen relics" (*Toronto Star*) and "Underground movies! Can you dig it, man?" (*Toronto Sunday Sun*). The *London Times* announced the find with a more reserved caption: "Klondike Film Hoard," while the *Los Angeles Times* proclaimed, "Silent Film Eureka in the Yukon."

Sam Kula and Clifford Thomson were both interviewed by Ron Adams on the nationally broadcast CBC radio show *Sunday Magazine*. In an interview with Barbara Frum of the CBC program

As It Happens, Kula said, "I'm going from what is on the labels on the cans, and from reports from Dawson, and it's absolutely maddening until we get the stuff shipped down here [to Ottawa] and get it in our own hands and view it ourselves. We're standing on one leg and shifting to the other."[7]

"Dawson has by now fielded inquiries from France, Germany and England, as well as a host of calls from places closer to home, such as New York and Los Angeles," reported the *Whitehorse Star*, "and all because some fill was needed for a swimming pool back in 1929."[8] Archivists around the world opined that this might be the last major collection of silent films to be uncovered.

With Dawson work completed as far as it could be taken, the next challenge was to get the reels to Ottawa. Jones planned to ship the films to Whitehorse by White Pass and Yukon Route Transport (better known as White Pass), but the company refused the move because cellulose nitrate is considered a hazardous good. Hauling them to Whitehorse in a pickup truck was contemplated, but by a stroke of luck, I spotted a Pacific Northwest moving van on the street and approached the drivers. They happened to be heading for Whitehorse with a half load, and they had room in their van to accommodate the seventy-seven boxes of film that had been prepared for shipping, so they were picked up from the root cellar at Bear Creek and hauled along with the belongings of a Dawson family that was moving south.

Meanwhile, Jones prepared a lengthy article for the *Whitehorse Star* that was published in its October 13 edition. "Among the films documented," she reported, "are serials such as *The Red Ace* (1917), *The Girl and the Game* (1916), and *The Seven Pearls* (1917). Dramas such as *Wildfire* (1915) headlined Lillian Russell and Lionel Barrymore; *Polly of the Circus* (1917) starred Mae Marsh; *The Inspector's Double* (1916) was directed by William Beaudine and *The Dancer's Ruse* was a 1915 Biograph Company production."

Jones went on to address a big question that had been posed by Yukon residents:

> Interest has been expressed within the Yukon as to why these films are being shipped outside. It should be explained that the composition of cellulose nitrate film makes it highly flammable and inherently unstable. Burial for 50 years has deteriorated the film quality and shrunk it.
>
> Now that it is excavated, deterioration will be rapid.
>
> Fungus, in fact, has been found on a number of the reels that cannot be documented. It would be irresponsible to assume that because we have found them in the Yukon they must not leave. The image would deteriorate rapidly and copying onto safety stock can only be undertaken by two Canadian companies—neither of which are in the Yukon.[9]

In addition to this, not one frame of the films recovered contained any Yukon content. Jones stipulated that as part of the agreement, the National Film Archives would refer to the collection as the Dawson Film Find, and they would supply a complete set of copies of the films to the Dawson Museum. She also got a commitment from Sam Kula that the first screening of the restored films would be in the Palace Grand Theatre at some future date.

The National Film Archives estimated that copying costs would be around $250,000.[10] "Our job now," reported Kula, "is to identify those films which can be salvaged and to transfer them onto safety stock, conserving as much of the image with as much fidelity to the surviving original as we can. It is slow work, since most of the film will be substandard in size due to shrinkage and damage to the sprocket holes and will probably have to be accomplished on a step-printer, literally duplicating one frame at a time."[11]

But first the films had to be transported to Ottawa. On business in Whitehorse in October, I made the rounds of the transport companies to make arrangements. But moving companies, airlines, long-distance haulers and even Greyhound all responded in the same way—that it was illegal to transport such dangerous goods. I still remember the response of the agent when I inquired: "I've heard all about your films. I know what they are, and we can't transport them because it's against the law. Sorry." In the Yukon, the films were too well known to attempt any deception.

I returned to Dawson without having made suitable arrangements. Lamenting the fact at a meeting of Parks Canada site managers, our head of finance and personnel, Jim Reilly, a former military man, suggested that we contact the Armed Forces, who are accustomed to handling explosives and other dangerous materials. The military flew planes into Whitehorse on a regular basis. I passed this suggestion along to Sam Kula, who contacted the Department of National Defence (DND). The DND agreed to pick up the films during one of their regularly scheduled flights to Whitehorse. Pacific Northwest Moving built large wooden crates for the move.

On November 11, Remembrance Day, a Canadian Armed Forces Hercules C-130 transport landed at Canadian Forces Base Uplands near Ottawa with its valuable payload, met by a team of specialists from the National Film, Television and Sound Archives (NFTSA) who transferred the crates onto a five-ton truck to move to the nitrate storage vaults at the Rockcliffe Air Base. As the plane taxied into position and came to a halt, the rear cargo bay door lowered and out dashed a squad of paratroopers on the double. One witness to this asked, "Was the cargo that valuable?"[12]

Once the films arrived in Ottawa, the team of film specialists from the NFTSA went into high gear. When they were removed from their icy tomb in Dawson City permafrost, the metal reels were heavily rusted; some of the films were coated with orange dust and others were caked in mud. The reels were too damp to place in cannisters, and by the time they arrived in Ottawa the specialists found them to be in shocking condition—the emulsion could be wiped off the film with a rag. Now that the films had been removed from the ground, it was feared they would deteriorate at a rapid rate. A speedy response was necessary. It was of utmost importance to find a safe and efficient means of drying them and cleaning them without losing or damaging the emulsion.

Drying film under such conditions had never been attempted before, so several approaches were experimented with to determine the best approach. One test involved microwave bombardment, but this was not successful. Another approach was to use liquid freon, but the emulsion loss was high using this approach. A third experiment involved the use of an Oxberry optical printer, but this too resulted in an unacceptable loss of emulsion, and the process created so much dust that it rendered the workspace unbreathable.[13] At Graphic Film Laboratories, a subsidiary of Crawley Films, collaboration between Bill O'Farrell (a Crawley Films veteran), newly hired NFTSA staff member Dennis Waugh and consultant Klaus Linnenbrueger produced the most practical solution.[14]

Within a week, Graphic Film Laboratories was contracted to undertake the cleaning of the films. Using a film processor that was adapted from 16 millimetre to 35 millimetre format (to accommodate the Dawson films), the developing end of the machine was converted into a prewash tank filled with water and a Photoflo solution.[15] This softened the accretions on the outside of the reels and allowed the successive layers of film on the reels to separate without damaging the emulsion. As the film came out of this tank, rust and dirt were removed manually from the edges of the film before subjecting it to a spray wash, and then spooling it into a third tank, where it was immersed in a fixing solution for three minutes to reharden the emulsion. The film progressed to a fourth tank, where it was subjected to a seven-minute spray wash before being dried in a climate-controlled drying chamber. According to Dennis Waugh, "This process took months to complete, due to rolls being gelled together (resembling hockey pucks!), splices parting, debris, broken perforations, curvature, distortion, and disintegration of the metal reels that the film was wound on. Sometimes, a good day would be completing one or two rolls. Some of the films were seventy years old, and the fragile splices in particular had to be monitored constantly as they tended to separate during the washing. During the process, cleanliness was of utmost importance to eliminate adding more dirt to the emulsion layer."[16] After that procedure, it took almost a month to clean the rust and dirt that penetrated every nook and cranny of the processing machine.[17] This rewashing process halted the deterioration of the film and allowed the conversion of the films to proceed at a normal rather than urgent speed.

The task of copying over five hundred reels of film was beyond the capacity of the NFTSA, so Kula turned to the Library of Congress in Washington, DC. Both institutions were signatories to an international convention that agreed to return films to their country of origin. Three hundred and eighty-nine reels of Hollywood footage from the Dawson Film Find were transferred to the Library of Congress for conversion.[18] Larry Karr from the American Film Institute had compared the list of titles against known copies to determine the priority for restoration. Unique titles were given priority for treatment over titles already known to exist elsewhere.

Copying of the Canadian newsreel footage progressed over the following years, but it was far from routine; each reel had to be inspected and broken sprocket holes repaired. The material had to be re-spliced and dimensional distortion accommodated. By August of 1980, half of the collection had been converted; by December of 1982, the work was essentially complete.[19]

In August 1980, twenty-six additional reels of film from the Dawson burial site were recovered from Wendell Farr and shipped to Ottawa. This brought the total of films recovered to 533, six of which could not be salvaged.

Public interest in the Dawson collection continued unabated after the first press release in September of 1978. Film buffs, historians, archivists and members of the general public were all clamouring to see what had come out of the permafrost in the Klondike. A carefully curated selection of films was assembled to be shown at a premiere event at the Palace Grand Theatre in Dawson City, followed by a touring program through Canada and the United States. Wherever possible, Kula toured with the films, speaking about the remarkable circumstances of their discovery, how they had been salvaged and the restoration process that followed. In the end, half a million feet of important silent film heritage was preserved, often being copied one frame at a time!

The Dawson Film Find is unique. Nothing like it had happened before, and nothing like it will ever happen again. "The Dawson City cache is one of the most exciting finds ever for the people at the [National] Film Archives," stated Ron Adams of the CBC program *Sunday Magazine* in October 1978. The British Canadian Pathé newsreels of Ernest Ouimet (1919–21), which are of particular interest to Canadian film historians, were not known to have survived before the Dawson City Film Find. The 1917 film *Polly of the Circus*, starring Mae Marsh, was the first film known to bear the name of film producer Samuel Goldwyn, and it did not exist in any archive before it was uncovered in Dawson. The 1915 film *Wildfire* is the only film in which actress Lillian Russell ever appeared. Her leading man was Lionel Barrymore. The list of unique discoveries is long and noteworthy.

Sam Kula wrote:

> To the film scholar, the fascination of the collection may lie in the possible significance of little-known productions by established figures (PRINCESS VIRTUE, with May Murray, BLISS, with Harold Lloyd and Bebe Daniels; THE SCANDAL MONGERS, written and directed by Lois Weber; THE INSPECTOR'S DOUBLE directed by William Beaudine), but to the archivist and historian the appeal is probably the unknown quantity represented by some 75 reels of newsfilm. Produced primarily between 1913 and 1922 under such titles as Universal Screen Magazine, Guamont's "The Reel of Real News," Universal Animated Weekly, Pathé Animated Gazette, Universal Current Events, and British Canadian Pathé News, these actualities, as their titles suggest, range far and wide for their subject matter. The majority were produced between the war years (1914–1918) and, along with the several reels of "British Government Official News" in the Collection, provide coverage of that conflict and the impact it was having in Canada, England, France and the U.S. The editions of British Canadian Pathé News that turned up in Dawson City are of particular interest because this assemblage of original Canadian "items" and items drawn from Pathé Frères world-wide network was one of the few successful attempts to introduce Canadian content into the theatrical newsreel.

No-one familiar with the considerable resources now accessible through the work of film archives throughout the world would seriously argue that the Dawson Collection, or any one cache of early film, will lead to a wholesale re-write of the histories. Nevertheless, we have learned over the years that, given the harsh reality that more than half the films that were produced in the world prior to 1930 are not known to exist and every film from the silent era is a valuable piece of the mosaic, even when it is at least partially complete, it will constitute a vital segment of our common cultural history.[20]

Since its discovery more than forty years ago, the Dawson Film Find has continued to captivate subsequent generations of silent film enthusiasts. It was featured as the letter Y (Yukon Film Find) in the 2004 Peter Rowe production of *Popcorn with Maple Syrup: Film in Canada from Eh to Zed*, and more notably, the 2016 feature-length documentary film *Dawson City: Frozen Time*, directed and co-produced by New York filmmaker Bill Morrison. In the film, Morrison traces the history of the Klondike capital from the gold rush until the film discovery in 1978. Relying heavily upon footage recovered in Dawson, Morrison weaves the narrative in the form of a silent movie with captions and a musical score by composer Alex Somers.

According to Morrison:

I first heard of it [the Dawson Film Find] as an art student at the Cooper Union in the late 1980s. It seems that film archivists and cinephiles who are my age and older (fifty plus) have some vague familiarity with the story, while most of those who are younger than me have never heard of the story. There was only one academic article about the collection by Sam Kula, director of audiovisual archives in the National Archives of Canada, entitled "Up from the Permafrost: The Dawson City Collection." Ever since I first heard of the Find, for me it had always been one of those great projects out there that I would keep in my sock drawer, hoping to one day get a chance to make it in the style that I made *The Film of Her*.

Then in March of 2013, Paul Gordon invited me to screen some of my work at the Bytowne Cinema in Ottawa, for a film series he organized with friends called the Lost Dominion Screening Collective. Paul also mentioned that he also worked as a film conservator for Library and Archives Canada, and that if I ever wanted to work with their collection, he could be a good point of contact. I asked him about the Dawson City Collection, and he confirmed that they had all the original 145 nitrate rolls that had Canadian content, and a 35mm safety of the entire collection of 533 reels. A light went off and I realized the moment had arrived to make the Dawson City film.[21]

Dawson City: Frozen Time made its North American debut at the New York Film Festival in October of 2016 and its Canadian premiere in Dawson City the following spring. Since then it has been screened widely around the world, spreading the story of the Dawson City Film Find to a new generation of viewers.

Morrison's careful scrutiny of the archival collection while preparing *Dawson City: Frozen Time* yielded more interesting discoveries that illustrate the potential that the Film Find has for research. The first discovery was footage of the infamous World Series from the year 1919. This series will be remembered for the banning of several members of the Chicago White Sox for life for fixing the World Series. When Morrison announced his find, the footage went viral.[22]

Here is another example. While creating a short film using footage of newsreels from the Dawson collection, Morrison made another connection that advanced historical inquiry. Within the newsreel collection, he found film footage depicting the 1920 race riots in the United States, which he incorporated into a thirteen-minute short film titled *Buried News*. While researching it, he referred to Peter Brackney's recent book, *The Murder of Geneva Hardman and Lexington's Mob Riot of 1920*, in which Brackney stated, "One of the most popular rumors, memorialized in Coleman's death at the courthouse, was that a newsreel cameraman had excited the already electric crowd by riling them up. Allegedly, the cameraman yelled to those nearby to 'shake your fists and yell.' This added fire to the 'highly charged atmosphere'... Yet today, the reels may exist in a lost archive or could be damaged and destroyed."[23] Imagine Brackney's surprise when Morrison contacted him to tell him that the films referred to were part of the Dawson collection![24]

Morrison's interest in the Dawson Film Find had not yet abated. Inspired by hints of more film, he returned to Dawson City in August of 2019, accompanied by an ally. Michael Goi is a film director and cinematographer who is interested in the preservation and restoration of old films. During his forty-year career in film, Goi has had four Emmy nominations for his work on the television series *Glee*, *My Name Is Earl* and *American Horror Story*. He is past president of the American Society of Cinematographers. Of the Dawson Film Find, Goi said, "They are a historical record of both American and Canadian cinema at a time when cinema was just being born." To him, the recovery of even one more reel would represent an important piece of film history.

CHAPTER 8

Morrison and Goi are determined that if there are any more salvageable reels of old film somewhere in Dawson, they are going to find them. Goi sees the potential for a long-term project. If anything remains to be recovered, he says, it could take five to ten years and millions of dollars to restore these film treasures. With his credentials, he may be able to deliver the goods.

The site where the original film discovery was made is now covered by Dawson City's recreation centre between Fourth and Fifth Avenues. During their visit to Dawson, Morrison and Goi met with then-mayor Wayne Potoroka to determine whether more films remain buried under the current recreation facility. Together, Morrison, Goi and Potoroka inspected the site where the films were buried, pored over city records of past recreation centre construction and talked to people who were involved with previous work at the site. They made a reconnaissance of the waterfront, speculating about where more old films might have been dumped in 1932.

During their visit, Morrison and Goi were granted access to the underbelly of the recreation building to examine the foundation, but until the building is removed from the site, there is no chance to excavate for more films. There is the possibility that a new recreation centre looms on the horizon. "If they ever raze that rec centre," said Morrison, "I'll be on the next plane faster than you can say Sam Kula!"[25]

The two filmmakers had planned to return to Dawson City in the spring of 2020 when, if there was a repeat of the record low-water level of 2019, they hoped to find what they were looking for buried in the silt along the shore of the Yukon River. The COVID-19 pandemic erased that possibility, but there is still hope that in the future, yet more films may be recovered.

EPILOGUE

Frank Barrett, the person who had originally prevented the films from being thrown away, was awarded a Letter of Commendation by the Commissioner of the Yukon on April 15, 1980, for "his assistance in saving films in Dawson." In acknowledgement of her involvement and accomplishments relating to the Dawson Film Find, Kathy Jones was recognized by the tourism industry with the 1979 Yukoner Award, and in 1984 she received a Heritage Award from the Yukon Historical and Museums Association (YHMA). I continued to work for Parks Canada until retirement in 2008. It's been a long and fulfilling adventure, and it's not over yet.

In early September 1979, slightly more than a year after the initial discovery of the films, true to his word, Sam Kula supplied two reels of restored footage from the Film Find for the world-premiere screening of a selection of the most interesting of the films, to be held in the Palace Grand Theatre in Dawson City.

A lot had happened in the meantime. In the spring of 1979, the swollen waters of the Yukon had flowed into Dawson and flooded the gold-rush town. Eighty per cent of the town was under water. Buildings had floated from their foundations and settled in the streets. Lives were in turmoil as the community struggled to recover from the chaos created by Mother Nature. But Dawson City residents proved to be resilient, and buildings were quickly set right. Mud and debris were cleaned up and Dawson was open for business when the tourist season began, if in a somewhat modified state. People worked double time to recover their homes and their lives, while at the same time continuing their daytime jobs.

The atmosphere of the community was upbeat and positive in its recovery, although a general state of exhaustion prevailed as the summer turned to autumn. The premiere of the films was the exclamation point at the end of a remarkable summer. The first screening of the films was part of the annual meeting of the YHMA, which had been planned before the flood occurred. The two reels of film sent by Kula were slow to reach Dawson, and there was considerable anxiety over whether they would arrive in time. "On Friday afternoon, all we knew for sure," said Jones, "was that they had left Edmonton. We were afraid that they'd been lost somewhere in between there and Whitehorse, but they finally showed up at 2:00 a.m. Saturday, thanks to David Ashley [a friend], who drove to Dawson with them from Whitehorse."[1]

Veteran musician and showman Fred Bass flew in from Vancouver to provide musical accompaniment to the films. Bass had been performing in front of live audiences for most of his eighty-two years. He began his career in show business "in the pit" in the old vaudeville days and graduated to playing piano for silent movies. He was a pioneer in Canadian broadcasting (he was an announcer for CKWX radio in Vancouver from 1928 to 1961) until he retired.[2] After that, he worked with stage impresario Fran Dowie in his Gold Rush Review in Barkerville, British Columbia, and in the Gaslight Follies in Dawson's Palace Grand during the 1960s.

"Sourdough Sue" Ward, who had performed with Bass in Barkerville and in the Gaslight Follies, took the stage at the Palace Grand in a gold-rush costume bedecked in feathers and sequins and served as master of ceremonies for the afternoon. The program was a ninety-minute selection from the more than five hundred reels recovered from the frozen depths the year before. To screen them all would have taken roughly ninety hours, not including popcorn breaks and trips to the washroom.

The theatre was jammed as an audience consisting of Dawson residents, YHMA conference delegates and visitors from as far away as Germany and Israel took their seats. As the lights dimmed and the screen flickered to life, Fred Bass pounded out the appropriate music from his mental jukebox for each sequence. For harvest time in the Annapolis Valley, it was "I'll Be with You in Apple Blossom Time." When a huge World War I battleship come on the screen, he hit a sustained dark and sinister chord.

Bass had been given an opportunity to view the films before the screening, but dismissed the idea. "I didn't do it then," he assured me when we offered him the preview, "and I don't intend to start now." His fingers darted over the keys for more than ninety minutes, with only brief interruptions when Kathy Jones and I introduced each film segment, giving us a glimpse of what it was like sixty or more years before when he had performed the same duty as a young man. Bass was bathed in sweat by the end of the performance, but still smiling he graciously returned to the keyboard so photographers and a CBC film crew sent to Dawson from Vancouver for the occasion could capture the moment.

Many of the films showed the effects of decomposition of the original nitrate-based 35-millimetre stock, or the effects of water seepage or chemical damage while the films were buried. As a result, a good number of the scenes ended abruptly and the margins of other scenes were damaged. Considering the conditions of the originals, it was amazing that so much of the imagery was restored and that the quality in many of the reels matched that of films from the period that had been stored in studio vaults for seventy-five years.

EPILOGUE

Thirty-eight years after recovering the film from the permafrost in Dawson City, Kathy and I celebrated our thirty-seventh wedding anniversary in New York City, during the North American premiere of *Dawson City: Frozen Time* at the 54th New York Film Festival. Gates collection.

Starting with a British Canadian Pathé newsreel, the program included episodes of the serial *Pearl of the Army* starring Pearl White, another serial titled *The Red Ace*, the rollicking comedy *All Jazzed Up*, the drama *Half Breed* starring Douglas Fairbanks, and *Polly of the Circus*, Sam Goldwyn's first movie.

The evening was a big success, which was a great relief to Kathy Jones and me, as we had worked continuously on the project for the previous year. We had first come together professionally, and then personally, and we had quickly fallen in love.

Only five weeks after the film premiere in the Palace Grand, on October 13, 1979, Kathy and I were married in St. Paul's Church in Dawson City. Forty-plus years later, we remain married and are still actively involved in exploring the Yukon's colourful and intriguing history. In October 2016, we enjoyed a reprise of sorts when we were invited to attend the North American premiere of Bill Morrison's film *Dawson City: Frozen Time*, which screened at the Lincoln Centre for the Performing Arts during the 54th New York Film Festival. We enjoyed our time in the Big Apple and celebrated our thirty-seventh wedding anniversary a few days early with shopping and sightseeing, including a carriage ride through Central Park. We visited Times Square at high noon, and again at midnight. What an incredible and fitting experience that trip was!

The film *Dawson City: Frozen Time* made its North American debut at the New York Film Festival in October, 2016.
Gates collection

APPENDIX

GOLD-MINING TECHNIQUES AND TERMINOLOGY

Hand Mining for Placer Gold

Gold is commonly found in **hard rock** deposits, where it is incorporated into the rock, or in unconsolidated gravel (**placer**) deposits of more or less free particles (nuggets). In the latter form, the recovery of gold in such deposits is known as **placer mining**.

Ranging from tiny, almost microscopic granules, or **dust**, to large **nuggets** weighing many ounces, gold's density (nineteen times that of water) causes it to settle quickly to the bottoms of streams, even where the water is moving at a rapid speed. It tends to concentrate in small backwaters or eddies, and it can lie in these deposits for tens of thousands of years, awaiting discovery.

A **prospector** will investigate stream beds looking for gold, testing the bottom materials with a **gold pan**, which has a circular, flat bottom, and broad, sloping sides. Mixed with water, the gold in the gravels will settle to the bottom of the pan when agitated vigorously. The pan is normally agitated at a slight incline, causing the dense yellow particles to be trapped in the angle formed by the bottom and side of the pan.

Once gold is found in a stream bottom, the material is mined in a man-made device that emulates nature. The **sluice box** is a long, narrow, open-ended box, slightly inclined so water will flow through it. The placer gravel is excavated and dumped in the upper end, where it is mixed with generous quantities of water. As this mixture flows down the incline, the gold falls to the bottom of the box and is trapped between rows of ribs, or **riffles**, that are placed at right angles to the current.

Another form of gold recovery involves the use of the **rocker**, which is a handmade box-like device that is rocked back and forth like a child's cradle. While rocking this device with one hand, a placer miner would scoop water with the other, using a small homemade ladle, into a hopper through the screened bottom of which the finer material would pass with the water. In the lower portion of the rocker, gold would be trapped on a canvas apron, or in riffles lining the bottom.

Once a deposit is discovered by an individual, it is **staked**, or marked out with stakes, and then **claimed** or documented with the mining recorder, a government official for the district. The size of the claims was prescribed in the government mining regulations, and was subject to occasional change.

The gold found in the Yukon Valley is usually trapped in ground that is permanently frozen (**permafrost**). Before the gold can be removed, the ground has to be thawed. This can be achieved naturally with water or the heat of the sun, or it can be achieved artificially. In the days before the gold rush, fire was used to thaw permafrost.

Every miner dreamed of finding the **pay streak** in a placer deposit. This is the zone where the gold is the most heavily concentrated and thus the richest. The pay streak was seldom near the surface, however; nor was it always found beneath the existing stream bed. To locate it, the miners had to excavate large quantities of gravel from an **open pit** until the zone was located. This work, which was performed in the summer, was both extensive and expensive for the miner, and could be hampered by the presence of permafrost.

Once the method of thawing frozen ground was perfected, miners could work through the winter, sinking vertical shafts down through the frozen ground until bedrock was reached, then excavating small adits or **drifts** horizontally until the pay streak was intercepted. This method, known as **drift mining**, was more efficient as it was not necessary to remove extensive quantities of **overburden** to get to the gold-bearing gravel. By thawing ground and working through the winter, the miner could accumulate a large amount of gravel, known as a **dump**, by spring. With the spring runoff, this material would be sluiced in a spring **cleanup**. During a cleanup, the introduction of water and gravel is stopped, and the riffles are removed. The material trapped between the riffles, which has a large concentration of gold, is scooped up and taken away to be refined.

Mechanized Mining for Placer Gold

Early mining in the Klondike was by hand methods, which were very expensive. But despite that, the deposits of gold were so rich in the Klondike that claim holders on Eldorado Creek became instant millionaires.

Within three years, mechanized mining employing steam-powered equipment was brought to the Klondike, reducing the hand labour that was required. Mechanized mining was more efficient and therefore made it profitable to work placer deposits that were not money makers when mined by hand.

Boilers fired by local wood produced steam to thaw frozen ground, or to power pumps, hoists, saws and other equipment. One device that was common in the Klondike was the **self-dumper**, which had a large bucket on a cable that hoisted pay dirt from winter diggings or open-pit summer mines, carried it a short distance to where a mechanical device was tripped and the excavated pay dirt was deposited in a pile next to a sluice box. Pumps would bring water to wash the gold.

Water was essential to the sluicing process, and a sufficient supply was not always immediately available. The problem could be rectified by building small dams or by diverting water through flumes or ditches from nearby streams. In some cases, water was used to remove the overburden, or even placer gravels, leaving the gold concentrated on the washed ground. This was known as **ground sluicing**. Water was also supplied under pressure to some claims to remove overburden by **hydraulicking**. In this process, the ground would be cut away along a vertical exposure by the pressure of the water. This process was not common before the Klondike discovery.

The water required for industrial-scale hydraulic mining often came from distant streams, transported through ditches and pipelines to where it was needed. Constructing such ditch systems required the investment of great sums of money that came from foreign investors located thousands of kilometres away.

Similar investment was required to finance the other efficient mining method: dredges. **Dredges** were large floating excavators that washed the gold from large volumes of gravel. They had a large bucket line with a continuous chain of steel buckets at the bow that dug thawed placer ground and carried this material to a large rotating perforated steel cylinder, through which the gold was washed from the gravel using high velocity pumps. The gold was captured below this cylinder, or **trommel**, in a series of sluice boxes. The gold-washed gravel was carried on a conveyor belt some distance from the stern of the dredge and deposited behind it. Three shifts of four men worked the dredges around the clock during the summer months.

A dredge operation required extensive infrastructure to support its work. A power crew maintained the electrical grid that provided the machinery with energy. A bull gang did the work on shore around the dredge, where cables that stabilized the dredges were anchored.

The ground in front of the dredge had to be prepared for mining. Vegetation was removed, then surface material was washed away using hydraulic monitors. Networks of pipes and hoses were then laid out over the cleared ground that injected steam or water into the frozen ground to thaw it for the dredges. The Yukon Consolidated Gold Corporation operated a fleet of dredges spread out over two thousand square kilometres for nearly forty years. At its peak, it employed eight hundred workers, including cooks, surveyors, engineers, machinists, blacksmiths, drivers and others to support the operation of the dredges. The last of these giant machines ceased operation in 1966.

ACKNOWLEDGEMENTS

There are many people I would like to thank for the assistance they provided me on my long journey to writing this book.

Alex Somerville and Angharad Wenz, Dawson City Museum, provided me with encouragement and their extensive knowledge of Klondike history. They opened their files and introduced me to several excellent collections that helped put flesh on the bones of this story. To them I am exceptionally grateful.

The staff of the Energy Mines and Resources Library have always been of great assistance during my research. This time, it was to track down obscure articles in distant libraries. The Yukon Archives, which was established fifty years ago, has become the bedrock upon which Yukon history is being preserved. Materials in its collections, especially the early newspapers, were always a reliable source to turn to. Generously sharing their extensive knowledge of their collections, they aided me many times.

Former and present staff of the National Film Archives in Ottawa were very helpful. First of all, Sam Kula saw the potential in these films and flew in person to Dawson to examine the site. Without his leadership at every step of the recovery and restoration of the collection, this story would never have been written, and a tremendous film treasure would simply have gone to the dump. Paul Gordon, senior film conservator, Digital Operations and

ACKNOWLEDGEMENTS

Preservation Branch of Library and Archives Canada, has been an excellent aid, leading me to resources at the Ottawa archive, as well as many of those who were involved in the Film Find restoration, including Dennis Waugh, Klaus Linnenbrueger and Kayley Kimball.

I have special thanks to extend to filmmaker Bill Morrison. It was he who demonstrated that there was widespread interest in the Dawson collection. Bill reignited my interest in telling the story of the Film Find, and showing how, in a bigger way, it reflects a century of change for Dawson City. It was a pleasure to help him create his masterful film, *Dawson City: Frozen Time*. Another filmmaker, Madeleine Olnek, brought an obscure dissertation on gold-rush theatre to my attention. It proved to be a useful reference.

Various individuals over the past several years willingly imparted their knowledge and memories of life in Dawson. Palma Berger, Dave Robertson, Ben Warnsby, Sue Parson and Debbie Nagano all shared their collective knowledge with me, especially about the Orpheum Theatre in its later years. Irene Crayford shared her involvement in recovering another film treasure: a collection of E. A. Hegg glass-plate negatives.

For those who helped me on the path to completing this story but whose names I forgot to write down at the time, you will no doubt draw my attention to that fact. I owe you all a drink for not paying closer attention.

Karen Routledge, Parks Canada historian, Whitehorse, proved to be a great sounding board when I questioned why I was doing this. Dylan Meyerhoffer of Parks Canada, Dawson City, was also welcoming and helpful whenever I asked him questions or sought assistance.

Arlene Prunkl, my editor, helped me to turn this story into a crisp narrative. Her eagle eye caught my errors and guided me in the production of a professional account. Being an outsider, she was able to point out the many instances where I needed to clarify and explain things that seemed obvious to me but might not have been so clear to readers unfamiliar with Yukon history. Thank you for your attention to my work.

I owe a thank you to Anna Comfort O'Keefe and numerous others at Harbour Publishing who saw the potential in this and the many other stories I have written. They take my uncut stones and turn them into top-quality gems. It is always a pleasure working with them.

A special thanks goes to my wife, Kathy. She was there when this story started more than forty years ago, and she is still with me today. She gets to see my work before anybody else does, and I can't thank her enough for her collaboration and support.

BIBLIOGRAPHY

Newspapers

Aurora Daily Express
Baltimore Evening Sun
Bioscope, The
Boston Globe
Chicago Daily Tribune
Dawson Daily News
Great Falls Tribune
Klondike Korner
Klondike Miner and Yukon Advertiser
Klondike News
Klondike Nugget
Los Angeles Evening Express
Los Angeles Times
Modesto News-Herald
Oakland Tribune
Ogden Daily Commercial
Philadelphia Inquirer
Sacramento Bee
Salt Lake Herald
San Francisco Call
San Francisco Examiner
Santa Anita Register
Santa Rosa Press Democrat
Syracuse Herald
Toledo Blade
Tucson Citizen
Vancouver Sun
Victoria Colonist
Victoria Times
Whitehorse Star
Yukon Sun
Yukon World

Books and Articles

Adney, Tappan. *The Klondike Stampede.* New York: Harper Bros., 1900.
Allen, A. S. "Dawson, Yukon Territory," *American Journal of Industry* (2000).
Archibald, Margaret. "Thomas William Fuller (1865–1951): A Preliminary Report." *Research Bulletin* 105 (1979). Parks Canada, Ottawa.

Armstrong, Nevill A. D. *Yukon Yesterdays: Thirty Years of Adventures in the Klondike.* London, UK: John Long Ltd., 1976.

Backhouse, Frances. *Women of the Klondike.* North Vancouver: Whitecap Books, 1995.

———. *Children of the Klondike.* North Vancouver: Whitecap Books, 2010.

Beardsley, Charles. *Hollywood's Master Showman: The Legendary Sid Grauman.* Cranbury, New Jersey: Cornwall Books, 1983.

Berton, Laura. *I Married the Klondike.* Toronto: McClelland and Stewart, 1961.

Berton, Pierre. *Klondike: The Last Great Gold Rush 1896–1899.* Revised edition. Toronto: McClelland and Stewart, 1972.

———. *Hollywood's Canada.* Toronto: McClelland and Stewart, 1975.

———. *My Times: Living with History 1947–1995.* Toronto: Doubleday Canada, 1995.

Black, Martha. *My Seventy Years.* Toronto: Thomas Nelson and Sons, Ltd., 1938.

Bodeen, DeWitt. "Marjorie Rambeau 1889–1970." *Films in Review* 29, no. 3 (March 1978): 129–142.

Booth, Michael. "Gold Rush Theatres of the Klondike." *The Beaver* 41, no. 4 (1962): 32–37.

Brackney, Peter. *The Murder of Geneva Hardman and Lexington's Mob Riot of 1920.* Mount Pleasant, South Carolina: Arcadia Books, 2020.

Burley, David and Michael Gates. "The Dawson Film Discovery: An Outline of Parks Canada's Involvement." *Research Bulletin* 140 (August 1980). Parks Canada, Ottawa.

———. "Old films were news." *Contact* 5, no. 1 (1981): 5. Environment Canada.

Clifford, Dorothy. *Klondike Childhood: Memoirs of Dorothy Dorris Miller Clifford.* Unpublished manuscript, author's collection, n.d.

Clifford, Howard. *The Skagway Story.* Anchorage: Alaska Northwest Publishing Co., 1980.

Coates, Ken and William R. Morrison. *The Sinking of the Princess Sophia: Taking the North Down with Her.* Toronto: Oxford University Press, 1990.

Council of the Yukon Territory. *Yukon Local Ordinances 1898–1901.* Printed under the direction of the Commissioner of the Yukon Territory, Dawson City, 1902.

———. *Consolidated Ordinances of the Yukon Territory 1902.* Printed under the direction of the Commissioner of the Yukon Territory, 1903.

———. *Consolidated Ordinances of the Yukon Territory 1914.* Printed under the direction of the Commissioner of the Yukon Territory, 1915.

Coutts, Robert. "The Palace Grand Theatre Dawson City, Y.T.: An Interpretive History." *Manuscript Report* 428 (1981). Parks Canada, Ottawa.

BIBLIOGRAPHY

Craig, Lulu Alice. *Glimpses of Sunshine and Shade in the Far North or, My Travels in the Land of the Midnight Sun.* Cincinnati, OH: The Editor Publishing Co., 1900.

Cunynghame, Francis. *Lost Trail.* London, UK: Faber and Faber Ltd., 1953.

Davis, Mary Lee. *Sourdough Gold: The Log of a Yukon Adventure.* Boston: W. A. Wilde Company Publishers, 1933.

DeArmond, R. N. *Movie Man: The Life and Times of William David Gross 1879–1962.* Editing and epilogue by Karleen Alstead Grummett. Sitka: unpublished paper, 2000. Photocopy in author's collection.

De Windt, Harry. *Through the Gold-Fields of Alaska to Bering Straits.* London, UK: Chatto and Windus, 1898.

Dill, W. S. *The Long Day: Reminiscences of the Yukon.* Ottawa: The Graphic Publishers, 1926.

Dobrowolsky, Helene. *Hammerstones: A History of the Tr'ondëk Hwëch'in.* Dawson City: Tr'ondëk Hwëch'in in Publication, 2003.

Evans, Chad. *Frontier Theatre.* Victoria, BC: Sono Nis Press, 1983.

Faulkner, Victoria. "Interim Report. Subject: Auditorium Theatre (Palace Grand), Dawson City, Yukon Territory." Typescript report prepared for National Historic Sites Division, National Parks Branch, Department of Northern Affairs and National Resources, Ottawa. Yukon Archives Acc# 82/86 GOV 1313, 1961.

Ferry, Eudora Bundy. *Yukon Gold: Pioneering Days in the Canadian North.* New York: Exposition Press, 1971.

Foster, Charles. *Once Upon a Time in Paradise.* Toronto: Dundurn Press, 2003.

Garcia Martin, Pedro. "The Lumières: Sires of the Cinema." *National Geographic* (January/February 2019): 6–9.

Gates, Michael. 1982: "The Dawson City Film Find: A Major Co-operative Film Conservation Project." *Journal of the International Institute for Conservation, Canadian Group* 5, nos. 1–2 (1982): 13–17.

———. *Gold at Fortymile Creek.* Vancouver: UBC Press, 1994.

———. *Dalton's Gold Rush Trail.* Madeira Park, BC: Harbour Publishing, 2012.

———. *From the Klondike to Berlin: The Yukon in World War I.* Madeira Park, BC: Harbour Publishing, 2017.

———. "Two Little Girls Linked to a Tragic Tale." *Yukon News*, March 8, 2019.

Giroux, Robert. *A Deed of Death.* New York: Alfred A. Knopf, 1990.

Grafenstadt, Daniel K. *The Diary of a Goldminer: Daniel K. Grafenstadt.* Volumes 1 and 2. Typescript of original diaries, transcribed by Heidi Toppel, n.d.

Green, Leonard. "The Dawson File." *The Journal of the British Kinematograph, Sound and Television Society* (May 1983): 224–227.

———. "The Dawson File." National Film Board of Canada. *Perforations* (September/October 1984): 54–59.

Green, Lewis. *The Gold Hustlers*. Anchorage: Alaska Northwest Publishing Co., 1977.

Guest, Hal. *A History of the City of Dawson, Yukon Territory, 1896–1920*. Parks Canada Microfiche Report no. 7. Ottawa, n.d.

Hackett, Yvette. "The Dawson Collection: Summary of Event Relating to the Dawson Film Find." Unpublished report, author's collection, 1984.

Hamlin, C. S. *Old Times on the Yukon*. Los Angeles: Wetzel Publishing Co., 1928.

Hayne, M. H. E. *The Pioneers of the Klondyke: Being an Account of Two Years Police Service on the Yukon*. London: Sampson Low, Marston & Co., 1897.

Herbert, J. D. "The Palace Grand Theatre, Dawson City." *Theatre Notebook* XVI, no. 2 (Winter 1961–62): 57–58.

Highet, Megan J. "Cheechakos, Sourdoughs and Soiled Doves: Men, Women and Community in a Klondike Gold Rush Boomtown." PhD Dissertation, Department of Anthropology, University of Alberta, Edmonton, 2015.

Hiscock, Francis William. *A Kiwi in the Klondike*. Waiuku, New Zealand: W. J. Dodds Printing, 1993.

Hitchcock, Mary E. *Two Women in the Klondike*. New York: G. P. Putnam's Sons, 1899.

Jones, Kathy. "Film Mystery Solved! Not Worth Saving in 1928." *Whitehorse Daily Star*, Friday, October 13, 1978.

King, Jean. *Arizona Charlie*. Phoenix, AZ: Heritage Publishers, 1989.

Kirchhoff, M. J. *Clondyke: The First Year of the Rush*. Juneau: Alaska Cedar Press, 2010.

Kirchhoff, Mark. "Dawson's Boom is Over: When the Klondike Gold Rush Ended, and Why it Matters." *Pacific Northwest Quarterly* 110, no. 2 (2019): 55–65.

Kirk, Robert C. *Twelve Months in the Klondike*. London, UK: Wm. Heinemann, 1899.

Kirkwood, John. "Klondike Kate's Romance." *Vancouver Sun*, December 16, 1959.

Knowles, Josephine. "Gold Rush in the Klondike: A Woman's Journey in 1898–99." Fresno, CA: Quill Driver Books, 2016.

Kula, Sam. "Rescued from the Permafrost: The Dawson Collection of Motion Pictures." *Archivaria* (Summer 1979): 141–148.

———. "There's Film in Them Thar Hills!" *American Film* IV, no. 9 (July/August 1979): 14–19.

Lucia, Ellis. *Klondike Kate*. New York: Hastings House Publishers, 1962.

Lynch, Jeremiah. *Three Years in the Klondike*. London, UK: Edward Arnold, 1904.

Macleod, Rod. *Sam Steele: A Biography*. Edmonton: University of Alberta Press, 2018.

Mallory, Enid. *Under the Spell of the Yukon*. Surrey, BC: Heritage House Publishing, 2006.

McLachlan, Robin. "Shaping a New Life in the Midnight Sun." Paper presented at the 2019 Annual Conference of the Independent Scholars Association of Australia, Canberra.

Mizner, Addison. *The Many Mizners*. New York: Sears Publishing Company, 1932.

Morgan, Lael. *Good Time Girls of the Alaska-Yukon Gold Rush*. Fairbanks, AK: Epicenter Press, 1998.

Morrison, David R. *The Politics of the Yukon Territory 1898–1909*. Toronto: University of Toronto Press, 1968.

Nerland, Andrew. "Something about Dawson City" *Norwegian-American Studies* 16, no. 4 (1898).

Norris, Frank. "Popular Images of the North in Literature and Film." *The Northern Review* 8/9 (Summer 1992): 53–81.

North, Dick. *Jack London's Cabin*. Whitehorse, YT: Willow Printers, 1986.

O'Connor, Richard. *Gold Dice and Women*. London, UK: Alvin Redman Ltd., 1956.

Oderman, Stuart. *Roscoe "Fatty" Arbuckle: A Biography of the Silent Film Comedian, 1887–1933*. Jefferson, NC: McFarland and Company, 1994.

Parker, Bert. "Kid in the Klondike: Girls, Gold and Gamblers." *Maclean's Magazine*, parts 1 & 2, November 1 and November 15, 1953.

Phillips, Clare M. Stroud Boyntan. *Klondike Tenderfoot: From the Diaries of Clare M. Stroud Boyntan Phillips, 1898–1902*. Walton, NY: The Reporter Co., 1993.

Public Archives Canada. "Historic Film Discovery." *The Archivist* 5, no. 6 (November/December 1978): 11–12.

Reddick, Don. *Dawson City Seven*. Fredericton, NB: Goose Lane Editions, 1993.

Rodney, William. *Joe Boyle, King of the Klondike*. Toronto: McGraw-Hill Ryerson, 1974.

Ross, Victor. *A History of the Canadian Bank of Commerce, Volume II*. Toronto: Oxford University Press, 1921.

Samuels, Charles. *The Magnificent Rube: The Life and Gaudy Times of Tex Rickard*. New York: McGraw-Hill Book Company, 1957.

Sanborn, Wallis R. *The Klondike Stampede as It Appeared to One of the Thousands of Cheechacos Who Participated in the Mad Rush of 1898–1899*. Jefferson, NC: McFarland and Co., 2017.

Snodgrass, Mary Ellen. *Frontier Women and Their Art*. Lanham, MD: Rowman and Littlefield, 2018.

Stevens, Gary L. "Gold Rush Theater in the Alaska-Yukon Frontier." PhD diss., University of Oregon, 1984.

Sullivan, Edward Dean. *The Fabulous Wilson Mizner*. New York: The Henkle Co., 1935.

Taylor, Leonard. *The Sourdough and the Queen*. Toronto: Methuen, 1983.

Thompson, Judy, and David Leverton. *SS Princess Sophia: Those Who Perished*. Victoria, BC: Maritime Museum of British Columbia, 2018.

Thrapp, Dan L. *Encyclopedia of Frontier Biography*. Vol. II: G-O (1991).

Tollemache, Stratford. *Reminiscences of the Yukon*. Reprint. London, UK: Edward Arnold, 1912.

Trelawney-Ansell, E. C. *I Followed Gold*. New York: Lee Furman, Inc., 1939.

Tuxford, Brig. General G. S. "The Trail of the Midnight Sun." Vol. 2 of George S. Tuxford Memoirs Vol. 1–4. n.d. Saskatchewan Archives Board, University of Regina, Microfilm R 2.247.

Walker, Franklin. *Jack London and the Klondike*. San Marino, CA: The Huntington Library, 1978.

Wickersham, James. *Old Yukon: Tales, Trails, and Trials*. Washington, DC: Washington Laws Book Company, 1938.

INDEX

Page numbers in bold indicate an illustration; page numbers in the form 275n72 refer to note 72 on page 275.

actors/actresses in Yukon
   amateur, 75, 153–59, **158**, 165
   background, 37–38, 71
   income, 70, 71, 91, 119
   professional, 91, 97, 165
   and prospectors, 28
   See also theatres in Dawson City, live performance
Adams, Ron, 239, 245
Adney, Tappan, 39, 41, 70–71, 228
Alaska
   gold rushes, 111, 132
   misidentified as site of Klondike, 5, 6, 225
   prospectors, 24
   route to Klondike, 103, 124
   setting for movies, 231–32
   theatres, 29, 72, 111, 225
   World War II, 198
   See also Circle City (AK)
Alaska Commercial Company, 25, 28, 29, 40, 41, 56
Albertson, C. H., 113
Allison, Byron, 29
American Film Institute, 244
American Photoplayer, 174–75
Amphitheatre, The, 110, 111
Anchorage (AK), 5
Apple, George, 121
Arbuckle, Roscoe "Fatty," 5, 150, 207, 211–13, **212**, 214
Arctic Brotherhood Hall, 149, 154, 159, 167, 196. *See also* Palomar Theatre and Dance Hall

Ash, Harry, 46
Ashley, David, 252
Atwood, Fred, 153–54
Auditorium Theatre
   in 1900s, 137–39, 142
   announcement of World War I, 177–78
   last years, 180–84
   movie theatre, 176, 181–83
   name changes, 113, 137, 176
   occasional use, 146, 148–51, 154, 159
   professional actors, 143–45, **144**, 146, 149, 212
   rebuilt in 1962, 202
   renovations, 139–40, 181
   shows movies, 149, 159, 166–67
   See also Palace Grand Theatre; Savoy Theatre

Bakke, Gus, 118
"Ballad of the Brand, The" (Service), 165
"Ballad of the Ice Worm Cocktail, The" (Service), 162
Ballads of a Cheechako (Service), 163, 165
banks in Dawson City, 107, 132, 161–62.
   See also Canadian Bank of Commerce
Bara, Theda, 19
Barkerville (BC), 252
Barlow, Mrs., 82
Barrett, Frank, 10, 11, 12–13, 251
Bass, Fred, 252–53
Beach, Rex, 217, 229, 231
Bear Creek (YT), 1, 130, 176
Bear Creek industrial complex, 20, **21**, 237, 238–40
belly dancing, 108–9

Bennett (YT), 52, 103
Berger, Fred and Palma, 199
Berton, Laura, 111, 188–89, 205
Berton, Pierre, 227–28, 232
Bittner, William "Willie," 137–40
Black, George, 177–78, 185, 188
Black, Martha, 177–78, 185, 205, 282n72.
   See also Purdy, Martha
Blei, Robert, 75, 82
Blossom (actress), 119, 126
Blumkin, Rose, 118
Boardman, Paul, 118
Bompas, Bishop, 55
Bonanza Creek (YT), 1, 31, 32, 104, 130, 131, 225, 280n13. *See also* Rabbit Creek (YT)
Bonanza King (steamer), 100–102, 108
Bonine, R. K., 124
Bonnifield, "Silent Sam," 46
boxing matches, 42, 43, 84–85, 87, 89, 115, 122, 166, 209
Boyd, George W., 142
Boyle, Joseph "Joe," **50**, 50–51, 129–30, 176, 204, 209, 228
Brackney, Peter, 249
Brand, The (movie), 165
Breen, Fred, 63, 70, 71, 72, 85, 108, 126, 135, 175
Brennan, William, 121
British Canadian Pathé News, 245, 246, 254, 289n100
Brocee, Florence and Myrtle, 85, 98–99, 117
Buel, Arthur, 114
Buried News (movie), 249
Burley, David, 13
Burning Daylight (London), 231

270

INDEX

Caine, Pauline, 115
Call of the Wild, The (London), 48
Call of the Wild, The (movie), 217, 231
Cammetta, Blanche, 120
Canadian Bank of Commerce, 107, 159–60, 161–62, 235, 295n3
Canadian Klondyke Mining Company, 176
Canadian Memorial Chapel, 206
Cantwell, George, 153
Caprice (actress), 63, 72, 76
Carmack, George, 30–31, 46, 279n7
Carpenter, Professor, 175, 177
Caruso, Enrico, 212
Caskey, Mrs. J. Harmon, 186, 223
Casley, Vernon Dunwood, 204
cellulose nitrate film stock, 14–15, 17, 235, 240–41. *See also* Dawson City Film Find: restoration
Chambers, Edith, 147–48
Chandon, Bessie, 143
Chaplin, Charlie, 213–14, 224, 230, 294n53
"cheechako," 280n10
Chicago White Sox, 248
Chilkoot Trail, 46, 47, 48, 52, 88, 103, 112, 215, 216, 231
Chisholm, Tom, 100
Circle City (AK), 25, 28–29, 33, 99
Claire, Pauline, 76
claqueuse, 90, 283n73
Clarke Taylor Stock Company, 149
Clondyke News, **37**
Coates, Daniel, 236, 237
Columbia Pictures, 220, 222, 224
Combination Music Hall, 69–70, 75, **76**, 86–87, **87**. *See also* Tivoli Theatre (Dawson City)
commissioner, of Yukon, 132, 134–35, 180
Conchita (actress), 121
Congdon, Frederick, 134, 135
Connor, Roddy, 65
Constantine, Charles, 31, 55
Cooper, Joe, 75, 107
Coutts, Robert, 91
Crahan, Thomas, 124
Crawford, Jack, 82
Crawley Films, 243
Creamer, Walter, 169–70, 174, 177, 183, 184 187
"Cremation of Sam McGee, The" (Service), 161

Criterion Theatre, 83–84, **84**. *See also* Family Theatre
Cummings, Ralph, 138, 139

dance hall girls
 about, 90–92, 95–98
 deaths, 99–100
 income, 44, 67, 68, 71, 91–92, 94–95, 96, 134
 marriage, 92–94
 morality, 91, 96–97, 99, 142, 221–22, **222**
 in motion pictures, 215, 221–22
 and prospectors, 43–45, 65–67, **68**
dance halls
 after gold rush, 132
 in Circle City, 29
 closed down, 134–35
 contain saloon and gambling area, 45, 66–67, 83, 111–12, 134
 in Dawson City, 37–38, 39, 43–45, 59–60, 65–67, **68**, 110–12
 fundraising events, 85
 at Grauman's Chinese Theatre, 216
 importance to Dawson, 60, 100, 102, 111–12, 133
 musicians, 110
 regulations, 45, 110, 133–34
 show movies, 87, 196
 See also Combination Music Hall; Criterion Theatre; Horseshoe Saloon; Monte Carlo; Pavilion Theatre Dance Hall; theatres in Dawson City, live performance
Dante-Durwood Company, 149
Daugherty, James "Nigger Jim," 29, 108, 204
D'Avara, Daisy, 108, 136
Davenport, Dick, 120
Davis, Ben, 82
Davis, Harry, 100
Dawson, George Mercer, 32
Dawson Amateur Athletic Association (DAAA) building
 about, **168**, 168–71, **169**, **170**, **171**
 baseball team, **182**
 Dawson City Film Find, 235–36
 destroyed by fire, 193, **195**, 235
 shows movies, 17
 See also Family Theatre
Dawson Amateur Operatic Society, 153, **154**, 154–55

Dawson City (YT)
 in 1890s, 1, 2
 in 1897, 33, 35, **36**, 38–41
 in 1898, 56–61, **57**, **58**
 in 1908, **150**
 in 1910, 165
 in 1920s, 188–89
 in 1978, 10–11, **11**
 after gold rush, 103–5, 109–10
 demolishes old buildings, 11, 199, 201
 electrification, 79–80
 established, 32
 fire (April 26, 1899), 105–7, **106**
 fire (January 9, 1900), 63, 117
 fire (November 25, 1897), 45
 fire (October 14, 1898), 80–82
 first motion picture, 86–87
 first "talkie," 188
 first theatre, 42 (*see also* Opera House (Dawson City))
 flood (1979), 251–52
 Great Depression, 189
 hockey team, 204
 hospital, 188
 location, 32, 55
 loses status of capital, 198–99
 in motion pictures, 185, 186–87, 226–27, 247–48
 national historic sites, 4–5
 newspapers, 6–7, 8, 37, 105
 population, 4, 10, 33, 56, 104, 111, 131, 155, 189, 199
 premiere showing of Dawson City Film Find, 252–54
 real estate values, 35, 42
 services for miners, 32–33, 35–36, 39–41, 56, 104–5
 sinking of *Princess Sophia*, 180
 subsidizes satellite television, 199
 supply centre for industrial mining, 131–32
 threat of famine, 40, 41
 travel to, 7–8, 10, 79, 84, 185, 186, 227
 World War I, 179–80, 188
 World War II, 197–98
 See also banks in Dawson City; dance halls; firefighting in Dawson City; gambling; hotels in Dawson City; North-west Mounted Police; prostitution in Dawson City; saloons; theatres in Dawson City

271

INDEX

Dawson City Film Find
  about, 1–2, 14, **14, 15,** 17–18, 234–37
  catalogued, 239
  discovery, 11, **12**
  and Frank Barrett, 10, 12–13
  legacy, 247–50
  media coverage, 239–41, 242
  no films of Yukon, 233, 241
  number of reels, 238, 245
  premiere showing, 245, 251–54
  recovery, 20–21, 237–38
  restoration, 16, 20–21, 241, 243–45, 253, 295n13
  significance, 245–47, 249
  storage in Dawson City, **21**
  transportation to Ottawa, 240, 241, 242
Dawson City: Frozen Time (movie), 247–48, 255, **255**
Dawson City Museum, 4, 20, 21, 234, 235, 237–38, 241. *See also* Jones, Kathy
Dawson Daily News
  about, 6, 8
  Alexander Pantages, 118, 142
  American Photoplayer, 174–75
  Auditorium Theatre, 138, 181
  burning of silent films, 190
  consolation of theatres and dance halls, 110–11
  dance hall girls, 95–98, 142
  Dawson City Film Find, 237
  De Luxe Theatre, 183
  filming of *The Trail of '98*, 186
  ice worm cocktail, 162
  last issue, 295n1
  Lillian Hall's productions, 143
  Margie Newman, 145
  Marjorie Rambeau, 150, 151, 152, 208
  movie advertisements, **16, 17, 172,** 175, 185–86, 193, **193**
  movie news, 123, 173–74, 185
  murder of William Desmond Turner, 224
  New Year's Eve 1906, 152
  Orpheum Theatre, 121, 138, **138,** 167, 187
  Palace Grand Theatre, 122
  Robert Service, 164
  theatre coverage, 7
  William Bittner's departure, 140
  World War I, 177, 185
Dawson Dramatic Club, 75

Dawson Electric Light and Power Company, 79
Dawson Festival, 202
De Luxe Theatre, 113, 183. *See also* Auditorium Theatre; Palace Grand Theatre
Deane-Tanner, William Cunningham, 223
Department of Indian Affairs and Northern Development. *See* Parks Canada
Department of National Defence, 242
Dietrich, Marlene, 217–18
Dill, W. S., 37, 155–58
Dines, John, 172
Dionne Quintuplets, 193
Dolan, Eddie, 122, 136
Dominion Saloon, 39, 45, 64, 106
Dowie, Fran, 252
Drake, Charley, 181
drift mining, 258
Drummond, Myrtle, 63, 108
Dunham, Sam, 110
Dyea (AK), 72, 103, 225

Eads, Murray, 136
Edison, Thomas, 23, 24, 86–87
Edison Company, 123–24, 166
Edwards, Harry, 100
Eggert, Theodore, 118, 126, 128, 136, 140
Eldorado Creek (YT), 32, 49, 93, 104, 130, 131, 258, 280n13
Elks Club, 82, 85
Elliott, Fred, 187, 190, 236
Elliott, Lucille, 69
Evans, Dave, 100

Fairbanks (AK), 132, 146
Fairview Hotel, 72, 90, 201
Falkenburg, Jinx, 220, **221**
Family Theatre
  in 1898–1899, 82–84, **83, 84**
  competition with other theatres, 175, 177, 182, 190, 193
  destroyed by fire, 193–94, **195**
  fundraising events, **181**
  only theatre in Dawson, 184, 187
  renovation for talkies, 190–91
  reopens in DAAA building, 168, 170–72, **171, 182**
  shows movies, 17, 175, 177, 182, 190
  World War I, 177, 180, 182, 185
  See also Dawson Amateur Athletic Association (DAAA) building

Fanning, Frank, 143
Far Country, The (movie), 231
Farr, Wendell "Windy," 238, 245
Faulkner, Victoria, 141
Fawcett, Charles, 126
Film Find. *See* Dawson City Film Find
Film of Her, The (movie), 248
film stock. *See* cellulose nitrate film stock
firefighting in Dawson City, 45, 80–81, 105–7, 117, 194
Forest, Emma, 63, 72, 76
Forty Mile (YT), 25–28, **26,** 33, 99
Fortymile River (YT), 25
Fox. *See* Twentieth Century Fox
Fraternal Order of Eagles, 184
Frawley Theatre Troupe, 149
Frum, Barbara, 239
Fuller, Thomas W., 13, 131
fundraising events, 85–86, 115, **116,** 122, 139, 145, 148, 150, 154–55, **181,** 206

Gaisford, C. C., 185
Gale, Franklyn, 143
gambling
  fines as form of licensing, 132–33
  importance in Dawson economy, 112, 133, 134
  orderly management, 60
  popular games, 114
  on river steamers, 45
  shut down, 134–35
  Sunday closure, 45
  See also saloons
Gardner, Frank, 117, 218
Garrett, Miss, 122
Gaslight Follies, 202, 252
Gates, Gladys, 135
Gates, Michael, 2, 3–4, 16–19, **22,** 235, 240, 242, 253–55, **254**
Gates, Swiftwater Bill, 48, 49–53, **50,** 69, 203–4, 228
George, "Professor," 82
Gilbert and Sullivan, 153, 154, 158
Gleaves, Harry, 195–96, 199, 200
Glycerine and Vaseline, 63, 65
Goethe, Johann Wolfgang von, 117
Goi, Michael, 249–50
gold
  about, 256
  in Alaska, 111, 132
  in ashes of Orpheum Theatre, 196

272

INDEX

fixed price, 198
industrial-scale mining, 129–31, 180, 259–60
price of, 7, 189
production in Yukon, 25, 31, 103–4, 129, 189, 256–60 (*see also* gold dredges; hydraulic mining)
staking a claim, 31, 257, 279ch1n7
See also Klondike gold rush
Gold Bottom Creek (YT), 30, 104
gold dredges, 130–31, 189, 197–98, 204, 259–60
Gold Rush, The (movie), 213, 214, 230
Gold Rush Review, 252
Goldwyn, Samuel, 214, 246, 254
"Goodbye Little Cabin" (Service), 152, 164–65
Goodman, Zella, 176, 177
Goodwin, Nat, 121
Gordon, Paul, 248
Gould, John, 295n5
Grand Forks (YT), 131
Grand Opera House, 112, **113**, 113–17. *See also* Palace Grand Theatre
Graphic Film Laboratories, 243–44, 296n14
Grauman, David, 211
Grauman, Sid, 210–11, 213–14, 216, 217
Grauman's Chinese Theatre, 213, 216, 217
Gray, Charles, 199, 200
Gray, Corinne B., 110
Gray, Tommy, 200
Great Depression, 189
Green, Danny, 177
Green Tree Hotel, 39, 80, 81, 201
Gross, William David, 225–26
Gross-Alaska Enterprises, Ltd., 225
Guichard, Jennie, 135

Hall, James L. "Arkansaw Jim," 93–94, **94**, 136–37, 139
Hall, Lillian, 93–94, **94**, 140, 143–44
Harper, Inspector, 59–60
Hart, Stephen C., 205–6
Hartshorn, Hazel, 177
Haynes, Lillian, 135
Hearst-Selig, 182, 289n100
Henderson, Robert, 30
Henderson Creek (YT), 47–48
Hewett family, 146–48, 166
Hightower, Mamie, 118, 126, 175
Hill, Charlie, 99–100
Hill, Stella, 99–100

Hillyer, George, 117
Hippodrome Amusement Company, 154
Historic Sites and Monuments Board of Canada, 4–5, 202
Hodgkin, Grace, 174
Hoffman, Archie, 84–85
Holden, Helen, 105
Holgate, Nellie, 82, 126
Hollywood, view of Klondike gold rush, 221–23, 227, 230–32. *See also Trail of '98, The* (movie)
Hollywood Walk of Fame, 207, 226
Hooley, Mike, 140
Hopkins, Grace, 176
Hopper, Hedda, 5, 152
Horseshoe Saloon/Dance Hall, 66, **66**, 69, 79, 108, 117, 118, 121. *See also* Orpheum Theatre
hotels in Dawson City, 26, 35, 39, 56, 81, 84, 132, 201. *See also* Fairview Hotel; Green Tree Hotel; Yukonia Hotel
Houck, Mertie, 75, 153
Howard, Frank, 72
Howard Stock Company, 149
Howell, Ida, 126
Huley, Pete, 224–25, 294n53
Hull, Emma, 69, 122
Hunker Creek (YT), 1, 104, 129–30, 190
hydraulic mining, 130–31, 259

I Married the Klondike (Berton), 111, 188–89
Imperial Order, Daughters of the Empire, 185, 186
Indigenous peoples, 24, 28, 30, 54–55, 56
Iseman, Mrs., 183

Jackson, W. R., 125, 136
Jacqueline and Rosaline, 63, 65, 72, 118, 281n14
Jennings and O'Brien, 110, 125
Jewel Theatre, 184. *See also* Orpheum Theatre
Jimmy's Place, 173, **173**, 187, 191, **192**
Johnson, Mrs. Gus, 176
Jones, Kathy, 20, 21, 234–35, 239, 240–41, 251, 252, 253, **254**, 254–55
Jory, Victor, 225–26, 230
Juneau (AK), 27, 146, 149

Káa Goox. *See* Tagish Charley
Karr, Larry, 244

Keish. *See* Skookum Jim
Keyes, Evelyn, 220, **221**
Kimball, Charlie, 62–63
Klondike (television series), 231–32
Klondike City (YT), 55, 133
Klondike gold rush
about, 1, 227–29
as American event, 5, 6, 59, 152, 229–30
begins, 30–31, 32–34
in books, 228–29
commemoration, 202
ends, 103
facts and fiction, 5–6, 44, 152, 210–12, 221–23
historical accounts, 228–29, 232
law and order, 59–60 (*see also* North-west Mounted Police)
in movies and tv shows, 123–24, 226–27, 229, 230–32
national historic sites, 4–5
photographs, 228
predicted, 32
threat of famine, 40, 41
travel to, 7–8, 32–33, 41, 50–51, 60, 103, 112–13, 227
and Tr'ondëk Hwëch'in, 54–55
women, 33, 89–91 (*see also* dance hall girls)
See also Dawson City (YT); gold; Yukon
Klondike Kate, 218–21, 228. *See also* Rockwell, Kate
Klondike Kate (Lucia), 140, 220
Klondike Kate (movie), 230
Klondike Korner, 234, 295n1
Klondike Miner and Yukon Advertiser, 6, 75, **81**
Klondike National Historic Sites, 2, 4–5
Klondike News, 113
Klondike Nugget, 6, 7, 86–87, 88, 102, 108–09, 114–15, 127–28
Klondike River (YT), 1, 30–31, 32, 54–55, 129. *See also* Dawson City (YT); Klondike gold rush
Klondike Stampede, The (Adney), 228
Klondike Visitors Association, 201–2
Knowles, Josephine, 278n3
Kula, Sam, 16–21, **19**, **22**, 235, 239–40, 241–42, 244, 245, 246–48, 251

La Mont, Blanche, 108
Ladue, Joe, 32, 38–39

273

INDEX

Lahr, Bert, 202
Lamore, Grace, 52
Lamore, Gussie, 49–50, 52, 69, 74, 118
Lamore, Nellie "the Pig," 63–64, 69, 74, 82, 108
Law of the Yukon, The (movie), 215
"Law of the Yukon, The" (Service), 215
Layne, Alf, 126, 128, 136, 138, 139
Leon, Beatrice, 72, 281n31
Levie, A. B., 110
Levy, Ben, 121, 167, 172
Lewis, P. C., 135
libraries in north, 29, 132, 236
Library and Archives Canada, 16, 248. *See also* Public Archives of Canada
Library of Congress, 4, 244
Linnenbrueger, Klaus, 243
Linton, John, 69, 76, 108, 122
London, Jack, 47–48, 210, 216–17, 229, 231, 278n3
Lorne, Beatrice, 93, 118, 119–20, 121, 136, 206, 281n31
Los Angeles theatres, 213–14
Lost Dominion Screening Collective, 248
Lousetown. *See* Klondike City (YT)
Lovejoy, Mae Isabel ["Diamond Tooth" Gertie], 9, 93, 118, 205–6, 228
Lovell, Lucy, 118, 126, 138–39
Lucia, Ellis, 140, 220
Lumière brothers, 23–24
Lynch, Jeremiah, 90, 92

Mack, Willard, 220
MacKay, Lucille, 174
Mackenzie, D. R., 192
Magnum, Sam, 152
Malchin, Ivan, 98
Mallory, Enid, 162
Maloof, Freda, 72, 108–9
Marchbank, J. W., 108
Marcus, H. B. S., 70
Marion, Cecil, 121, 136
Mascot Theatre, 72, **73**
Matson, Johnny, 196, 220
Matson, Kate Rockwell. *See* Rockwell, Kate
Maurettus, Dick, 63, 69, 70, 108, 122, 135, 136
McCook, James, 205
McDonald, Jack, 143
McFarland, Warren H. S., 189
McHenry, Harry, 181

McInnes, William, 150
McQuesten, Jack, 29
Meadows, "Arizona Charlie," 112–13, 115–17, 120, 136, 137, 195, 206–7, 286n12. *See also* Grand Opera House
Meadows, Mae, 112, 115–16
Melville, Madge, 139
Messenger, Frank, 186
Metro-Goldwyn-Mayer, 186, 193
Miller, Len, 199
Miner, May, 135
Mitchell, Dolly, 136
Mitchell, Jack, 78–79
Mizner, Wilson, 85, 207, 209–10
M&N Saloon, 39, 45, 162, 194
Monte Carlo
   about, 50, 70–72
   boxing matches, 84–85, 204
   in Chaplin's *The Gold Rush*, 214
   electrification, 79
   fire, 117–18, 205
   live theatre, 72, 73, 75, 108, 119
   murders and suicides, 99–100
   redecorated, 111
   shows movies, 88, 89
   theatre closes, 120
Montgomery, Frank, 143
Moosehide Mountain (YT), 30, 55
Moran, Casey, 29
Moran, Chris, 143
Morrison, Bill, 247–50
movie theatres. *See* theatres in Dawson City, motion pictures
movies, silent
   end of era, 216
   fire hazard, 14–15, 235
   first, 23–24
   loss of, 15, 19–20, 247
   projectors, 23–24, 86–88, 123, 136, 141, 187, 285n38
   replaced by "talkies," 188, 190–91, 216
   win Academy Award for best picture, 187
   See also Dawson City Film Find
Mullen, Billy, 126, 175–76
Mulligan, John, 69, 75, 76, 82, 108, 122, 136
Mulroney, Belinda, 72, 90, 131
Murder of Geneva Hardman and Lexington's Mob Riot of 1920, The (Brackney), 249

music halls. *See* dance halls; theatres in Dawson City, live performance
musicians in Dawson City, 71, 96, 110, 174–75, 176, 177, 183, 252–53
My Seventy Years (Black), 178
Myers, Josie, 118

National Film, Television and Sound Archives (NFTSA), 4, 16, 235, 241, 242–44, 296n14, 296n15. *See also* Kula, Sam
New Pavilion, 108
New Theatre, 113, 176. *See also* Auditorium Theatre
New York Film Festival, 248, 255
New York Rangers, 209, **210**
Newhard, Bob, 186
Newman, Margie, 72–74, **73**, 82, 85, 88, 142–43, 144–46
Newman family, 63, 72–74, **73**, 85, 108, 140, 144–45
newsreels, 177, 184, 245, 246, 249, 254, 289n100
nitrate film stock. *See* cellulose nitrate film stock
Nome (AK), 111, 123, 132, 133, 149
Norris, Frank, 231
North American Transportation and Trading Company (NAT&T Co.), 28, 41, 56, 131
Northern, The, 47
North-west Mounted Police
   arrest men to prevent marriage, 93–94
   crack down on gambling, 132–33
   in Dawson City, 56, 59, 80, 107
   establish Canadian presence, 230
   in Forty Mile, 27, 31, 32
   maintain order, 38, 45, 59–60, 112, 133, 222
   record mining claims, 31
   register Klondikers, 90
   and Tr'ondëk Hwëch'in, 55
   See also Steele, Sam
Novelty Theatre, 108–9, 111. *See also* Tivoli Theatre (Dawson City)
Noziglia, Hal, 183, 290n8
Nugget Dance Hall, 113
Nutty Club, 234, 295n1

Oatley Sisters (Lottie and Polly), 65–69, 85, 87, 108, 144, 204–5
O'Brien, Ed, 119, 120, 121

INDEX

O'Brien, Steve, 125, 136
O'Brien family, 118, 125
Oderman, Stuart, 5
O'Farrell, Bill, 243
Ogilvie, William, 32, 134–35
Oglow, James "Apple Jimmy," 173, **173**, 187, 191–92, **192**, 194–95
Olsen, Olaf, 172, 187
Oneel, Tip, 183
Opera House (Dawson City)
   about, 39, 42–45, **63**
   electrification, 79
   fire, 45, 106–8, 117–18
   first theatre, 42
   live theatre, 42–43, 69, 119
   stock company, 118–20, 121 (*see also* Orpheum stock company)
Orpheum stock company, 121, 135, 136, 148–49
Orpheum Theatre
   about, **120**, 121
   after World War II, 199–200
   appeals to families, 167, 172, **172**
   competition with other theatres, 122, 127, 137–38, 167, 172, 175, 190, 193
   demolished, 199
   fire, 194
   grand opening, **119**, 121
   live theatre, 121, 122, 126–27, 135, 136, 137–38, **138**, **150**, 155–58, 159
   name changes, 136, 184
   rebuilt in 1940, 195–96, **197**
   renovations, 167, 173, 192–93, **193**
   reopens as movie theatre, 187–88
   sells sound equipment, 191
   shows movies, 123, 159, **166**, 166–67, **172**, 172–74, 175, 177, 190
   during World War I, 180, 181, 184
   See also Oglow, James "Apple Jimmy"; Pantages, Alexander
Orpheum Theatre (Victoria), 140–42
Othman, Frederick C., 218
Ouimet, Ernest, 245

Pacific Northwest Moving, 240, 242
Page, Tony, 80
Palace Grand Theatre
   competition with other theatres, 122
   Dawson City Film Find, 241, 245, 251–54
   derelict, 195
   fundraising events, **116**, 122

live theatre, 69, 70, 117, 120–21, 122, 125, 202
   name changes, 113
   purchased for Lillian Hall, 94
   reconstructed by Parks Canada, 113, 202
   shows movies, 123
   special events, 117, 122
   tourist shows, 202, 252
   See also Auditorium Theatre; De Luxe Theatre; Grand Opera House; Meadows, "Arizona Charlie"
Palomar Theatre and Dance Hall, 196–97. *See also* Arctic Brotherhood Hall
Pantages, Alexander
   about, 118–19, **213**
   after leaving North, 141, 142, 211, 219
   and Kate Rockwell, 135, 141, 142, 219
   at Opera House, 118, 119
   at Orpheum, 121, 123, 126, 135, 136, **138**
Paradise Alley, 36, 81–82, 110
Parker, Bert, **66**, 67
Parkes, Walter, 88, 89, 123, 136, 282n62
Parks Canada, 13, 20–21, **21**, 113, 202, 238
Parsons, Louella, 221
Pathé, 177, 245, 246, 254, 289n100
Patterson, Shirley, 220, **221**
Paulton, Edward, 220
Pavilion Theatre Dance Hall, 62–63, **64**, 72, 118, 122, 126. *See also* Standard Theatre
permafrost, 1, 11, 12, 169–70, 233, 238, 257, 258
Perry, A. B., 133
Peterson, Bert, 187
Peterson, Ramps, 118
Phoenix Dance Hall, 108, 205
Pioneer Hall, 75, 87–88
Pioneer Saloon, 39, 99
Placell, "Professor," 139
placer deposits, 25, 32, 104, 256
placer mining, 104, 256–57
Popcorn with Maple Syrup: Film in Canada from Eh to Zed (Rowe), 247
Post, Jim, 135
Post, Wiley, 192
Potoroka, Wayne, 250

Princess Sophia (ship), 180, 188, 290n2
Pringle, Eunice, 219
prospectors
   about, 256–57
   arrive in Yukon, 24–25
   and dance hall girls, 28, 43–45, 65–67, **68**
   give way to industrial mining, 129, 258–59
   hardships, 31, 40–41, 57, 60–62, 84, 89
   health problems, 57, 89
   and Indigenous women, 28, 30
   mining process, 31, 104, 256–59
   and theatres, 4, 73, 83, 145, 147
prostitution in Dawson City, 36, 90, 105, 110, 133, 282n72, 286n3
Public Archives of Canada, 16, 237, 238, 239. *See also* Library and Archives Canada
Purdy, Martha, 90, 282n72. *See also* Black, Martha
Pyne, Babe, 135

Rabbit Creek (YT), 30–31. *See also* Bonanza Creek (YT)
Rambeau, Marjorie, 5–6, 149–52, **151**, 155, 207–8, **208**, 212, 220, 230, 288n58
Rappe, Virginia, 213
Raymond, Maude, 108
Reilly, Jim, 242
Rhodes, Louis, 32
Rhymes of a Rolling Stone (Service), 164, 165
Richardson, Stanley, 238
Rickard, George Lewis "Tex," 46–47, 85, 209, **210**
river steamers, 25, 33, 40, 45, 100–102, 108, 125
Robertson, Dave, 199
Robinson, Gracie, 63, 72
Rockwell, Kate
   and Alex Pantages, 135, 141, 142, 219
   arrives in Dawson City, 125
   daughter, 142
   "Klondike Kate," 6, 218–20, **221**
   last appearance in Dawson, 142
   movie of her life, 218, 220–21, 222–23, 230
   at Orpheum, 135, 136
   pans gold from Orpheum ashes, 196

275

INDEX

Rockwell, Kate (*cont.*)
    reality of Klondike, 221–22
    tableaux, 138
    in Victoria, 140–41
Rockwell, Lotus, 142
Rogers, Will, 112, 192, **192**
Rooney, Pat, 42
Rooney, Tom, 118
Rooney and Forrester, 139
Roselle, Maude, 63, 100
Ross, J. H., 135
Rowe, Peter, 247
Ruggles of Red Gap (Wilson), 219
Russell, Curly, 196
Ryan, "Klondike Kate," 219

saloons
    after gold rush, 132, 149
    in Circle City, 28–29
    closed after 1899 fire, 107
    and dance halls, 45, 66–67, 83
    in Dawson City, 33, **37**, 39, 45, 47, 56, 59, 60, 61–62
    declining business, 132
    in Forty Mile, 25–26, 28
    importance to Dawson economy, 111–12, 132–33
    in Klondike gold rush, 27
    in movies, 215
    regulations, 112, 132–34
    in theatres, 45, 70, 82, 83, 114, 126, 132
    See also Gates, Swiftwater Bill; Grand Opera House; Horseshoe Saloon; M&N Saloon; Monte Carlo
Samuels, Charles, 46
San Francisco (CA), 33, 51–52, 93, 95, 211
Sarantis, George, 191
Savage, Ann, 223, 230
Savoy Theatre, 113, 125–26, 127–28, 135, 136. *See also* Auditorium Theatre; Palace Grand Theatre
Savoy Theatre Company, 125–26, 136
sawmills, 32, 38, 55, 104
schools in Dawson City, 132, 133
scurvy, 48
Seattle (WA), 33, 51, 52
Sennett, Mack, 212
Service, Robert
    about, 159–60, **160**
    fictitious encounters with, 5–6, 152, 210, 278n3

film adaptations, 165, 186, 215, 216, 231
shapes perception of Klondike, 229
in *The Spoilers*, 217–18
writing, 160–63, 164–65
in Yukon, 160–64
Shaaw Tláa, 30
Sharp, Becky, 92, 283n79
Shaw, George Bernard, 119
Shooting of Dan McGrew, The (movie), 231
"Shooting of Dan McGrew, The" (Service), 161, 218
Shriners, 176–77
Sifton, Clifford, 134
silent movies. *See* movies, silent
Silver Fox Company, 185
Simons, Frank, 110, 115, 125
Sixtymile River (YT), 25
Skagway (AK), 72, 103, 112, 146, 149, 232
Skookum Jim, 30–31
Slavin, Jim [Frank], 42, 84–85, 204, 209
Smith, Bill, 50, 53
Smith, George, 93, 206
Snow, George T., 27–28, 29, 38–39, 203
Somers, Alex, 247
Songs of a Sourdough (Service), 161
"sourdough," 47, 48, 162,188, 215, 280ch2n10
Southard, Ray, 138, 139, 150
Sparks, Ned, 208–9
Sparks, Thomas, 100
Spoilers, The (movie), 217, 231
Standard Theatre, 126, **127**, 127–28, 135–36, 137, 203, 291n45. *See also* Pavilion Theatre Dance Hall
Stanley Cup, 204
Staton, Claude, 118
steamers. *See* river steamers
Steele, Sam, 107, 108–10, 132–33
Steins, John, 226
Stewart River (YT), 25, 47
Stillwater Willie. *See* Gates, Swiftwater Bill
Strange Case of Mary Page, The, 16, **16**, 17, 183
Straub, Kittie, 99–100. *See also* Hill, Stella
Stutter, Mike, 199
"Such a Nice Girl, Too" (Seldon and Anderson), **77**, 78
Sutovich, Nick, 196
Suttles, Jack, 185

Swanson, Frank, 83

Tabor, Charles W. C., 93, 205
Tagish Charley, 30–31, 279ch1n5
Taylor, William Desmond, 223, **224**
telegraph, 104, 132
Thalberg, Irving, 216
theatres in Alaska, 28–29, 72, 111
theatres in Dawson City, live performance
    after gold rush, 132, 140, 143–44
    amateur, 75, 149, 151, 153–59, **158**, 165, 171
    based on local events, 69, 71, 108
    becomes a summer event, 146, 202
    declining value, 137
    description, 27–28, 37–38, 42–43, 70–71, 95–98
    exodus of talent, 111, 140–42, 143–45
    for families, 75, 82–83, 121, 128, 146
    first, 42–45
    fundraising, 85–86, 115, **116**, 122, 139, 145, 148, 150, **154**, 154–55, **181**, 206
    historical accounts, 7
    importance to Dawson City, 1, 2–3, 60, 100, 102, 111–12, 133
    map, **viii**
    newspaper coverage, 7, 205
    professional, 82, 110, 111, 114, 117, 125–26, 128, 146, 159 (*see also* Bittner, William "Willie")
    for prospectors, 4, 73, 83, 145, 147
    regulations, 45, 108–9, 110, 112, 127–28
    "sacred" concerts, 45, 86, 115, 136
    and saloons, 70, 82, 114, 125–26, 132
    secondary to movies, 175
    theatre boxes, 42, 71, 76, 96, 114, 127, 139
    travelling troupes, 38–39, 110, 146, 149–50, 166, 212 (*see also* Hall, Lillian; Hewett family; Savoy Theatre Company; Simons, Frank)
    in winter, 84–86, 89
    See also Auditorium Theatre; dance halls; Family Theatre; Monte Carlo; musicians in Dawson City; Opera House (Dawson City); Orpheum Theatre; Palace Grand Theatre;

INDEX

theatres in Dawson City, motion pictures — *continued*
  Pavilion Theatre Dance Hall; Tivoli Theatre (Dawson City); vaudeville
theatres in Dawson City, motion pictures
  admission fee, 183, 192–93
  competition between theatres, 136, 167, 176, 190
  dispose of films, 190, 236, 250 (*see also* Dawson City Film Find)
  at end of distribution chain, 184–85, 193, 236
  fires, 14–15, 181, 193–94
  first show in Dawson City, 81, 86–89
  and live theatre, 123, 146, 148, 159, 165–68, 175, 184
  musical accompaniment, 174–75, 176, 177, 183, 252–53
  newspaper advertising, **16**, 17, **81**, 87, 88, 167, **172**, 174, 175, 185–86, 193, **193**
  novelty, 2, 87, 89, 226
  show movies of local interest, 123–24, 185–86
  subjects, 87, 88–89, 123, 166–67
  "talkies," 188, 190–91
  See also Auditorium Theatre; Family Theatre; Orpheum Theatre; Palace Grand Theatre
Thompson, Mollie, 76
Thomson, Clifford, 235–37, 239
Thorne, Dick, 150
Thorne-Southard Company, 149
Three Years in the Klondike (Lynch), 90
Tivoli (Circle City), 29
Tivoli Theatre (Dawson City)
  in 1898–1899, 75–76, **76**, 78–79, 82, 99
  advertisement, **81**
  destroyed by fire, 105, 107
  electrification, 80, 81, 88
  fundraising events, 85
  shows movies, 81, 88
  See also Combination Music Hall; Novelty Theatre
To Build a Fire (movie), 231
Tozier, Leroy, 82
Tracy, Fred, 87–88
Trail of '98, The (movie), 186–87, 215–16, 231
Trail of '98, The (Service), 163, 165, 186
Treadgold, Arthur Newton Christian, 129–30

Trelawney-Ansell, Edward, 61–62
Troberg, Eric, 190–91, 194
Troberg, Ralph, 194
Troberg, Walter, 191
Tr'ochëk, 5, 54, 55
Tr'ondëk Hwëch'in, 30, 54–56
Tr'ondëk Hwëch'in Final Agreement, 56
Troxwell, George, 136
Turner, Tom, 47
Tuxford, George, 74
Twentieth Century Fox, 19–20, 208
typhoid, 57, 89
Tyrrell (steamer), 100–102, 108

Unger, Frank, 176

vaudeville
  about, 42
  before dances, 38, 45
  mainstay in live theatre, 71, 82, 86, 121, 145, 184
  and motion pictures, 24, 141, 184, 211
  in Nome, 111
  on river steamers, 45
  travelling troupes, 136
  See also theatres in Dawson City, live performance
Victor, Ed, 172, 173, 181, 290n5
Victoria (BC), 51, 98, 140–42
Victoria, Queen, 136
Vining, Mrs., 183
Vorhees and Davis, 115

Ward, "Sourdough Sue," 252
Warnock, Harry, 75
Warnsby, Ben, 199
Waugh, Dennis, 243, 244, 296n14
Weber, Harry, 220
White, Libby, 100
White Fang (movie), 231
White Pass and Yukon Route, 103, 104, 160, 240
Whitehorse (YT), 104, 146, 149, 159–61, 186, 198–99, 288n1
Whitehorse Rapids (YT), 123, 187, 216
Whitehorse Star, 160, 240–41
Wickersham, Judge, 278n3
Wickman, Len, 187–88, 190
Wilson, Cad, 77–79, **77**, 86, 94, 108, 126–27, 202–3
Wilson, Harry Leon, 219
Wilson, Henry, 143

Wilson, Tom, 118
Wilson, W. M., 70
Winchell, Carrie, 139
Winchell Sisters, 136
Wolf, Doctor, 52–53
Wondroscope Company, 87, 88, 136
Woolrich, Harry, 111
World War I, 177–80, 204, 246
World War II, 197–98

Yukon
  about, 6, 24
  accessibility, 7–8, 10, 160 (*see also* Yukon River (YT))
  becomes Canadian territory, 104
  first prospectors, 24–25
  first theatre, **26**, 27–28
  government presence, 27, 32, 132, 134–35, 180 (*see also* Northwest Mounted Police)
  in motion pictures, 123–24, 186–87, 215, 233
  population, 104, 111, 165
  telecommunications, 18, 104, 132
  window in Canadian Memorial Chapel, 206
  World War I, 177, 179–80, 185, 186
  World War II, 198
  See also Dawson City; Klondike gold rush; Whitehorse (YT)
Yukon Act (1898), 104, 132
Yukon Consolidated Gold Corporation (YCGC), 189, 197–98, 260
Yukon Field Force, 230
Yukon Film Commission, 226
Yukon Gold Company, 130, 223, **224**
Yukon Historical and Museums Association (YHMA), 251, 252
Yukon River (YT)
  access route for Klondike, 33, 39, 79, 84, 103, 105, 227 (*see also* river steamers)
  discarded films, 190, 236, 250
  flood (1979), 251–52
  gold mining, 25
  in *The Trail of '98*, 187
Yukon Sun, 6, 7, 87, **87**, 137, 143–44, 154–55
Yukonia Hotel, 194, 205

277

NOTES

Abbreviations

DDN: *Dawson Daily News, Dawson Weekly News, Dawson News*
KMYA: *Klondike Miner and Yukon Advertiser*
KN: *Klondike Nugget*, semi-weekly and daily
NYT: *New York Times*
WS: *Whitehorse Star*
YS: *Yukon Sun*
YW: *Yukon World*

Preface

1. Oderman, *Roscoe "Fatty" Arbuckle*, 13.
2. "Marjorie Rambeau Recalls Early Alaska," *Chicago Daily Tribune*, March 10, 1959, B4.
3. Josephine Knowles remembers travelling to Skagway aboard a steamer with Jack London, who lived near her in Dawson—an impossible feat, as London had left the Yukon before Knowles set foot in it. Knowles, *Gold Rush in the Klondike*, 15, 30–31. Judge Wickersham reported meeting Robert Service in Skagway "in one of the banks," where he was introduced to Wickersham as a writer of poetry. Wickersham, *Old Yukon*, 30.

Introduction

1. Recorded interview, Kathy Jones and Sam Kula, Dawson, July 1978. Author's collection.

NOTES

2   Burley and Gates, *The Dawson Film Discovery*, 2.

Chapter 1: Two Worlds

1. For a more detailed description of the life of early miners, see Gates, *Gold at Fortymile Creek*, 1994.
2. De Windt, *Through the Gold-Fields of Alaska*, 139–140.
3. Hayne, *The Pioneers of the Klondyke*, 89.
4. Hamlin, *Old Times on the Yukon*, 24.
5. Although known as Tagish Charley at the time of "Discovery," within a few years, he became more well-known as Dawson Charley both in newspaper accounts and his home community of Carcross.
6. Kirchhoff, *Clondyke*, 18–26.
7. Claims were numbered in relation to the first, or "Discovery," staked in a watershed. Thus, Claim Number 21 Above Discovery on Bonanza Creek was the twenty-first sequential claim staked above Carmack's original discovery claim.

Chapter 2: The Gold Rush Begins

1. https://www.washington.edu/uwired/outreach/cspn/Website/Classroom%20Materials/Curriculum%20Packets/Klondike/Documents/78.html.
2. Dill, *The Long Day*, 159–161.
3. "Ladue's Story," *Boston Globe*, August 6, 1897, 1–2.
4. It is possible that the M&M saloon referred to by Adney is the M&N referred to elsewhere.
5. Adney, *The Klondike Stampede*, 179–82.
6. Adney, 182–83. For more information about those who went south over the Dalton Trail to escape the famine, see Gates, *Dalton's Gold Rush Trail*, 104–110.
7. Kirk, *Twelve Months in the Klondike*, 95–99; for more descriptions of the Opera House, see Adney, *The Klondike Stampede*, 338; Stevens, "Gold Rush Theater in the Alaska-Yukon Frontier," 468–69.
8. Samuels, *The Magnificent Rube*, 42.
9. Samuels, 45.

10 The minimum requirement for someone to become a "sourdough," or veteran prospector, was to have stayed in the Yukon watershed for at least a year, and have seen the Yukon River freeze in the fall and break up in the spring. A *cheechako* was a new and inexperienced arrival in the Yukon watershed.
11 See North, *Jack London's Cabin*.
12 Walker, *Jack London and the Klondike*, 165; Gates, *Dalton's Gold Rush Trail*, 107.
13 Eldorado Creek was a tributary of Bonanza Creek. Because a discovery claim existed on Bonanza, there could not be a second discovery. The claims on Eldorado creek were therefore numbered sequentially, starting with Number 1 at the confluence with Bonanza Creek.
14 Berton, *Klondike*, 77.
15 "Swiftwater Bill Gates," *KN*, June 25, 1902, 4.
16 Gates, *Dalton's Gold Rush Trail*, 107.
17 *Victoria Colonist*, November 28, 1897, 2.
18 Berton, *Klondike*, 303–304.
19 Ross, *A History of the Canadian Bank of Commerce*, 180–181.
20 "Swiftwater Bill," *KN*, April 1, 1898, 25.
21 "No Love for Her Husband," *NYT*, December 26, 1898.
22 "Swiftwater Bill Drowned," *The Caribou Sun*, May 16, 1898, 1.
23 Berton, *Klondike*, 303.
24 "Monte Carlo Closed," *KN*, July 20, 1898, 1.

Chapter 3: The Boom Year

1 For a more detailed account of the impact upon the Tr'ondëk Hwëch'in, refer to Dobrowolsky, *Hammerstones*, Chapter 3.
2 Library and Archives Canada, RG 85 C-1-3, Vol. 655, File 3008.
3 LAC, RG 85 C-1-3, Vol. 655, File 3008.
4 Kirchhoff, *Is Dawson's Boom Over*, 57.
5 Craig, *Glimpses of Sunshine and Shade*, 62.
6 Cunynghame, *Lost Trail*, 34.
7 Report of the North-west Mounted Police 1898, Queen's Printer, Ottawa, 1899. Appendix D: Annual Report of Inspector F. Harper, Fort Herchmer, Dawson, Yukon Territory, December 29, 1898.
8 Trelawney-Ansell, *I Followed Gold*, 176.
9 Armstrong, *Yukon Yesterdays*, 48.
10 "How Dawson Amuses Itself," *KN*, August 13, 1898, 4.

NOTES

11   Trelawney-Ansell, *I Followed Gold*, 173.
12   "Better Ventilation," *KN*, November 19, 1898, 2.
13   "Grand Opening of the Pavilion," *KN*, June 16, 1898, 3.
14   Jacqueline and Rosaline are frequently mentioned in the newspapers. Berton, *Klondike*, p. 366 refers to them as Jacqueline and Rosalinde, and in *Klondike Kate*, pp. 125–126, Lucia names them Jacqueline and Evaline.
15   Mizner, *The Many Mizners*, 129.
16   Lucia, *Klondike Kate*, 125–126.
17   "Novelty Theatre," *Ogden Daily Commercial*, December 25, 1890, 12; "Saltair Notes," *Salt Lake Herald*, August 1, 1893, 6; *Tucson Citizen*, October 30, 1897.
18   "Dawson's Amusements," *British Colonist*, March 25, 1899, 7.
19   "Something about Dawson City," Andrew Nerland to *Washington posten*, December 30, 1898.
20   Parker, "Kid in the Klondike," part 2, 80.
21   Berton, *Klondike*, 367.
22   Stevens, *Gold Rush Theater*, 111.
23   "Combination Music Hall," *KN*, August 3, 1898, 1.
24   *KN*, August 3, 1898, 1.
25   *KN*, November 23, 1898; Berton, *Klondike*, 360.
26   "The Combination," *KN*, September 21, 1898; Evans, *Frontier Theatre*, 245.
27   "The Klondike Theater," *Kansas City Journal*, December 4, 1898, 11.
28   "The Klondike Theater," *KCJ*, December 4, 1898, 11.
29   "Dawson's New Theatre," *KN*, August 3, 1898, 4.
30   Adney, *The Klondike Stampede*, 427–428.
31   "Dawson's New Theatre," *KN*, August 3, 1898, 4. Beatrice Leon might, in fact, be Beatrice Lorne, the Australian soprano known as the "Klondike Nightingale."
32   Personal communication with Mark Kirchhoff, August 26, 2021, citing the *Dyea Press*, May 24, 1898.
33   Tuxford, *Trail of the Midnight Sun*, 138.
34   Davis, *Sourdough Gold*, 152.
35   "First Snow of the Season," *KN*, September 14, 1898, 3.
36   "A New Theatre Proposed," *KMYA*, September 17, 1898, 1.
37   "Dawson Dramatic Club," *KMYA*, October 21, 1898, 2.
38   "Something about Dawson City," Andrew Nerland to *Washington posten*, December 30, 1898.
39   Berton, *Klondike*, 368.
40   Morgan, *Good Time Girls*, 74.
41   "Electric Lights for Dawson," *KN*, October 8, 1898, 3.

42 "Dynamos Stuck at Indian River," *KN*, November 2, 1898.
43 "The First Man to Cross," *KN*, November 5, 1898, 1.
44 "The Tivoli," *KMYA*, January 20, 1899, 1.
45 "Dawson on Fire," *KN*, October 15, 1898, 1; "Jury Decides Who Caused the Fire," *KN*, October 22, 1898, 1.
46 Yukon Archives, poster P-421.
47 "Elk's Social," *KMYA*, December 30, 2.
48 Phillips, *Klondike Tenderfoot*, 47.
49 Phillips, 47.
50 "Grand Opening," *KN*, May 3, 1899, 4.
51 "Presto Change," *KN*, May 3, 1899, 4.
52 "The Criterion," *KN*, May 20, 1899, 4.
53 Armstrong, *Yukon Yesterdays*, 174.
54 Armstrong, 174–178.
55 "Was It Clean?" *KN*, October 29, 1898, 2.
56 "A New Thing," *KN*, August 31, 1898, 1.
57 Hitchcock, *Two Women in the Klondike*, 284.
58 Hitchcock, 355.
59 O'Connor, *Gold, Dice and Women*, 151.
60 "The Wondroscope," *KN*, November 19, 1898, 4; "The Wondroscope," *KN*, November 23, 1898, 3.
61 "Wondroscope," *KN*, November 26, 1898, 4.
62 Parkes is also referred to as Parks, Sparks and Sparkes in other newspaper accounts of the period.
63 "A Fine Entertainment," *KN*, December 14, 1898, 1.
64 "A Fine Entertainment," *KN*, December 14, 1898, 1.
65 "Local Brevities," *KN*, January 18, 1899, 1.
66 "The New Tivoli," *KN*, January 14, 1899, 4.
67 "The Monte Carlo," *KN*, February 4, 1899, 4. Parkes is named as Sparkes in another article in the *Klondike Nugget* from December 14, 1898.
68 "The Monte Carlo," *KN*, February 4, 1899, 4.
69 *Klondike Nugget*, February 4, 1899, as cited in Stevens, 1984, 188.
70 A cleanup is the process of washing the pay dirt in a sluice box in order to recover the gold it contains.
71 Black, *My Seventy Years*, 115.
72 Black, 134. For a thorough exploration of the distinction between entertainers, dance hall girls and prostitutes, see Highet, *Cheechakos, Sourdoughs and Soiled Doves*, Chapter 5. Martha's special mission was to act as an agent for a man named Lambert, whose uncle had died in the Klondike and bequeathed

a million dollars in gold dust to his family. Martha was to receive half of this gold dust for going to the Klondike and collecting the gold. Black, *My Seventy Years*, 90.

73 Lynch, *Three Years in the Klondike*, 179. *Claqueur* is French for men who clap for the entertainers, presumably to provide support for them and build excitement in the audience. Although the word *claqueuses* could not be located in a French or English dictionary, it's probably safe to assume it refers to women who do the same.

74 Sanborn, *The Klondike Stampede*, 169.

75 Coutts, *The Palace Grand Theatre*, 25.

76 Hiscock, *A Kiwi in the Klondike*, 50.

77 Sanborn, *The Klondike Stampede*, 170.

78 Sanborn, 171.

79 Becky Sharp was the main character in William Thackery's novel *Vanity Fair*. Sharp is portrayed as a social climber who uses her charms to seduce upper-class men.

80 Lynch, *Three Years in the Klondike*, 56–57.

81 McLachlan, "Shaping a New Life in the Midnight Sun."

82 "Protected from Himself," *DDN*, December 9, 1899, 1.

83 "Jim Hall is Married," *DDN*, December 12, 1899, 1.

84 "Man Who Made Millions in the Klondike," *WS*, September 20, 1918, 3; "Suicide Identified," *Napa Journal*, August 20, 1918, 1.

85 "Half Million on the Cutch," *San Francisco Chronicle*, August 29, 1899, 3; "Variety Actress Wins a Fortune," *San Francisco Call*, August 29, 1898, 9.

86 "Wicked Side of Dawson," *DDN*, March 6, 1900, 01.

87 "Romance of Baron," *Spokane Chronicle*, October 17, 1898, 8; "A Bold, Bad Baron," *Victoria Times*, October 10, 1898, 3.

88 "Blew out Her Brains," *Vancouver Province*, January 5, 1899, 5.

89 "Victorian on Board," *Vancouver Province*, November 25, 1898, 7.

90 "She Blew out Her Brains," *KN*, December 14, 1898, 3; see also "Blew out Her Brains," *Vancouver Province*, January 5, 1899, 5.

91 "Is It Epidemic?" *KMYA*, December 23, 1898, 1.

92 "A Bad Murder and Suicide," *KN*, February 4, 1899, 4.

93 LAC MG 30 Series E 529, Vol. 1, North-west Mounted Police Activities Summary 1896–1932, 11.

94 "Dawson's Big Joke," *KN*, May 31, 1899, 1.

95 "Dawson's Big Joke," *KN*, May 31, 1899, 1.

96 "Dawson's Big Joke," *KN*, May 31, 1899, 1.

NOTES

Chapter 4: The Busy Years

1. Lynch, *Three Years in the Klondike*, 137.
2. "Worst Is Known," *KN*, April 29, 1899, 1.
3. "Opera House," *KN*, May 13, 1899, 3; "Opera House," *KN*, May 20, 1899, 3.
4. "Grand Opening," *KN*, May 24, 1899: 2; Dawson City Museum, Fred Atwood Fonds, 2015.3.16, Queen's Birthday programme for May 24, 1899.
5. "Fun at the Novelty," *KN*, July 12, 1899, 1; "The Novelty," *KN*, June 7, 1899, 1.
6. "Muscle Dance Tabooed," *KN*, July 1, 1899, 1.
7. "The New Tenderloin," *KN*, May 10, 1899, 1.
8. Stevens, *Gold Rush Theater*, 115; "An Emotional Actress," *KN*, July 8, 1899, 7.
9. Stevens, *Gold Rush Theater*, 112–113.
10. "People About Town," *DDN*, September 20, 1899, 1.
11. "Relics in the Klondike," *Aurora Daily Express*, July 20, 1899, 4.
12. "Side Lights of Dawson," *DDN Midsummer Edition*, August 30, 1899.
13. There are several articles describing this discovery on the front pages of the June 14 and June 17, 1899, editions of the *Klondike Nugget*.
14. Kirchhoff, "Is Dawson's Boom Over," 60.
15. Stevens, *Gold Rush Theatre*, 156–157.
16. "Local Brevities," *KN*, July 22, 1899, 3.
17. "Opens This Monday," *DDN*, August 17, 1899, 2.
18. Coutts, *The Palace Grand Theatre*, 23.
19. "Charley's Grand Opening," *KN*, July 22, 1899, 1.
20. "Charley's Grand Opening," *KN*, July 22, 1899, 1.
21. "Charley's Grand Opening," *KN*, July 22, 1899, 1.
22. "Charley's Grand Opening," *KN*, July 22, 1899, 1.
23. Coutts, *The Palace Grand Theatre*, 30–31.
24. "The Grand Changes Hands," *DDN*, October 13, 1899, 1; "New Management the Palace Grand Theatre," *DDN*, October 31, 1899, 4; Coutts, *The Palace Grand Theatre*, 32–34.
25. "St. Andrew's Night," *DDN*, November 30, 1899, 2; "Ladies' Bazaar Now Entered upon Its Career," *DDN*, December 23, 1900, 1; "Fun for Sourdoughs," *DDN*, January 2, 1900, 6; "Was a Musical Treat," *DDN*, January 8, 1900, 1; "City News in Brief," *DDN*, January 12, 1900, 4.
26. Detailed accounts of the fire can be found in "Destroyed Again!" *KN*, January 10, 1900, 1; "Yesterday's Big Fire," *KN*, January 11, 1900, 1; "Half Million Dollars," *DDN*, January 10, 1900, 1; "Dawson's Annual Fire," *DDN*, January 11, 1900, 1; "A Block Sweeper," *YS*, January 10, 1900, 1.
27. "The Big Fire Two Years Ago," *DDN*, May 3, 1901, 9.

28　Lucia, *Klondike Kate*, 101.
29　"Strange Success," *DDN*, July 27, 1907, 2.
30　"The Stage," *DDN*, January 2, 1900, 4.
31　"Stage Notes," *DDN*, April 24, 1900, 3.
32　"Palace Grand to Reopen," *DDN*, January 12, 1900, 4.
33　"A New Opera House," *DDN*, January 13, 1900, 1.
34　"The Stage," *DDN*, February 27, 1900, 4; "The Orpheum," *YS*, March 6, 1900, 5.
35　"Stage Gossip," *DDN*, February 27, 1900, 4.
36　"Re-opening of the Palace Grand," *YS*, March 20, 1900, 1.
37　"Dawson's Circus Parade," *DDN*, May 8, 1900, 3. There is no elaboration on the giraffes and camels, but it is not believed that these were actual live animals.
38　"The Orpheum All This Week," *DDN*, June 26, 1900, 4. I could find no historical record of an Armatuograph projector. It's possible that either the reporter or the typesetter made a mistake and was really referring to the Animatograph, which was a well-known competitor to Edison's device at the time.
39　"Moving Pictures at the Orpheum," *DDN*, August 28, 1900, 1.
40　"Parkes' Lecture a Success," *DDN*, July 9, 1900, 1.
41　"In Gay New York," *Weekly Wisconsin*, November 11, 1899, 2; "Moving Pictures of Klondike," *Los Angeles Times*, November 26, 1899, 20.
42　"In Gay New York," *Weekly Wisconsin*, November 11, 1899, 2.
43　"Broom at Mast," *KN*, August 9, 1900, 1.
44　"O'Brien-Jackson Company," *KN*, August 12, 1900, 5.
45　"Upstairs Booze," *KN*, August 24, 1900, 1.
46　"Orpheum To-Nite," *DDN*, August 21, 1900, 4.
47　Atwood scrapbook, Dawson City Museum, #2006.33, Standard Theatre Programme for September 3, 1900.
48　"Hannah Arrives," *DDN*, June 4, 1900, 3; "The Orpheum," *DDN*, June 9, 1900, 4; "The Stage," *DDN*, June 19, 1900, 4.
49　"The Local Play Houses," *KN*, November 29, 1900, 7.
50　"Standard Theatre Reopens," *KN*, January 24, 1901, 7.

Chapter 5: The Twilight Years

1　For more information about T. W. Fuller, see Archibald, "Thomas W. Fuller (1865–1951): A Preliminary Report."

NOTES

2. Sir Sam Steele Collection, University of Alberta, #2008.1.2.1.3.6.1, "NWMP Undercover Report—Criminal Activity in the Gold Fields."
3. Guest, *A History of the City of Dawson*, 219–232; Highet, *Cheechakos, Sourdoughs and Soiled Doves*, 192, states that in September of 1898 there were at least 150 prostitutes in Dawson's red-light district.
4. Consolidated Ordinances for the Yukon Territory, 1902, Chapter 76, Section 59, 611.
5. Guest, *A History of the City of Dawson*, 209–210.
6. Morrison, *The Politics of the Yukon Territory 1898–1909*, 39.
7. Guest, *A History of the City of Dawson*, 206–207; Morrison, *Politics of the Yukon*, 39–40.
8. Morrison, *Politics of the Yukon*, 40.
9. "At the Theatres," *YS*, January 5, 1901, 1. Note that this name has been rendered as Troxell in other sources, e.g., in the Juneau Opera House theatre programme of September 13, 1897, 1, 3, Gates collection.
10. "Grand Sacred Concert," *YS*, February 9, 1901, 6; "Grand Sacred Concert," *YS*, February 16, 1901, 6; "Grand Sacred Concert," *YS*, March 9, 1901, 8; "Late Dawson News," *WS*, January 9, 1901, 7.
11. The New Savoy Programme, January 27, 1902, Dawson City Museum, Barber Collection.
12. "Value of Property," *DDN*, October 24, 1901, 3; Coutts, *A History of the Palace Grand*, 49–50, states that Meadows and Hall played cards to determine whether the payment was to be made in gold dust or hard cash, and Meadows is stated to have won the bet for cash.
13. "At the Auditorium," *YS*, April 19, 1902, 1.
14. "David Harum This Week," *YS*, April 22, 1902, 4; "Orpheum Theatre," *YS*, April 22, 1902, 4.
15. "Border Life on the Stage," *YS*, April 29, 1902, 3.
16. "Border Life on the Stage," *YS*, April 29, 1902, 3.
17. "He Finds It Does Not Pay," *YS*, May 27, 1902, 3.
18. "Enlarging Theatre," *DDN*, July 3, 1902, 3.
19. "Waterfront Notes," *DDN*, July 6, 1902, 8.
20. "Actors Depart," *DDN*, October 14, 1903, 4.
21. "Actors Depart," *DDN*, October 14, 1903, 4.
22. "Fine Sunday Concert," *YS*, July 8, 1902, 4.
23. "Passengers," *Victoria Daily Times*, November 24, 1902, 3.
24. "Manager W. J. Stevenson," *Victoria Daily Times*, December 23, 1902, 5.
25. "Theatre Manager in the Toils," *Victoria Colonist*, February 8, 1903; see also "Johnson Is Freed," *Victoria Colonist*, February 12, 1903, 5. There are conflicting

accounts as to who acquired the theatre and named it the Orpheum: "Victoria Theatres Are Pride of City," *Victoria Colonist*, July 1, 1917, 24; "City's First Movie House," *Victoria Colonist*, July 1, 1917, 27; and "Pioneer Owner of Movie House Dead," *Victoria Daily Times*, May 19, 1920, 7.

26 Faulkner, "Interim Report: Auditorium Theatre (Palace Grand)."
27 "The Orpheum," *Victoria Colonist*, April 29, 1903, 2; "The Orpheum," May 12, 1903, 2; "Precautions Taken Against Fire," August 8, 1903, 8.
28 For example: *Victoria Colonist*, September 23, 1903, 5; December 7, 1903, 3.
29 "Empire Theatre," *Tacoma Times*, February 9, 1904, 3.
30 "New Plea Is Refused in Thompson Libel Case," *DDN*, November 17, 1904, 3.
31 "Yukoners Outside," *DDN*, May 20, 1904, 3.
32 "New Company Reaches City," *DDN*, June 19, 1903, 8.
33 "Warmly Welcomed," *DDN*, June 23, 1903, 5.
34 "Excellent Closing Show at the Auditorium," *Dawson Record*, August 25, 1902, 2; "Closing Night," *DDN*, August 24, 1903, 8.
35 "Hall Company Is to Go to Nome," *YS*, August 2, 1903, 12.
36 "Mixed Bill at Auditorium," *DDN*, September 29, 1903, 8.
37 "Farewell to Little Actress," *YW*, June 7, 1904, 3.
38 "Thursday Farewell," *DDN*, June 6, 1904, 4.
39 "Newmans Leaving," *DDN*, June 13, 1904, 4.
40 "Died in Portland, Buried in Tacoma," *DDN*, July 21, 1906, 1.
41 "The Great Hewett Co.," *DDN*, June 5, 1905, 4.
42 Clifford, *Klondike Childhood: Memoirs of Dorothy Dorris Miller Clifford*, 64.
43 "Mystery Rampant," *DDN*, June 9, 1905, 4.
44 Clifford, *Klondike Childhood*, 64.
45 "Mystery Rampant," *DDN*, June 9, 1905, 4.
46 "Hewett Pleased," *DDN*, June 30, 1905, 4.
47 "The Hewett's Pass Rampart," *DDN*, August 5, 1905, 4.
48 "Body Has Been Found," *DDN*, September 12, 1905, 3; "Dr. Chambers Effects Positively Identified," *DDN*, October 4, 1906, 1.
49 "Auditorium," *YW*, June 9, 1907, 4; "Hewett Draws Large Gathering," *DDN*, June 23, 1908, 2.
50 "Opens in City Tonight," *DDN*, June 20, 1910, 4.
51 "Big Company Here Soon," *DDN*, June 7, 1906, 4.
52 "Marjorie Rambeau's Adventurous Career," *Boston Daily Globe*, January 7, 1923, 50.
53 Coutts, *The Palace Grand Theatre*, 56.

54 "Drama Opens Here Tonight," *DDN*, June 14, 1906, 4; "A Week of Drama," *DDN*, June 14, 1906, 4; *YW*, June 17, 1906, 1.
55 "Pleased with Play," *DDN*, June 19, 1906, 4.
56 "Auditorium," *DDN*, June 25, 1906, 4.
57 "Pleasant Evening," *DDN*, July 20, 1906, 2.
58 "Factory for Making 'Stars.'" *YW*, July 29, 1906, 4, suggests that Rambeau's many Dawson friends persuaded her to remain for the winter.
59 "To Open Season," *DDN*, September 10, 1906, 4.
60 "To Open Season," *DDN*, September 10, 1906, 4.
61 "Ready for the Play," *DDN*, November 15, 1906, 4; "Show Is Success," *DDN*, November 21, 1906, 4; "Auditorium," *DDN*, February 19, 1907, 4; "Will Not Be Sleepy," *DDN*, February 22, 1906, 4.
62 "Will Stay in Dear Old Dawson," *DDN*, March 9, 1907, 4; "Rambeaus Leave for Outside," *DDN*, April 1, 1907, 4.
63 "Marjorie Rambeau Recalls Early Alaska," *Chicago Daily Tribune*, March 10, 1959, B4.
64 "Marjorie Rambeau, of Dawson, Has Arrived—Gives Gotham Guff," *DDN*, November 21, 1916, 2.
65 "The Actor's Christmas," *NYT*, December 19, 1915.
66 "Carnival Triumph," *DDN*, January 1, 1907, 3.
67 HMS *Pinafore* programme, Atwood scrapbook, Dawson City Museum, #2006.33.
68 Atwood scrapbook, Dawson City Museum, #2006.33; also, information provided by Alex Somerville and Angharad Wenz of the Dawson City Museum.
69 For example, "Charity Entertainment," *DDN*, October 3, 1906, 3.
70 "Operatic Society's Statement," *YS*, June 22, 1902, 4.
71 "She Went a-Barnstorming in Cold, Far-Off Alaska," *NYT*, December 5, 1915; Dill, *The Long Day*, 165–171, appears to be describing the same event in comic detail.
72 Dill, *The Long Day*, 165–171.
73 Playbills and programs for these performances can be found in the Frederick Nelson Atwood fonds at the Dawson City Museum, #2015.3.
74 "The Little Old Log Cabin," *WS*, May 10, 1902, 3.
75 Mallory, *Under the Spell of the Yukon*, 64.
76 Mallory, 97.
77 Mallory, 98.
78 "Yukon's Beverage," *DDN*, April 27, 1906, 4.

NOTES

79   Mallory, *Under the Spell of the Yukon*, 109.
80   "In from a Long Journey," *DDN*, August 12, 1911, 4.
81   "Service on Trip," *DDN*, June 29, 1912, 4.
82   *Vancouver Daily World*, July 9, 1912, 9; "Service Has a Good Summer in Olympics," *DDN*, August 31, 1912, 4.
83   "Imperial Theater Today Only," *Great Falls Tribune*, June 20, 1912, 2.
84   "Orpheum Theatre Is Reopened," *DDN*, May 15, 1906, 4.
85   Frederick Nelson Atwood fonds, Dawson City Museum, #2015.3.45.
86   "Many at Show," *DDN*, June 13, 1907, 2; see also https://www.youtube.com/watch?v=LD57YNtuebo.
87   "Entirely New Moving Pictures," *DDN*, March 22, 1910, 4.
88   "Orpheum," *DDN*, January 19, 1911, 4.
89   "Improvements at the Orpheum," *DDN*, February 11, 1911, 4.
90   "Is Almost Prepared," *DDN*, May 30, 1908, 2; "Building Frame of the Tank," *DDN*, June 8, 1908, 2; "Open to Swimmers," *DDN*, June 25, 1908, 4.
91   "D.A.A.A. Theater Opens with a Bumper House," *DDN*, October 27, 1911, 4.
92   "Orpheum, Noted Picture House of Dawson City," *DDN*, December 23, 1913, 33.
93   "Seven Capital Sins at the Show Tonight," *DDN*, September 21, 1912, 4.
94   "Wonderful New Orchestra for the Yukoners," *DDN*, October 13, 1914, 4.
95   "Opening at the New Theater This Evening," *DDN*, December 22, 1913, 4.
96   "Waiting for Films," *DDN*, January 26, 1914, 4.
97   "Re-opening Auditorium Theatre Tonight," *DDN*, July 25, 1914, 4; "Auditorium Theater Tonight," *DDN*, August 1, 1914, 4; "At the Auditorium," *DDN*, July 31, 1914, 4.
98   "At Auditorium" and "Auditorium Theatre Tonight," *DDN*, August 3, 1914, 4.
99   "Special Attraction at DAAA Tonight," *DDN*, August 3, 1914, 4.
100 "Correct Tango Steps Shown at Orpheum," *DDN*, August 3, 1914, 4. Pathé was a company that produced newsreels commonly shown at the theatre at that time. Similar companies of the day included Gaumont and Hearst-Selig.
101 "Dawson Stirred by the News of the War," *DDN*, August 4, 1914, 4.
102 Black, *My Seventy Years*, 225.

Chapter 6: Movie Night in Dawson

1   For a detailed account of the Yukon during World War 1, see Gates, *From the Klondike to Berlin*.

NOTES

2 The accepted number of deaths had long been set at 354; however, further research by Thompson and Leverton, *SS Princess Sophia*, 13, has raised that number to 367.

3 For more information on this maritime disaster, refer to Coates and Morrison, *The Sinking of the Princess Sophia*, or Thompson and Leverton, *SS Princess Sophia*.

4 "Auditorium to Open Tomorrow—Plans Complete," *DDN*, April 9, 1915, 4.

5 "Orpheum Theater Reopened Tonight," *DDN*, August 17, 1915, 35. Victor is believed to be the same man who previously managed the Orpheum with Edwards.

6 "Moose Night at Auditorium Big Success," *DDN*, December 23, 1915, 18. The Moose were a fraternal order.

7 Both advertised on page 18 in the *Dawson News* Christmas special edition for December 23, 1915.

8 Hal Noziglia enlisted in the American military later in the war. Gates, *From the Klondike to Berlin*, 238.

9 "De Luxe to be Opened Tomorrow," *DDN*, April 5, 1916, 4.

10 "Auditorium," *DDN*, November 2, 1917, 4.

11 "New Moving Picture House Is Opened," *DDN*, November 5, 1917, 4.

12 "D.A.A.A.," *DDN*, November 2, 1917, 4.

13 "New Moving Picture House Is Opened," *DDN*, November 5, 1917, 4; see also *DDN*, November 2, 1917, 4.

14 "Special Entertainment at the Jewel Theater," *DDN*, April 11, 1921, 4; see also "The Jewel Tomorrow," *DDN*, April 14, 1921, 4, and "Free Show Tonight," *DDN*, April 28, 1921, 4.

15 Advertisement, *DDN*, April 7, 1917, 4.

16 "Movie Man to Tour Yukon This Season," *DDN*, April 3, 1916, 4.

17 "Hun" is a derogatory term for German soldiers or collectively for the enemy (Germany) during World War I.

18 "Pictures of Yukon Boys Tomorrow," *DDN*, January 16, 1917, 4; "Yukon Boys in Movies Cheered in Home Town," *DDN*, January 18, 1917, 4.

19 "D.A.A.A. Tonight," *DDN*, August 1, 1917, 4.

20 "Coming Soon at D.A.A.A. Theater," *DDN*, July 31, 1918, 4; "D.A.A.A.," *DDN*, August 10, 1918, 4; "Big Show to Start at 8:30 This Evening," *DDN*, August 14, 1918, 4.

21 "Yukon Boys Are Seen on Silver Screen," *DDN*, April 10, 1919, 4.

22 "D.A.A.A. Tonight," *DDN*, August 9, 1920, 4.

23 "Why Not Dawson?" *DDN*, May 5, 1927, 2.

NOTES

24 "Why Not Dawson?" *DDN*, May 5, 1927, 2.
25 It is possible that a film crew reached Dawson City. In the final version of *The Trail of '98*, there is a brief scene showing a fleet of boats floating toward Dawson, with the Moosehide slide clearly visible in the background.
26 "Local Men Run Miles Canyon and Whitehorse Rapids," *WS*, September 16, 1927, 3.
27 "Historic Orpheum Reopens Its Doors," *DDN*, October 30, 1930, 4.
28 "'Talkies' Pack Orpheum on the Opening Night," *DDN*, August 6, 1931, 4.
29 The residence was reopened briefly in early August 1922 to accommodate the vice-regal visit of the Governor General.
30 Laura Berton, *I Married the Klondike*, 143.
31 Coates and Morrison, *Land of the Midnight Sun*, 190.
32 "Silent Pictures Dumped into Yukon," *DDN*, July 28, 1932, 4.
33 "Silent Pictures Go Up in Flames," *DDN*, September 23, 1932, 4.
34 "Fred Elliott Writes from U[H]unker," *DDN*, January 7, 1933, 4.
35 "DAAA, Dawson Family Theatre, Reopens Tonite," *DDN*, April 8, 1933, 4.
36 "Man Who Is Busy All the Time," *DDN*, March 23, 1911, 4.
37 "Will Rogers and Wiley Post: Their historic visit to the Yukon," *Yukon News*, February 7, 2020, 27.
38 For example, "Damage Done to the D.A.A.A. Building," *DDN*, August 18, 1913; Dawson Museum, Dawson City Fire Department Report, Vol. 10–14, 1914–1945 for April 14, 1936.
39 "Family Theatre Destroyed by Fire, *DDN*, December 30, 1937, 1.
40 "Fire Destroys Historic M&N Corner," *DDN*, March 18, 1939, 1.
41 "Sourdough Merchant Sells Out," *DDN*, March 23, 1939, 4.
42 "Disastrous Fire Visits the City Again," *DDN*, May 23, 1940, 4.
43 "Pyromaniac Thought to Be in Dawson," *DDN*, May 30, 1940, 1; "Two Major Fires in Slightly Over 24 Hours," *DDN*, May 30, 1940, 4.
44 "Jimmy Oglow Passes Away," *DDN*, May 10, 1941, 4; "Jimmy Oglow Is Laid to Final Rest," *DDN*, May 15, 1941, 4.
45 The Standard Theatre, which stood beside the Auditorium, was torn down in 1925.
46 "Lumber Arrives for Orpheum Theatre and 'The News,'" *DDN*, June 27, 1940, 4; "Operations in Full Swing Orpheum Site," *DDN*, July 2, 1940, 4; "New Orpheum Building Rising Fast," *DDN*, July 13, 1940, 4.
47 "From Dawson," *The Mayo Miner*, June 15, 1940, 6.
48 "Klondike Kate Becomes a Miner," *DDN*, July 25, 1940, 4.

49 "New Picture Palace in Dawson Rises from Ashes of the Past," *The Mayo Miner*, September 21, 1940, 5.
50 "Orpheum Theatre," *DDN*, September 19, 1940, 4.
51 Letter from George Black to Ned Black, January 5, 1945, from Mary, Doug and Diane Black papers, author's collection; Green, *The Gold Hustlers*, 286–287.
52 "By Way of Change," *Klondike Korner*, September 9, 1954, 3.
53 Personal communication, Palma Berger, February 2016; "Theatre Sold," *WS*, March 16, 1967, 17.
54 "Orpheum Showed Its Last Reel 23 Years Ago," *WS*, August 12, 2002.
55 "Remembering Landmarks on Front Street," *WS*, September 27, 2002, 38.
56 "Dawson Bids Farewell to Historic Theatre," undated article by Palma Berger, *Yukon News*, author's collection.

Chapter 7: The Klondike and Hollywood

1 "Number Dilapidated Buildings Come Down," *DDN*, August 2, 1945, 6.
2 "Famous Man on Way Here," *Fairbanks Daily Times*, September 8, 1906, 4.
3 "Swiftwater Bill Is in Toils," *Reno Evening Gazette*, October 6, 1915.
4 Gates, *Dalton's Gold Rush Trail*, 107.
5 Reddick, *Dawson City Seven*.
6 Taylor, *The Sourdough and the Queen*; Rodney, *Joe Boyle, King of the Klondike*.
7 "The Case of the Drunken Diplomat," *Yukon News* online, May 29, 2009, https://www.yukon-news.com/letters-opinions/the-case-of-the-drunken-diplomat/.
8 Laura Berton, *I Married the Klondike*, 122.
9 "The Mesher Incident," *DDN*, August 20, 1904, 4; see also Backhouse, *Women of the Klondike*, 99.
10 "Klondike Nightingale," *DDN*, October 27, 1945, 2.
11 King, *Arizona Charlie*; Thrapp, *Encyclopedia of Frontier Biography*, 964–965.
12 National Board of Review, Best Supporting Actress Award, https://www.nationalboardofreview.org/award-names/best-supporting-actress/.
13 Bodeen, *Marjorie Rambeau 1889–1970*, 135–136.
14 "Brook, Rambeau, Shannon Collect 'Silence' Honor," *DDN*, April 5, 1934, 4.
15 "Orpheum Theatre Wednesday and Thursday," *DDN*, March 30, 1937, 4; "Marjorie Rambeau Returns to Dawson," *DDN*, September 9, 1944, 4.
16 "Orpheum Theatre Tonight," *DDN*, August 2, 1941, 4.

NOTES

17 Foster, *Once Upon a Time in Paradise*, 267–286.
18 For more on the colourful life of Wilson Mizner and his family, refer to Sullivan, *The Fabulous Wilson Mizner*, and Mizner, *The Many Mizners*.
19 Beardsley, *Hollywood's Master Showman: The Legendary Sid Grauman*, 28.
20 "Grauman's Theatre," *San Francisco Examiner*, January 11, 1903, 4.
21 "National Tent Show Theatre," *San Francisco Call*, May 28, 1906, 7.
22 Beardsley, *Hollywood's Master Showman*, 30–31.
23 Oderman, *Roscoe "Fatty" Arbuckle*, 10.
24 "Home Video; Arbuckle Shorts, Fresh and Frisky," *NYT*, April 13, 2001, https://www.nytimes.com/2001/04/13/movies/home-video-arbuckle-shorts-fresh-and-frisky.html.
25 Oderman, *Roscoe "Fatty" Arbuckle*, 86.
26 Beardsley, *Hollywood's Master Showman*, 32.
27 "Egyptian Theater Mecca," *LA Times*, June 26, 1925, 25.
28 Beardsley, *Hollywood's Master Showman*, 27.
29 "Shooting Snow for 'Trail' Was One Tough Job," *LA Evening Express*, May 12, 1928, 7, 9.
30 "Shooting Snow for 'Trail' Was One Tough Job," *LA Evening Express*, May 12, 1928, 9.
31 "'Trail of '98' Immense Hit," *LA Evening Express*, March 23, 1928, 18; "'Trail of '98' Seen at Astor, New York," *LA Times*, March 22, 1928, 11.
32 "Grauman Wins Fight for Film," *LA Evening Express*, April 18, 1928, 6; "Grauman Gets Alaska 'Super'; Opens May 4th," *LA Evening Express*, April 3, 1928, 10.
33 Beardsley, *Hollywood's Master Showman*, 114.
34 Beardsley, 114.
35 "Author Receives Copy of Film," *The Bioscope*, March 29, 1928, 41.
36 "Avalanche, Flood and Fire at the Tivoli," *The Bioscope*, August 15, 1928, 33.
37 https://www.imdb.com/name/nm0518711/.
38 "'Call of the Wild' Breaks Records," *LA Times*, July 26, 1935, 35.
39 "Behind the Scenes Hollywood," *Santa Rosa Press Democrat*, January 23, 1942, 14.
40 "Klondike Kate," *WS*, March 20, 1925, 2; "The Woman Called Klondike Kate," *Maclean's Magazine*, December 15, 1922, 64–65.
41 "Klondike Kate Not to Testify," *The Santa Anita Register*, October 10, 1929, 1; "Klondike Kate Tells of Trial," *SF Examiner*, October 20, 1929, Section 1-4; "Story of Kate Rockwell's Life Given," *DDN*, December 5, 1929, 1, 2;

NOTES

"Klondike Queen at Trial of Pantages," *Modesto News-Herald*, October 3, 1929, 1, 2.

42 "Romance of 'Klondyke Kate' Blossoms," *Vancouver Sun*, July 14, 1933, 1; "Klondike Kate to Wed Again," *LA Times*, July 14, 1933, 3; "Romance Is Concluded in Vancouver," *DDN*, July 18, 1933, 1.

43 "Klondike Kate Film Subject," *LA Times*, May 19, 1934, 26; *Sacramento Bee*, May 19, 1934, 7; "Film Gold to Help Pals of Klondike Kate," *Fresno Bee*, May 20, 1934, 1.

44 *SF Examiner*, December 25, 1941, 26.

45 "Klondike Kate Takes No Sass from Hollywood," *SF Examiner*, February 1, 1942, 25.

46 "Movies Got Dance Hall Girls Wrong, Says Klondike Kate," *Oakland Tribune*, May 16, 1942, 12.

47 "Says Dawson Days Weren't Really Wild," *Baltimore Evening Sun*, June 20, 1934, 18.

48 "Around Hollywood," *The Pampa News* (Texas), October 19, 1943, 4.

49 "Musicale on Upper Bonanza," *DDN*, May 21, 1904, 4; "Give Concert on Last Chance," *DDN*, February 18, 1904, 3.

50 Ferry, *Yukon Gold*, 106–107; Giroux, *A Deed of Death*, 69–70.

51 Giroux, *A Deed of Death*, 1990; see also "Klondiker Center of Murder Sensation," *DDN*, February 6, 1922.

52 "Pete Huley," *Toledo Blade*, February 10, 1973.

53 Charlie Chaplin first appears as the tramp in a movie made in 1914. If Pete Huley did not go to Hollywood until 1923, it seems unlikely that Chaplin was imitating a character created by Huley.

54 "Pete Huley, Movie Comedian, Returns Home," *DDN*, August 27, 1932, 4; "Klondike Pete Retires," *WS*, January 11, 1968, 7; "Klondike Pete Theatre Guest," *WS*, December 15, 1966, 13; "Grand Old Yukoner Passes On," *WS*, February 7, 1973, 11.

55 DeArmond, *Movie Man: The Life and Times of William David Gross 1879–1962*.

56 "Stock Proves Jory's Film 'Open Sesame,'" *The Syracuse Herald*, November 24, 1932, 14.

57 "Whirlwind Tinseltown visit," *WS*, April 5, 2007, 8.

58 Berton, *Klondike*, 412–414.

59 Norris, "Popular Images of the North in Literature and Film," 55.

60 Norris, "Popular Images," 53.

61 https://www.imdb.com/name/nm0785827/.

62 Berton, *My Times: Living with History 1947–1995*, 194.

63 Berton, 193–194.
64 Berton, 239.

Chapter 8: Recovery, Restoration and Inspiration

1   The Nutty Club got its name from the "Nuts"—No-one Under Thirty—which consisted of women from the community. They began producing a newsletter called the *Klondike Korner*. When Whitehorse became the capital on April 1, 1953, the *Dawson Weekly News* lost its patronage and issued its last edition the following year.
2   *Klondike Korner*, August 3, 1978, 1. Note that the DAAA building was destroyed by fire on December 30, 1937.
3   The Canadian Bank of Commerce became the Canadian Imperial Bank of Commerce in 1961 in a merger with the Imperial Bank of Canada.
4   "Hockey Meeting Sunday Shows Much Enthusiasm," *DDN*, November 19, 1929, 4.
5   "Children Finding Much Movie Film," *DDN*, October 1, 1938, 1. Resident John Gould, in personal communication with the author, remembered that the films would sometimes emerge from the ice, and children would delight in igniting these fragments.
6   "Memorandum of Agreement No. 80897," between the Public Archives of Canada and the Dawson City Museum, dated August 7, 1978. Copy in author's collection.
7   Interview with Barbara Frum and Sam Kula on *As It Happens*, October 1978. Copy in author's collection.
8   "Films Come Home for 'Icing on Cake,'" *WS*, May 25, 1979, 17.
9   "Film Mystery Solved!" *WS*, October 13, 1978, 14, 35.
10 https://www.inflationcalculator.ca/. Factoring inflation into that figure, it would be $855,000 in current figures.
11 "Film Mystery Solved!" *WS*, October 13, 1978, 14, 35.
12 Green, "The Dawson File," 54.
13 An optical printer is a device consisting of one or more film projectors mechanically linked to a movie camera. It allows filmmakers to re-photograph one or more strips of film. The optical printer is used for making special effects for motion pictures, or for copying and restoring old film material. From Raymond Fielding, *The Technique of Special-Effects*

NOTES

      Cinematography, Focal Press (1972). As cited in Wikipedia, https://en.wikipedia.org/wiki/Optical_printer#cite_note-1.

14   Dennis Waugh, personal communication, January 27, 2021, states: "I had just joined the NFTSA when the Dawson Film Find occurred. Having worked in film laboratories (Film House, then Deluxe Toronto and Graphic Films, [then] Crawley) for over 10 years, I was most familiar with the processes and equipment used for post production of Motion Picture Film. When I was at Graphic Film[s], I actually purchased the machine from Film House that was used in the salvage/rewash process."

15   Klaus Linnenbrueger (personal communication, July 6, 2021) confirmed details of the process that was developed. The National Film Archives subsequently acquired their own processing machine and modified it to treat decomposing nitrate film.

16   Dennis Waugh, personal communication, February 6, 2021. Waugh received a merit award for his efforts on this project.

17   Hackett, "The Dawson Collection," 12.

18   Hackett, 12; note, in correspondence with Dennis Waugh, he recalls events differently. He stated that the films were not transported to Maryland until after they had been washed and dried in Ottawa.

19   Hackett, "The Dawson Collection," 16–17.

20   Kula, "Rescued from the Permafrost," 147–148.

21   "NYFF Interview: Bill Morrison," *Film Comment*, October 6, 2016, https://www.filmcomment.com/blog/nyff-interview-bill-morrison/.

22   https://www.cbc.ca/news/canada/north/footage-of-scandalous-1919-world-series-saved-by-yukon-permafrost-1.2635519; https://www.glimmerglassfilmdays.org/news/unknown-and-unseen-newsreels-from-the-history-of-baseball; https://www.sabr.org/latest/rare-footage-of-1919-world-series-discovered-in-canadian-archive/.

23   Brackney, *The Murder of Geneva Hardman*, 77.

24   Personal communication, Morrison to Kathy Gates, March 29, 2021.

25   Personal communication, Morrison to Kathy Gates, March 29, 2021.

Epilogue

1   "Dawson Remembers Yukon History," *WH*, September 4, 1979, 23.

2   "Fred Bass, 87, dies," *Vancouver Sun*, February 22, 1985, 73.